THE STORY OF FLIGHT

The Story of Flight

COLIN HOLCOMBE

Darren Harbar

Colin Holcombe

Acknowledgemets

In reseaching information for this book, I am greatful to
the following individuals, organisations and pulications.

Aerospace Museum Bristol
David Bradley   formaly of Airbus
Graham Clark   formaly of Rolls-Royce
Combat Air Museum, Kansas, USA
Royal Aeronautical Society
Jane's All World Aircraft
Chard Museum
Otto Lilienthal Museum

Dedication

I should like to dedicate this book to David Bradley and the
rest of the restoration team at Bristol Aerospace Museum
and to all those dedicated volenteers around the country
who give up much of their presious tim to locate, save and
restore historic aircraft. Without them, many examples of
our rich aviation heritage would be lost for ever.

Contents

Introduction

Introduction

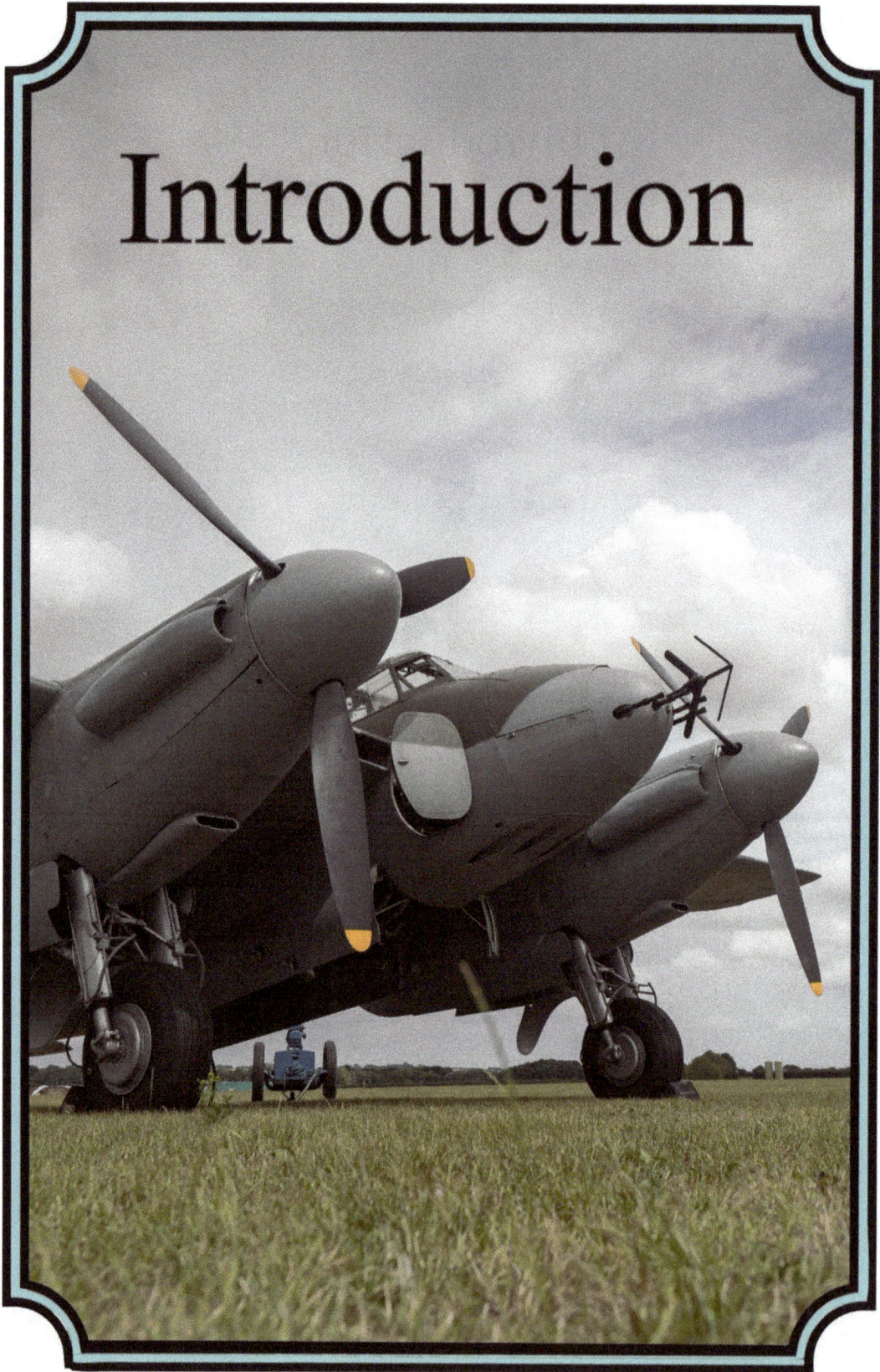

What exactly is the story of flight? It's not just the story of how the aeroplane evolved, in fact, it's just as much about people. Initially, the visionaries and romantics who just knew that one day man would fly, men like George Cayley, who first identified the four forces involved in heavier than air flight, Otto Lilienthall who eventually gave his life in the pursuit of flight and many more, including the Wright brothers who eventually achieved the first manned, heavier than air, powered flight. But the story doesn't end there, that was just the beginning, there are all the ones who came after, the people who have pushed things further, flown higher, longer and further and designed better, safer and more powerful machines. Louis Blériot, who showed that aeroplanes could cross both national and geographical boundaries and John Alcock and Arthur Brown, who showed that it didn't matter how wide the boundary was and that even oceans could be crossed. There are of course a great many more names, of both men and women who have written chapters for our story and we will look at some of them and their contributions in this book.

Growing up in central and North Bristol, I was exposed to aircraft and aeroplane manufacture from an early age, my father had spent the war on countless airfields around the country repairing Beaufighters and other aircraft, indeed the clock in our kitchen when I was growing up had once resided in just such a cockpit.

At the age of ten we had just moved into a flat over my father's second hand furniture shop in Chandos Road and it was around this time that I heard my first and only sonic-bang. I was outside the house, sorting out a tyre on my bike with my father, when we heard a loud double bang and the windows of our house shook. My father explained to me that we had just heard a plane going through the sound barrier, something that they wouldn't be allowed to do over a city now of course. I can only assume that something was being tested out of Filton aerodrome that was just a few miles away and home to Bristol Aeroplane Company (BAC) and Bristol Siddeley Engines (later Rolls-Royce,) easily Bristol's largest employers at the time.

Next door to us was a Green-grocer's shop and I became friendly with Alan Pegler, the son of the family who owned it and also lived over the shop. We became close friends and started senior school together in 1959. My bedroom at this time was filled with an array of both antique weaponry and models of aircraft, interspersed between the swords and muskets, I had everything from a Sopwith Pup to a Saturn Rocket and my friend Alan shared my interest in all things aviation.

We didn't think back then about how the aircraft flew, just how they were used and how cool they all were in their own ways. It was inevitable I suppose, that we would one day think about becoming pilots ourselves and when we were seventeen, we booked a week's gliding holiday at Nympsfield in Gloucestershire. We were both hooked and joined the club straight after.

Waiting for my first solo take-off in 1966

Some time ago, I was watching a news item on the television about some fashion models who were being flown off to an exotic destination to be photographed in the latest fashions. For some reason there was a large crowd seeing them off and they were being treated like celebrities, which I suppose they were.

As I watched one of them turned to wave at the crowd as they stepped through the door of the aircraft that was going to whisk them away and I remember thinking, why are people so enthralled with them? They're only going to have their pictures taken somewhere, that's not so difficult, why are we not celebrating the men and women who designed the incredible feat of engineering that was going to get them there, surly those people are much more worthy of our adoration?

Now OK, before I get lots of protests from celebrities or those in the fashion industry, I have to confess that as a young lad, even I would have been far more likely to have a picture of Bridget Bardot or Sophia Loren on my wall, than I would of Barnes Wallis or Frank Whittle, sorry chaps!

Of course, the full story of the development of heavier than air powered flight is not just about the great achievements, like the Wright brothers first flight or Alcock and Brown crossing the Atlantic, it is just as much about the failures, the things they got wrong, sometimes at great personal cost. Should the Wright brothers be remembered for their achievement more than George Cayley for his work, or Otto Lilienthal for his ultimate sacrifice to the cause. A matter of opinion maybe.

And what do we think about the way things have turned out? We can now fly faster than the speed of sound, we can fly none stop around the world, we can take off and land without a runway, we can even travel to the moon and back. Civil airliners carry us all over the world on our holidays, and if we pay for it, they can even do so in the hieght of luxury. But as with any great invention that has the potential to improve our lives, there is always the flip side of the coin. The world's great powers now have what America refers to as "Global reach", simply meaning that they can bomb anywhere on the planet from their home bases. The decendents of the Wright's aeroplane can now carry enough firepower to utterly destroy whole cities, continents even!

But let's try to be optimistic and say that international travel on the scale we see today can only really serve to bring us all closer together as a species, and slowly break down the barriers and mistrust that has always existed between the world's different races.

I'm sure it's what we all hope.
Colin Holcombe

Early Pioneers

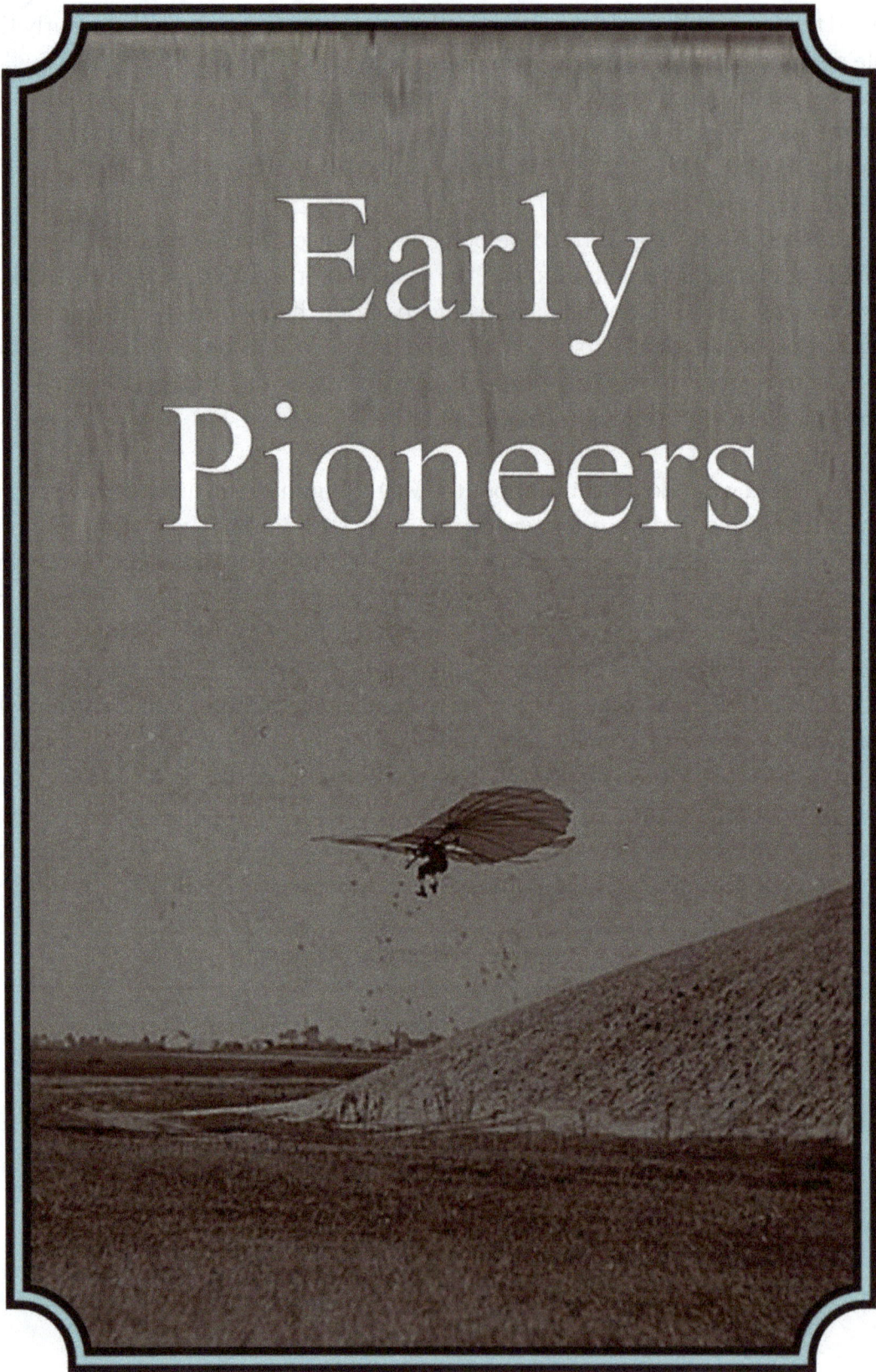

Chapter One

Early Pioneers

Nobody knows who or when it was that man first looked to the skies and dreamed of being able to fly like the birds but you can be sure it was a long time ago, ancient stories of Icarus flying too close to the sun, winged Gods, and men riding winged horses tell us that. We also know that the earliest attempts ended in failure, injury and in some cases death, some of which have been recorded but the vast majority probably not.

It's easy today to look at the old pictures of men and their strange flying machines, often with flapping wings, jumping off high structures and dismiss them as idiots and crackpots but many, if not all of those men who attempted flight in the early days were both brave and far sighted, knowing instinctively that one day man would master flight. We will never know how many people fashioned artificial wings from paper, material or feathers and jumped from high cliffs or towers to their death. But it's possible that the first time a man lifted off the ground, he was carried into the air by a kite. The kite may indeed have been the first form of man-made heavier than air aircraft but let's look first at something lighter than air.

The Balloon

The Chinese seem to have understood that warm air rises and to have been using what they referred to as "Sky Lanterns" from as early as the 3rd century BC. These lanterns were simply small hot-air balloons, made first from silk or oiled rice paper, under which a small lamp or candle was suspended.

The discovery of hydrogen gas in the 18th century led to the invention of the hydrogen balloon at around the same time that the Montgolfier brothers were experimenting with their hot air balloon. Balloons, both free-flying and tethered, began to be used for military purposes from the end of the 18th century, with the French government establishing Balloon Companies during the French Revolution.

The Kite

The kite first appears in China, possibly as far back as the 5th century BC and was possibly invented by philosophers Mozi (Mo Di) and Lu Ban (Gongshu Ban). Designs were often made to resemble flying insects, birds, and sometimes mythical animals. Ancient and medieval Chinese sources also describe kites being used to measure distances, test the wind, signal, and communicate and send messages as well as lift men into the sky.

The idea of kites eventually spread around the world to places like India and Japan, where they were used for all sorts of purposes both civil and military. One early recorded flight from the sixth century in China, was that of the prisoner Yuan Huangtou, who was the son of Yuan Lang of Northern Wei. At that time, Gao Yang took control of the court of Eastern Wei and set the emperor up as a puppet ruler. Finally, Yuan Huangtou was imprisoned by Gao Yang, and as a punishment, he was flown from the tower of Ye, China, strapped to a large kite. He apparently survived the ordeal but was later starved to death in prison.

In the 15th century in Italy, Leonardo da Vinci made drawings of flying machines, however there is no evidence that he ever attempted to make any of them but around 400 BC, again in China, a small toy existed, known as a bamboo dragonfly or bamboo copter, it consists of a helicopter like rotor that flies up when spun rapidly.

George Cayley (1773-1857)

George Cayley (1773-1857)

The Bamboo copter was the object of early experiments by George Cayley. In 1792, he began experimenting with helicopter toys, which he later called "rotary wafts" or "elevating fliers," and in his landmark article of 1809 "On Aerial Navigation" he pictured and described a flying model with two propellers (constructed from corks and feathers) powered by a whalebone bow drill. In 1835 Cayley remarked that while the original toy would rise no more than about 20 or 25 feet (6 or 7.5 metres,) his improved models would mount upward of 90 ft (27 metres) into the air. This then was the direct ancestor of the helicopter rotor and the aircraft propeller.

George Cayley identified the four forces involved in heavier than air flight, weight, lift, drag and thrust but must have been frustrated at the time by the lack of a powerful or light enough engine, so he concentrated his efforts on gliders, a sketch of one his model gliders, drawn by Cayley himself, is shown here.

His full-size glider had a large wing attached to a pole, at the rear of which was a horizontal tailplane and a vertical rudder and when anyone ran forward with it at full speed, Cayley stated that it would *"frequently lift them into the air and convey them several yards together"*. Cayley's calculations of lift and drag and his observations on stability and control of an aeroplane in flight were a solid base on which progress could be made but for some reason, progress stalled for some thirty years.

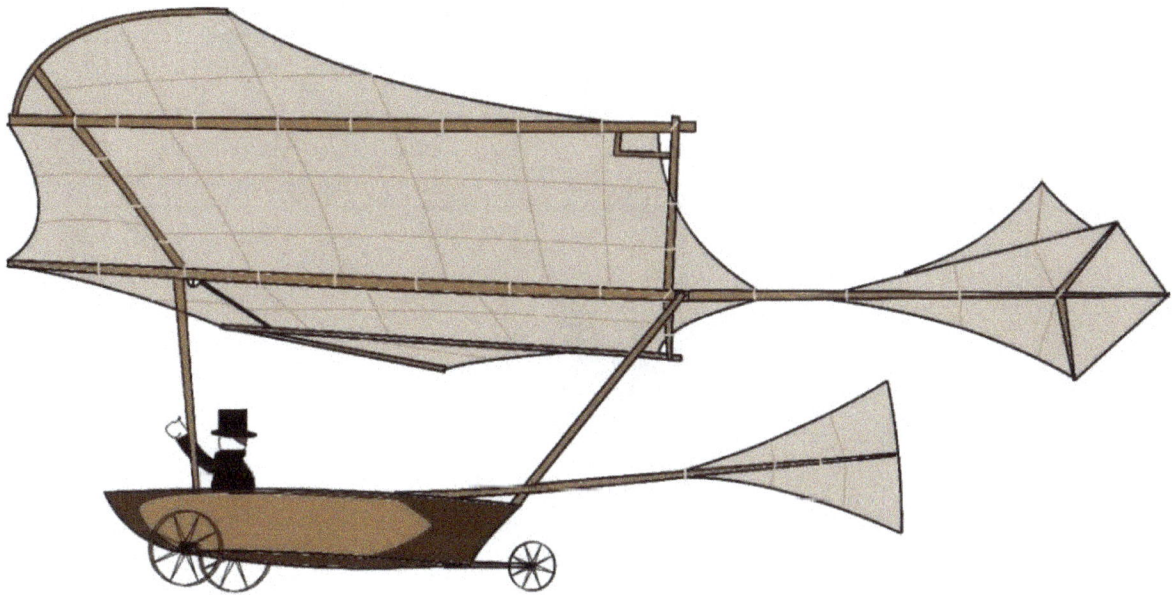

An impression of George Cayley's full-size glider

Henry Giffard (1825 – 1882)

In 1852 Henry Giffard flew the first steerable, steam powered airship or dirigible some 27 kilometres from Paris to Elancourt, but he was unable to make the return journey as intended because the wind was too strong. The hydrogen-filled airship was equipped with a 3 hp steam engine that drove a single propeller and the engine was fitted with a downward-pointing funnel. The exhaust steam was mixed in with the combustion gases and it was hoped by these means to stop sparks rising up to the gas bag; he also installed a vertical rudder.

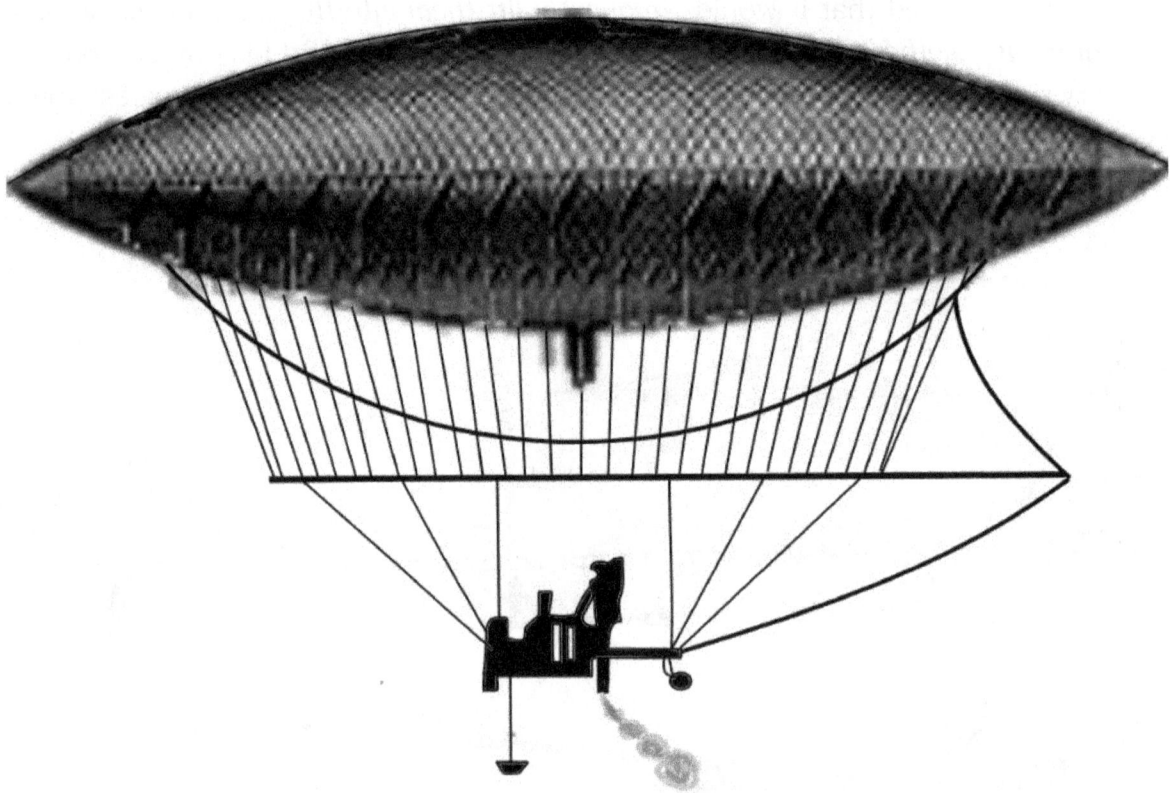

Gifford's Dirigible

Later that same year on the 19th October the Montgolfier brothers launched the first manned flight, a tethered balloon with people on board at the Folie Titon in Paris. The aviators in the balloon on that occasion were the scientist Jean-François Pilâtre de Rozier the manufacture manager Jean-Babyiste Réveillon and Giroud de Villette.

They later followed it up on 21st November 1783 with the launch of the first free flight with human passengers. King Louis XVI had originally decreed that condemned criminals would be the first pilots, but Jean-François Pilâtre de Rozier, along with the

Marquis François d'Arlandes successfully petitioned the King for the honour. They drifted 8 km (5.0 miles) in a balloon powered by a wood fire.

Jacques Montgolfier

Joseoh Montgolfier

On 1ˢᵗ December, Jacques Charles and the Robert brothers launched their manned hydrogen balloon from the Jardin des Tuileries in Paris, as a crowd of 400,000 watched in awe. They managed to ascended to a height of about 1,800 feet (550 m) and landed late in the evening at Nesles-la-Vallée, after a flight of over two hours and covering some 36Km. After Robert alighted, Charles decided to ascend again alone, and this time, with less weight on board, he ascended rapidly to an altitude of about 9,800 feet (3,000 m), where he saw the sun again but after suffering extreme pain in his ears he never flew again.

Montgolfier's hot air balloon

Ballooning became a major "rage" in Europe in the late 18th century, providing the first detailed understanding of the relationship between altitude and the atmosphere.

In 1808, with ballooning becoming ever more integrated in popular culture, possible the most elaborate duel in history took place in France. The dispute was between M. de Grandpre and M. le Pique and concerned a certain Mademoiselle Tirevit of the imperial opera, who apparently was unable to choose between her two suitors. On their orders, two identical hydrogen balloons were constructed and on the day of the duel, the two men entered the baskets of their respective balloons, along with their brave seconds.

The balloons were released some eighty yards apart from the grounds of the Tuilleries, watched by a large crowd. The gentlemen were to fire, not at each other, but at their opponent's balloon, and each was armed with a blunderbuss. When they reached a height of about half a mile the signal was given from the ground to fire.

Le Pique fired first but somehow managed to miss his opponent's balloon completely. De Grandpre on the other hand, scored a direct hit, collapsing Le Pique's balloon and sending it, together with Le Pique and his unfortunate second to the ground. De Grandpre then landed some miles away and hastened to the arms of Mademoiselle Trievit, whose mind was presumably, now made up.

Non-steerable balloons were employed during the American Civil War by the Union Army Balloon Corps and a young Ferdinand von Zeppelin first flew as a balloon passenger with the Army of the Potomac in 1863.

In the early 1900s ballooning was a popular sport in Britain. These privately owned balloons mostly used coal gas as the lifting agent, even though this had only half the lifting power of hydrogen, meaning that the balloon envelopes had to be much larger but coal gas was far more readily available than hydrogen and the local gas works sometimes provided a special lightweight formula for ballooning events.

The Age of Steam, Henson and Stringfellow

John Stringfellow
(1799-1883)

Two names stand out when it comes to steam powered flight, John Stringfellow, (1799 – 1883) and William Samuel Henson (1812 – 1888,) both man are remembered for their work on the Aerial Steam Carriage, illustrated here. The two men, who both worked in Chard, in Somerset, England, had visions of creating the Aerial Transit Company and designed an elaborate passenger carrying aircraft, the design stage was as far as it got however, but nevertheless, it was the first in history for a propeller-driven fixed-wing aircraft.

At first Henson managed to attract potential investors for his proposed company with his elaborate drawings of his carriage flying in exotic locations but in the end, he failed to persuade anyone to put up the necessary money for a full size aircraft and the project was abandoned.

In 1848 John Stringfellow achieved the first powered flight using an unmanned, steam-powered monoplane with a 10 ft wingspan. It was built in a disused lace factory in Chard, Somerset and employed two opposite hand propellers.

William Henson
(1812-1888)

A replica of John Stringfellow's successful aeroplane

On the first attempt, made indoors, the machine flew ten feet before becoming destabilised, damaging the craft. The second attempt was more successful however, the machine, following a guide wire to start with for stability, flew freely after release for some thirty yards of straight and level powered flight. A bronze model of that first primitive aircraft stands in Fore Street in Chard.

In 1866 the Aeronautical Society of Great Britain was founded and in 1888 they held their first aeronautical exhibition and awarded John Stringfellow a £100 prize for his invention of a steam engine with the best power-to-weight ratio.

Felix du Temple (1828 – 1890)

Felix du Temple(1828-1890)

In France in 1857 Felix du Temple proposed a monoplane with a tail plane and a retractable undercarriage, initially building a model, powered at first with clockwork but later with steam. In 1857 his model was able to take off under its own power, eliciting claims for the first powered flight, there were however competing claims for the first assisted powered flight with John Stringfellow's experiments in 1848.

With the help of his brother, M. Louis du Temple, he tried to build a machine capable of carrying a man but soon realized that steam engines lacked the necessary power and were too heavy. In 1867 they designed an original hot air engine but it too, proved unsatisfactory.

Francis Herbert Wenham (1824 – 1908)

Francis Herbert Wenham was a Council Member of the Aeronautical Society of Great Britain, and is generally credited with designing and operating the first wind tunnel in 1871, (see Appendix). It had a trunk 12 feet long and 18 inches square to direct the current horizontally, and in parallel course. A fan-blower upstream of the model, driven by a steam engine, propelled air down the tube to the model.

Francis Herbert Wenham
(1824-1908)

Using the wind tunnel Wenham mounted various shapes, measuring the lift and drag forces created by the air rushing by. For such a simple experiment, the results were of great significance to aeronautics. Wenham and his colleagues were astounded to find that, at low angles of incidence, the lift-to-drag ratios of test surfaces could be surprisingly high, roughly 5 at a 15 degree angle of attack. With such high lift-to-drag ratios, wings could support substantial loads, making powered flight seem much more attainable than previously thought possible.

Wenham presented a paper to the society, largely based on George Cayley's work on cambered wings but he had taken the work further and to test his ideas had built several gliders both manned and unmanned, some of which had as many as five stacked wings. Wenham realised that a long thin wing was better because it had more leading edge for its area and this is possibly the first reference to "aspect ratio".

With the arrival of the wind tunnel, aircraft designers finally began to understand the factors that controlled lift and drag, but they were still plagued by the question of model scale. Can the experimental results obtained with a one-tenth scale model be applied to the real, full-sized aircraft? Almost all wind tunnel tests were and still are performed with scale models because wind tunnels capable of handling full-sized aircraft are simply too expensive.

Towards the end of the nineteenth century, a lot of study and research was carried out by gentlemen of wealth who had in interest in the natural world and a passion to be the first to achieve manned powered flight.

Matthew Piers Watt Boulton

Among those people was one Matthew Piers Watt Boulton, a British classicist, member of the British Metaphysical Society, amateur scientist and inventor. Boulton studied the problems of lateral control and was the first person to patent an aileron control system in 1868, some 36 years before it was first employed in manned flight by Robert Esnault Pelterie in 1904.

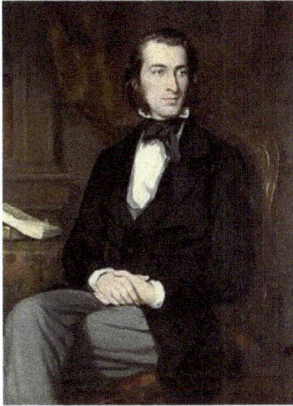

Matthew Piers Watt
Boulton

In 1873, five years after Boulton's aileron patent, the French military engineer and aircraft designer Charles Renard, built and flew a small unmanned multi-wing glider incorporating ailerons which he termed "winglets" at St.-Eloi, near Arras.

Boulton's British patent, completed in 1868, was issued more than 35 years before ailerons were "reinvented" in France, and ailerons were later re-patented in the United States by Glen Curtiss in 1911, Boulton's 1868 patent having become lost and forgotten until a few years before they came into general use in 1915.

Towards the end of the nineteenth century a large number of inventors, designers and scientists were focusing their attention on the problems of flight. Lacking a suitably powerful engine, they concentrated their efforts on being able to control the aircraft in flight. People like the Englishman Horatio Phillips.

Horatio Phillips

Phillips conducted extensive wind tunnel research on aerofoil sections, proving the principles of aerodynamic lift foreseen by Cayley and Wenham. His findings underpin all modern aerofoil design.

An English aviation pioneer, he was famous for building multiple flying machines with many more sets of lifting surfaces than are normal, like the one shown in. However, he made a more lasting contribution to aeronautics with his work on aerofoil design.

He devised and built a wind tunnel in which he studied a wide variety of aerofoil shapes. The tunnel was unusual in that the gas flow was provided by steam rather than air.

By 1884 he was able to register his first patent, and more were to follow. He demonstrated the truth of George Cayley's idea that giving the upper surface greater curvature than the lower accelerates the upper airflow, reducing pressure above the wing and so creating lift.

Phillips' 1904 flying machine

Karl Wilhelm Otto Lilienthal (1848 – 1896)

Otto Lilienthal (1848-1896)

Karl Wilhelm Otto Lilienthal was a German aviator who became known as the "flying man," and was the first person to make well-documented, repeated, successful flights with gliders. Lilienthal became something of a celebrity at the time, with newspapers and magazines publishing photographs of him gliding. This publicity captured the imagination of the wider general public and favourably influenced scientific opinion about the possibility of maned flight.

His gliders were carefully designed to distribute weight as evenly as possible to ensure a stable flight and he controlled them by changing the centre of gravity by shifting his body, much like modern hang gliders today. However, they were difficult to manoeuvre and had a tendency to pitch down, from which it was difficult to recover, the reason for which was that he held the glider by his shoulders, rather than hanging from it like a modern hang glider. Only his legs and lower body could be moved and this limited the amount of weight he could move.

Lilienthal about to fly a monoplane glider

In 1894 he filed a U.S. patent that directed pilots to grip the bar of an A-frame for carrying and flying the glider that sounds very much like the control frame of modern hang-gliders. With his brother Gustav Lilienthal, he made over 2,000 flights in gliders, until on 9th August 1896, the glider he was flying stalled and he was unable to regain control. Falling from about 15 m (50 ft), he broke his neck on landing and died the next day, 10th August 1896.

Robert Esnault Pelterie (1881 – 1957)

Pelterie's first experiments in aviation were not successful, being based on an incomplete understanding of the Wright brothers' 1902 glider.

Although using a version of the wing-warping which the Wright brothers had used to control their aircraft, his did not work properly and he abandoned it, considering it to be dangerous.

His later approach developed the concept of the aileron and he fitted a pair of mid-gap control surfaces in front of the wings.

In 1906 he began his first experiments in towed flight and on 19th September 1906 he flew 500 m (1,600 ft). He made his first powered flight on 10th October 1907, a distance of 100 m (330 ft) with the REP 1 that was driven by a seven-cylinder, 30 hp air-cooled engine of his own design.

Robert Palterie (1881-1957)

Pelterie in flight in his monoplane

Trials of the monoplane REP 2 began on June 8th, 1908. This aircraft set a record with a 1,200 m (3,900 ft) flight, reaching an altitude of 30 m (98 ft) and was possibly the first to be controlled with a joystick. After a modified version of this plane was flown for the last time in 1909 at Rheims, Pelterie stopped flying and instead focused on the development and manufacture of aircraft.

Pelterie later became interested in space travel and not knowing of Tsiolkovsky's 1903 work, produced a paper in 1913 that presented the rocket equation and calculated the energies required to reach the Moon and nearby planets and In 1929 he proposed the idea of the ballistic missile for military bombardment.

By 1930, Esnault-Pelterie and Barré had persuaded the French War Department to fund a study of the concept and in 1931, the two began experimenting with various types of rocket propulsion systems, including liquid propellants. The same year he ran a demonstration of a rocket engine powered with gasoline and liquid oxygen. During an experiment with a rocket design using tetra-nitromethane he lost three fingers from his right hand during an explosion and ultimately, their work failed to create an interest in rocketry within France.

Octave Chanute (1832 – 1910)

Octave Chanute (
1832-1910)

Octave Chanute first became interested in aviation after watching a balloon take off in Peoria, Illinois, in 1856 and after he retired from his railroad career in 1883, he decided to spend his time furthering the new science of aviation. Applying his engineering knowledge and background, Chanute collected all available data he could from around the world and combined it with the knowledge he'd gathered as a civil engineer. He published his findings in a series of articles in "The Railroad and Engineering Journal" from 1891to 1893, which were then republished in an influential book entitled "Progress in Flying Machines" in 1894. This was the most systematic global survey of fixed-wing heavier-than-air aviation research published up to that time.

Multi-wing glider of Chanute's design

Jean-Marie Le Bris (1817 – 1872)

Jean-Marie Le Bris
(1817-1872)

Le Bris built a glider, the design of which was inspired by the shape of the Albatross and named it unsurprisingly, "The Artificial Albatross".

In 1856 he flew it briefly on the beach of Sainte-Anne-la-Palud, the aircraft was launched by being placed on a cart that was towed by a horse. He actually managed to gain height, which was a first for a heavier-than-air flying machine, and reports state that he reached a height of 100 m (330 ft), for a distance of 200 m (660 ft). Some doubt has been expressed to me about the accuracy of these figures and after analysis they do seem remarkable. However, whether this account is accurate or not, is does seem credible that Le Bris did make a successful gliding flight in his machine on that date.

The Artificial Albatross photographed on it's carriage in 1868

In 1868, with the support of the French Navy, he built a second flying machine, which he tried out this time in Brest but without a great deal of success. It was almost identical to his first flying machine, except that it was lighter and had a system to shift weight distribution. His flying machine became the first ever to be photographed, albeit on the ground, in 1868.

Although the first well-documented glider was built by George Cayley and flown by an employee in 1853 and John Stringfellow had built some small unmanned models in 1848, Le Bris invented more effective flight controls, which could act on the incidence of wings and which were patented in March 1857.

Alphonse Pénaud (1850 – 1889)

Alphonse Pénaud was a 19th-century French pioneer of aviation, designer and engineer. He employed many of Cayley's ideas, including the use of twisted rubber to power model aircraft. He built a model aeroplane in 1817 which was the first aerodynamically stable flying model and then went on to design a full-sized aircraft with some advanced features such as dihedral wings, but failed to get backing for the project, and eventually committed suicide in 1880, aged 30. A dihedral wing is one that has an upward angle from horizontal so the wing tip is higher off the ground when not in flight. Having dihedral wings helps with lateral stability.

Victor Tatin (1843 – 1913)

Victor Tatin

In 1879, Victor Tatin flew a model aircraft which was a monoplane with twin tractor propellers but also had a separate horizontal tail. It was powered by compressed air and flown tethered to a pole. This was the first model to have taken off under its own power from the ground.

Taton's model plane 1879

Clément Ader (1841 – 1925)

In 1890 Clément Ader claimed to have solved the problem of powered flight but as far as can be ascertained, his bat-like looking craft only managed to skim the ground at a height of about 20cm for a distance of some 50 metres and this is not accepted as being sustained controlled flight.

Ader later published a very popular book on aviation called "L'Aviation Militare" in which he advanced his idea for an aircraft carrier. *"An aeroplane-carrying vessel is indispensable. These vessels will be constructed on a plan very different from what is currently used. First of all, the deck will be cleared of all obstacles. It will be flat, as wide as possible without jeopardizing the nautical lines of the hull, and it will look like a landing field"*.

Clément Ader

Alder's flying machine the "Eole" in 1890

Sir Hiram Maxim (1840 – 1916)

Hiram Maxim

Hiram Maxim was an American born English inventor best known for the invention of a fully transportable automatic machine gun.

He constructed a large machine with a wingspan of 32 metres, a length of 44 metres, fore and aft horizontal surfaces and a crew of three. Twin propellers were powered by two lightweight compound steam engines each delivering 180 hp. The overall weight was 8,000 pounds (3,600 kg) and it was intended as a test rig to investigate aerodynamic lift, so lacking flight controls, it ran on rails with a second set of rails above the wheels to restrain it.

It was completed in 1894, and when it tested it broke from the rails and became airborne for about 200 yards at two to three feet of altitude and was badly damaged upon falling back to the ground. It was subsequently repaired, but Maxim abandoned his experiments shortly afterwards.

Maxim's flyng machine and test track 1894

Lawrence Hargrave (1850 – 1915)

Lawrece Hargrave

Lawrence Hargrave experimented with and established the box kite as a stable aerial platform and in 1894 he linked four of his kites together and added a sling seat. He flew up to a height of 16 feet (4.9 m), the kite line was moored via a spring balance to two sandbags. Hargrave carried an anemometer and a clinometer with him to measure windspeed and the angle of the kite line.

Hargrave was an excellent experimenter and his models were well crafted and he always refused to patent his inventions, anxious only that he might succeed in adding to the sum of human knowledge

Hargrave reported the results of his experiments and these were seen by Abbott Lawrence Rotch of the meteorological observatory at Harvard University, who constructed a kite from the published particulars. This was then modified and adopted by the weather bureau of the United States. The use of box-kites for meteorological observations became widespread, after which the principle was applied to gliders, and in October 1906 Alberto Santos-Dumont used the box-kite principle in his aeroplane to make his first flight. Until 1909 the box-kite aeroplane was the usual type in Europe.

Hargrave had not confined himself to the problem of constructing a heavier-than-air machine that would fly, for he had given much time to the means of propulsion. In 1889 he invented a rotary engine. This form of engine was used a lot in early aviation but the weight of the required materials meant that he was unable to get sufficient power from his engines to build an independent flying machine.

Professor Richard Threlfall who was elected a fellow of the Royal Society in 1899 called Hargrave "the inventor of human flight."

Samuel Pierpont Langley (1834 – 1906)

On May 6th, 1896, Langley's Aerodrome No. 5 made the first successful sustained flight of a heavier-than-air unpiloted, engine-driven craft. It was launched from a spring-operated catapult that was mounted on top of a houseboat on the Potomac River near Quantico, Virginia. The idea of flying from and landing in the river was to save weight by not needing any landing gear. Two flights were made that afternoon, one of 1,005 metres (3,297 ft) and a second of 700 metres (2,300 ft), at a speed of approximately 25 miles per hour (40 km/h). On November 28th 1896, another successful flight was made with the Aerodrome No. 6. This flight, of 1,460 metres (4,790 ft), was witnessed and photographed by Alexander Graham Bell.

Samuel Pierport Langley

With the successes of the Aerodrome No. 5 and No. 6, Langley started looking for funding to build a full-scale man-carrying version of his designs. Possibly motivated by the Spanish American war, the U.S. government granted him $50,000 to develop a man-carrying flying machine for aerial reconnaissance. Langley planned on building a scaled-up version known as the Aerodrome A, and started with the smaller Quarter-scale Aerodrome, which flew twice on June 18th 1901, and then again with a newer and more powerful engine in 1903.

With the basic design successfully tested, he then turned to the problem of a suitable engine. He contracted Stephen Balzer to build one, but was disappointed when it delivered only 8 hp (6.0 kW) instead of 12 hp (8.9 kW) he expected. Langley's assistant, Charles M. Manly then reworked the design into a five-cylinder water-cooled radial engine that delivered 52 hp (39 kW) at 950 rpm, a feat that took years to duplicate. Now with both power and a design, Langley put the two together with great hopes but the resulting aircraft proved to be too fragile. Simply scaling up the original small models had resulted in a design that was too weak to hold itself together. Two launches in late 1903 both ended with the *Aerodrome* immediately crashing into the water. The pilot, Manly, was thankfully rescued each time. It was apparent that the aircraft's control system was too cumbersome to allow quick pilot responses, and it had no method of lateral control, added to which the *Aerodrome*'s aerial stability was marginal.

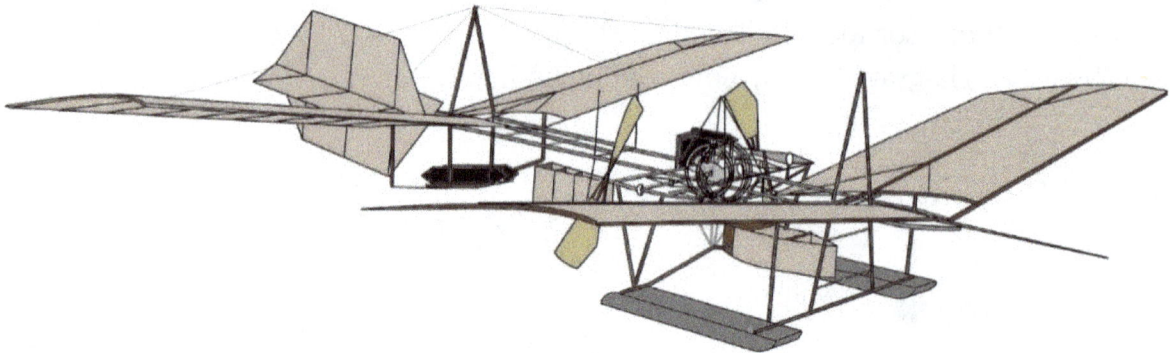

Impression of Langley's aerodrome

Langley's attempts to gain further funding failed, and his efforts ended. Nine days after his second abortive launch on December 8th, the Wright brothers successfully flew their *Flyer*.

Glen Curtiss then made 93 different modifications to the Aerodrome and flew this very different aircraft in 1914 and without acknowledging that any modifications had been made, the Smithsonian Institution stated that Langley's Aerodrome was the first machine to be built that was, "capable of flight."

This statement by the Smithsonian resulted in a feud with Orville Wright, (Wilbur having died in 1912) who accused the Smithsonian of misrepresenting flying machine history. Orville backed up his protest by refusing to donate the original 1903 Kitty Hawk Flyer to the Smithsonian, instead donating it to the extensive collections of the Science Museum of London in 1928. The dispute finally ended in 1942 when the Smithsonian published details of the Curtiss modifications to the Aerodrome and recanted its claims for the aircraft. A year later the Wright Flyer was returned to the United States from England and it now resides in the National Air and Space Museum in Washington D.C.

John Joseph Montgomery (1858 – 1911)

Between 1883-1900, the American John Joseph Montgomery (1858 – 1911) developed a series of three manned gliders, before conducting his own independent investigations into aerodynamics and circulation of lift. Montgomery devised different control methods for his gliders, including weight shifting for roll and an elevator for pitch in 1884. Subsequent designs used hinged, pilot-operated trailing edge flaps on the wings for roll control and later, a full wing warping system for both pitch and roll.

Montgomery in one of his gliders

First Flights

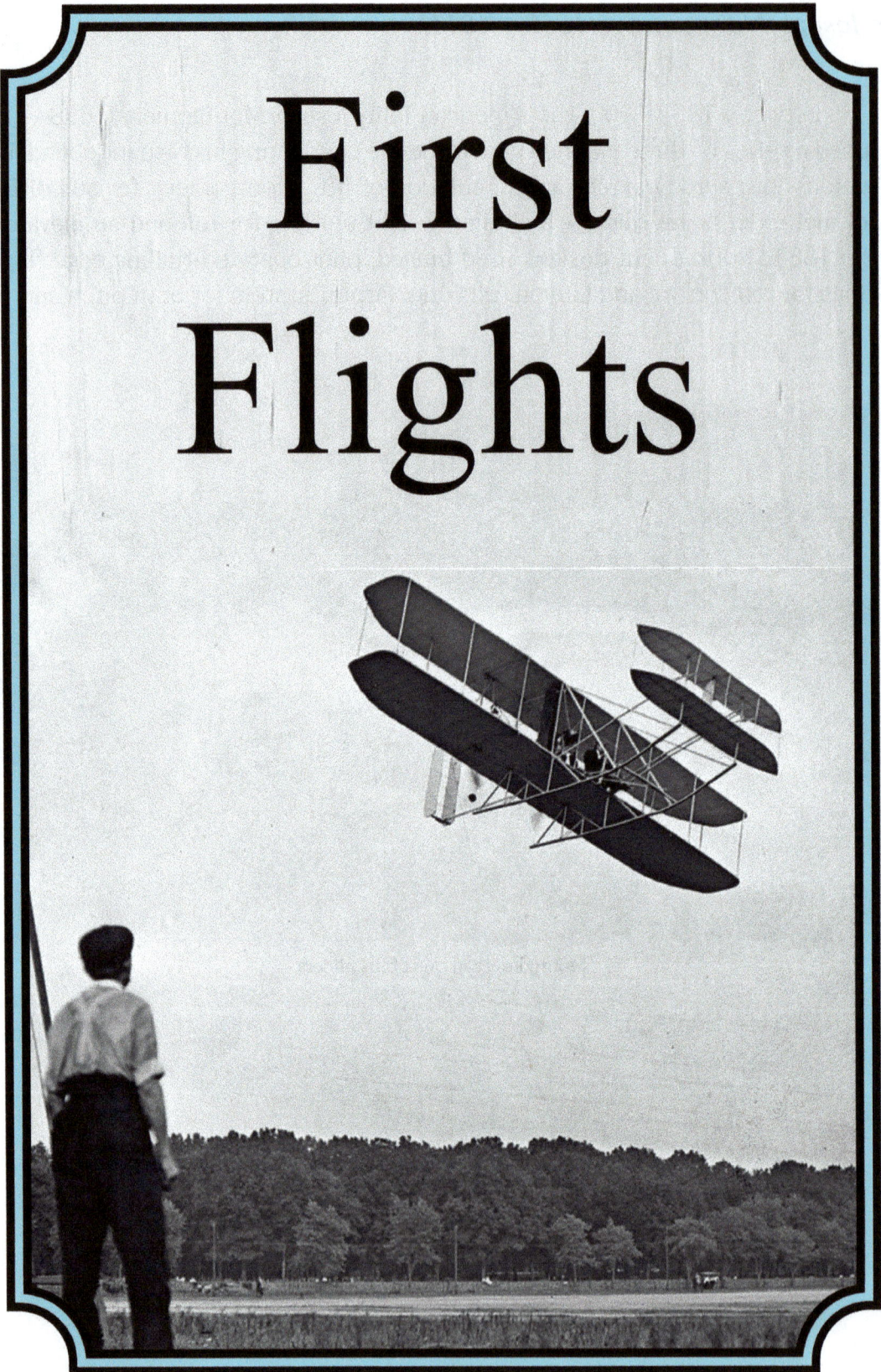

Chapter Two

First Flights

Who was first?

Ask anyone who achieved the first powered flight and the vast majority of people will declare that it was the Wright brothers in 1903, but is that correct? Certainly there is no doubt that the Wright brothers' "Flyer" rose into the air over Kitty Hawk, North Carolina on the 17th December 1903, it is too well documented not to have happened, but was it the first time man had taken to the air in a powered aircraft and flown?

Although the Wright brothers acknowledged the contributions of many others who had nearly succeeded before them, they quickly dismissed the claims of one Gustave Whitehead. In the 2013 edition of, "Jane's All the World's Aircraft," however, an editorial reveals that the Smithsonian Institute in Washington only secured possession of the Wright brothers' "Flyer" from Orville Write, after signing a legally binding document stating that, "the Smithsonian shall not state that any aircraft, earlier than the Wright aeroplane of 1903, was capable of carrying a man under its own power."

Many suggest that the signing of that document means the Smithsonian is unable to impartially investigate any claims of earlier flights.

Did Gustave Whitehead fly two years before the Wright brothers? We will probably never know for sure, because although, Jane's All the World's Aircraft, seems to give credit to Whitehead's claim, many other reputable aviation historians dispute it.

Gustave Whitehead (1874 – 1927)

Gustave Whitehead

Gustave Weißkopf was a German aviation pioneer who emigrated to the U.S. where he soon changed his name to Whitehead and from 1897 to 1915, he designed and built early flying machines and engines.

On August 14th, 1901, two and a half years before the Wright Brothers' flight, he claimed to have carried out a controlled, powered flight in his Number 21 monoplane at Fairfield, Connecticut. The flight was reported in the "Bridgeport Sunday Herald" a local newspaper and 30 years later, several people, who were questioned by a researcher, claimed to have witnessed that flight or others by Whitehead.

Whether Whitehead flew before the Wright brothers or not, one thing that he certainly deserves credit for, is his design of a light weight acetylene-fuelled engine.

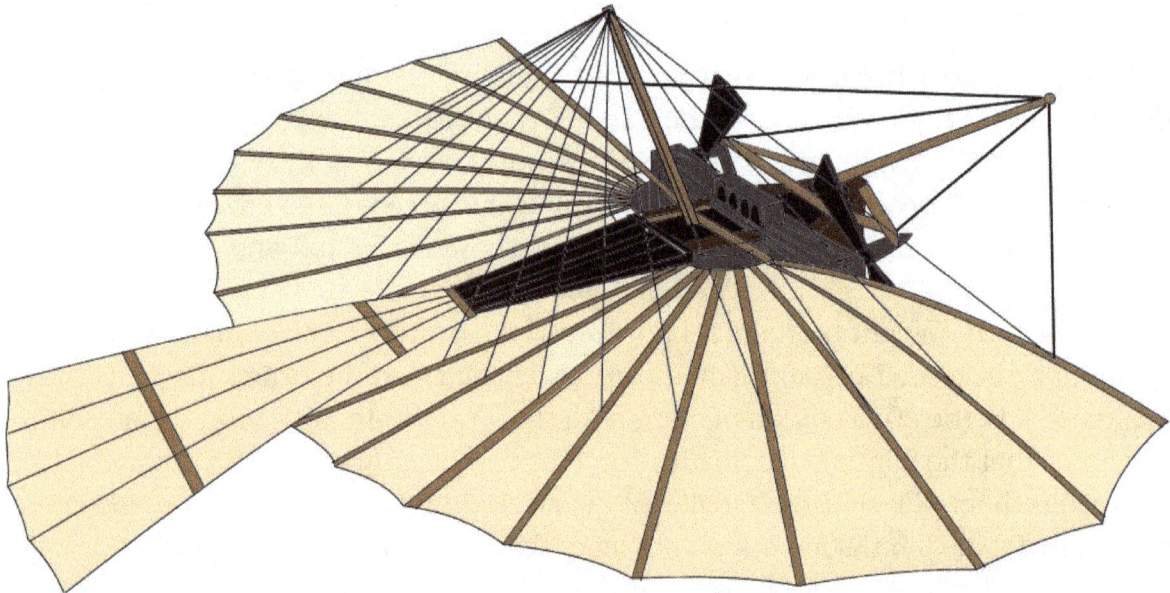

Impression of Whitehead's Aircraft No1

Whitehead did not see the achievement of the first flight as his only goal, he wanted to grow a business and thought that once flight became accepted, he could sell his aircraft to business men who would house their flying machines at their homes and drive them to a place to take off. He obviously did not foresee the development of aerodromes. Whitehead therefore equipped his machine, known as "aircraft No 21, with two acetylene-fuelled engines of his own design: a 10 hp engine for road wheels and 20 hp engine as the main power source of forward flight. At an appropriate moment during take-off and at the flick of a lever, he could transfer the road engine's output to boost the motor driving the twin propellers. He was by no means the only aviator to incorporate powered wheels into his designs but the practice soon died out.

The Wright Brothers

Wilbur Wright (1867 – 1912)
Orville Wright (1871 – 1948)

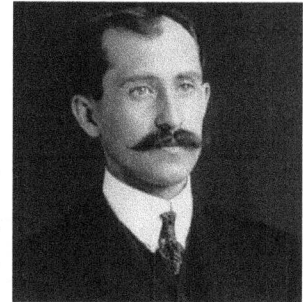

Wilber and Orville Wight are generally accepted as having invented and built the world's first, heavier than air aeroplane to accomplish a manned, sustained and controlled flight. It happened on the

Wilbur Wright

Orville Wright

17th December 1903 four miles south of Kitty Hawk, North Carolina and in 1904-05 they developed their machine into the first practical fixed wing aircraft, the Wright Flyer 111.

The brothers' breakthrough came with their creation of a three-axis control system which enabled the pilot to steer the aircraft effectively and to maintain its equilibrium. From the beginning of their aeronautical work, the Wright brothers had focused on developing a reliable method of pilot control as the key to achieving powered flight, whereas most others had concentrated more on developing more powerful engines. Their first patent for example, was not for a flying machine but for a system of aerodynamic control that manipulated a flying machine's surfaces.

in December 1892 the brothers, capitalising on the development of the safety cycle and the increased popularity of cycling, opened a cycle repair and sales shop "the Wright Cycle Exchange," and in 1896 they began manufacturing their own brand of cycle. They used the profits from this business endeavour to fund their growing interest in flight and in the early or mid-1890s they read newspaper or magazine articles about the dramatic glides that had been performed by Otto Lilienthal in Germany.

There were several events in 1896 that captured the interest of the brothers, Samuel Langley's successful flight of an unmanned steam powered model, Octave Chanute's glider flights and the tragic death of Karl Wilhelm Otto Lilienthal. The brothers later said that it was with the death of Otto Lilienthal that their interest in flight research really began, drawing on the work of Cayley, Langley, Lilienthal and Chanute.

Wilbur wright had noted, after observing birds in flight, that they changed the angle of the ends of their wings to make their bodies roll right or left. The brothers decided this would also be a good way for a flying machine to turn, to bank or lean into the turn just like a bird, and just like a person riding a bicycle, an experience with which they were thoroughly familiar. Equally important, they hoped this method would enable recovery when the wind tilted the machine to one side, thus restoring "lateral balance." They puzzled over how to achieve the same effect with man-made wings and eventually discovered wing-warping, illustrated here, when Wilbur idly twisted a long inner-tube box at their bicycle shop.

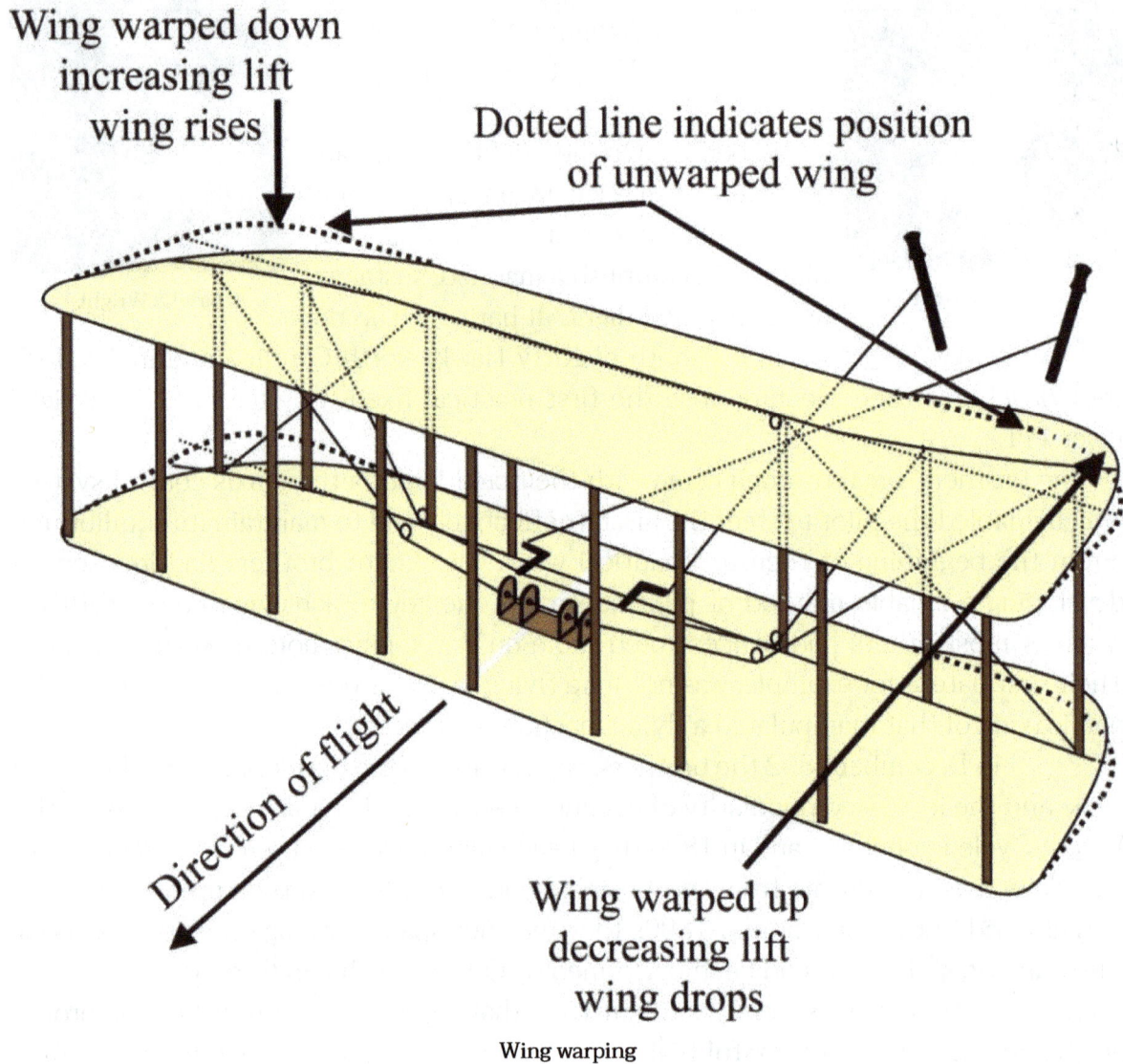

Wing warped down increasing lift wing rises

Dotted line indicates position of unwarped wing

Direction of flight

Wing warped up decreasing lift wing drops

Wing warping

Most designers at this time envisaged aircraft as steering in much the same way as other craft, like trains and boats, they thought a rudder would do the steering while the aeroplane stayed level in the air, the idea of deliberately rolling or banking to one side in order to turn seemed both dangerous and unnecessary. In 1899 the brothers built a biplane kite with wing warping capability; the warp being controlled by four cords attached to the kite and operated by the kite flyer.

A Wright brothers' kite

The Wright brothers based the design of their kite and full-size gliders on work done in the 1890s by other aviation pioneers. They adopted the basic design of the Chanute-Herring biplane hang glider or the "double-decker" as the Wrights called it, which had flown well in the 1896 experiments near Chicago, and they used the aeronautical data on lift that Otto Lilienthal had published.

The brothers designed the wings of their plane with camber, a curvature of the top surface. They had not been the ones to discover this principle, it's advantage over a flat one first being discussed by Sir George Cayley, but they took advantage of it. Lilienthal, whose work the Wrights had carefully studied, also used cambered wings in his gliders, proving its advantage over flat ones in actual flight.

The wooden uprights between the wings of the Wright glider were braced by wires and was their own version of Chanute's modified Pratt truss, a bridge-building design he used for his biplane glider. They mounted their horizontal elevator in front of the wings rather than behind, apparently believing this feature would help to avoid or at least protect them from a nosedive and crash, like the one that had killed Lilienthal. Wilbur however, incorrectly believed a tail was unnecessary and their first two gliders did not have one.

Wilbur lay flat on the lower wing, as planned, in order to reduce aerodynamic drag and as a glide ended, he was supposed to lower himself into a vertical position through an opening in the lower wing and land on his feet with his arms wrapped over the framework.

Within a few glides, however, they discovered that he could remain prone on the wing without undue danger when landing and they made all their subsequent flights in that position for the next five years.

In 1902, their third glider, after a few modifications, did use a trailing rudder for yaw and it responded well to the controls. They initially used wing warping to control roll and a forward elevator for pitch. The glider, however, delivered two major disappointments. It produced only about one-third the lift calculated and some-

Wilbur having just landed their 1901 glider

times pointed opposite to the intended direction of a turn when Wilbur used the wing-warping control, a problem later to become known as adverse yaw. On the trip home, a deeply dejected Wilbur remarked to Orville that man would not fly in a thousand years.

The poor lift experienced with the gliders led the Wrights to question the accuracy of Lilienthal's data, as well as the "Smeaton coefficient" of air pressure, a value which had been in use for over 100 years and was part of the accepted equation for lift.

(In 1759, John Smeaton, (1724 – 1792) an English civil engineer, had published a paper entitled, "An Experimental Enquiry Concerning the Natural Powers of Water and Wind to Turn Mills and Other Machines Depending on Circular Motion"). Smeaton developed the concepts and data which became the basis for the Smeaton coefficient, the lift equation used by the Wright brothers.

It has the form:

$L = kV2\ ACl$ where:
L is the lift
k is the Smeaton coefficient
V2 is the velocity squared
A is the area in square feet
Cl is the lift coefficient (the lift relative to the drag of a plate of the same area)

To learn whether errors existed in Lilienthal's data tables, the brothers used one of their bicycles for a new type of experiment. They made a model-sized aerofoil and a counter-acting flat plate, both according to dimensions Lilienthal had specified, and attached them to an extra bicycle wheel, which they mounted horizontally in front of the handlebars, an illustration of which is shown here.

Pedalling strenuously on a local street to create airflow over the apparatus, they observed that the third wheel rotated against the aerofoil instead of remaining motionless as Lilienthal's formula predicted. The experiment confirmed their suspicion that either the standard Smeaton coefficient or Lilienthal's coefficients of lift and drag or both of them—were in error.

The brothers then built a six-foot (1.8m) wind tunnel in their workshop and between October and December 1901 they conducted systematic tests on dozens of model wings. The "balances" they devised and mounted inside the tunnel to hold the wings may have looked crude, made of bicycle spokes and scrap metal, but they were as critical to the ultimate success of the Wright brothers, as were the gliders. The devices allowed the brothers to balance lift against drag and accurately calculate the performance of each wing. They could also see which wings worked well as they looked through the viewing window in the top of the tunnel.

Initial conditions

Model wing

Drag plate

s = spoke length
b = angle

s

b   b

Test conditions

Wind

Lift
L

A = rotation angle

a

b + a   b - a

Drag
D

$$L \sin (b+a) = D \cos (b-a)$$

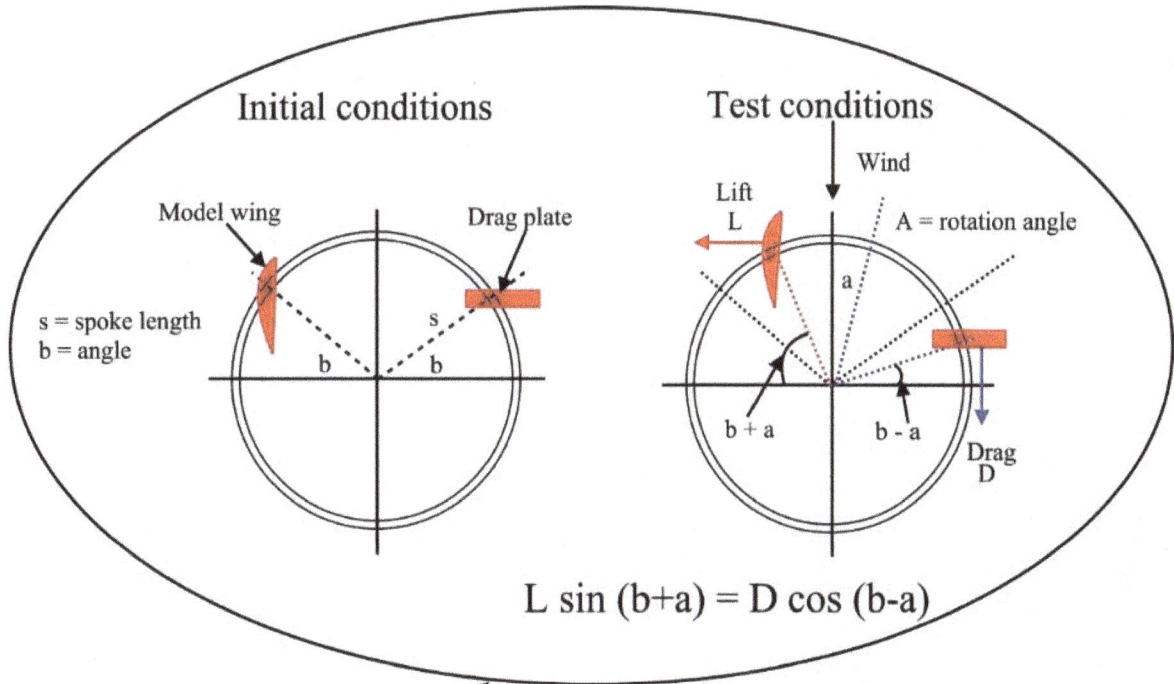

Wright brothers' bicycle wheel experiment

The tests provided them with a huge amount of valuable new data and showed that the poor lift of the 1900 and 1901 gliders was almost entirely due to an incorrect Smeaton value. They also established that Lilienthal's published data was fairly accurate for the tests he had done.

Over the years a wide variety of values had previously been measured for the Smeaton coefficient; Chanute identified some of them and Wilbur knew that Langley had used a lower number than the traditional one. Determined to confirm the correct

Smeaton value, Wilbur performed his own calculations using measurements collected during kite and free flights of the 1901 glider. His results correctly showed that the coefficient was very close to 0.0033 (similar to the number Langley had used), not the traditional 0.0054, which would significantly exaggerate predicted lift.

With typical caution, the brothers first flew their 1902 glider as a kite, the same as they had done with previous tests, and using the newly obtained figures, the 1902 glider flew at a much flatter angle of attack and held up its tether lines almost vertically, and thus clearly demonstrating a much better lift to drag ratio.

The 1902 glider flown as a kite

It was also in 1902 that they realised that it was the wing warping that caused the aircraft to turn away from the direction of bank, (adverse yaw). Increasing lift on one wing also increased the drag causing the front of the aircraft to point away from the direction of turn. It was for that reason that they incorporated a rear steerable double rudder to counteract the adverse yaw. In short, it was the Wright brothers that discovered that the real purpose of a rear steerable rudder, was not to change the direction of travel, as the rudder on a boat, but rather to align the aircraft correctly during a banking turn and eliminate adverse yaw. The actual turn was achieved by banking the aircraft with wing warping, and later with ailerons.

Their new glider with its steerable rudder performed so well that they were able to make numerous successful flights and it was the foundation of three axis control, wing warping for bank or roll, a forward sited elevator for pitch and a steerable rear rudder for yaw control, all they needed to do was add power and the true aeroplane had arrived.

They built their "Wright Flyer" from spruce and covered it in muslin, after which they looked for a suitable propeller and engine. They wrote to several engine manufacturers, but none could meet their need for a sufficiently lightweight engine, so they enlisted the help of their shop mechanic.

In the end, the wright brothers built their own 12 hp, four-cylinder engine in eight weeks with the aid of Charles Taylor, their shop mechanic and machinist, but without drawings. The engine weighed 170 lbs. including the radiator, water and fuel tanks, and 1.5 gallons of petrol. With no throttle, the four-stroke engine always ran at about 1,000 rpm. but output could be somewhat controlled by retarding or advancing the spark timing.

The crankcase, cylinder water jacket, mounting lugs, and part of the intake manifold were cast as a single piece of aluminum and because it was hand-made, there were no interchangeable parts, each piston for example, only fitted the cylinder it was made for.

The valves were of the poppet type and the camshaft was driven by a bicycle chain from their workshop. The fuel was gravity fed into the intake manifold where it was vaporized by the hot water jacket and sucked through the inlet valve and into the cylinders. The engine needed to be overhauled after every twelve hours of use.

The Wright brothers' engine

There were no established design formulae for either a marine or an air propeller at that time so they set about designing and carving their own. Working on the assumption that a propeller was simply an aerofoil mounted vertically, they used wind tunnel tests to design one and they ended up with a propeller that was over eight feet long and later discovered to be 66% efficient. They decided to use two counter-rotating propellers in order to cancel out torque and to transfer power from the engine to the propellers they devised a simple chain and sprocket arrangement running from the engine crankshaft to a pair of steel propeller shafts. To make the propellers rotate in opposite directions they simple twisted one of the two chains into a figure of eight.

At Kill Devil Hills, they endured weeks of delays caused by broken propeller shafts during engine tests and after the shafts were replaced, a process that required two trips back to Dayton, Wilbur won a coin-toss and made a three-second flight attempt on December 12th 1903, stalling after take-off and causing minor damage to the Flyer. December 13th 1903, was a Sunday so the brothers didn't make any attempts that day, even though the weather was good, so their first powered test flight happened on the 14th December 1903.

In a message to their family, Wilbur referred to the trial as having *"only partial success"*, stating *"the power is ample, and but for a trifling error due to lack of experience with this machine and this method of starting, the machine would undoubtedly have flown beautifully."*

Following repairs, the Wright brothers finally took to the air on December 17th 1903, making two flights, each from level ground into a freezing headwind gusting to 27 miles per hour (43 km/h). The first flight, by Orville at 10:35 am, of 120 feet (37 m) in 12 seconds, at a speed of only 6.8 miles per hour (10.9 km/h) over the ground, was recorded in a now famous photograph shown below.

The next two flights covered approximately 175 and 200 feet (53 and 61 m), by Wilbur and Orville respectively. Their altitude was about 10 feet (3.0 m) above the ground. The following is Orville Wright's account of the final flight of the day:

"Wilbur started the fourth and last flight at just about 12 o'clock. The first few hundred feet were up and down, as before, but by the time three hundred ft had been covered, the

machine was under much better control. The course for the next four or five hundred feet had but little undulation. However, when out about eight hundred feet the machine began pitching again, and, in one of its darts downward, struck the ground. The distance over the ground was measured to be 852 feet; the time of the flight was 59 seconds. The frame supporting the front rudder was badly broken, but the main part of the machine was not injured at all. We estimated that the machine could be put in condition for flight again in about a day or two."

Five people witnessed the flights: Adam Etheridge, John T. Daniels, who snapped the famous "first flight" photo using Orville's pre-positioned camera, Will Dough, all of the U.S. government coastal lifesaving crew; area businessman W.C. Brinkley; and Johnny Moore, a teenaged boy who lived in the area. After the men hauled the Flyer back from its fourth flight, a powerful gust of wind flipped it over several times despite the crew's attempts to hold it down. Severely damaged, the aeroplane never flew again. The brothers shipped it home, and years later Orville restored it and lent it to several U.S. museums and institutions for display, then to a British museum, before it was finally installed in 1948 in the Smithsonian Institution in Washington, D.C. where it currently resides.

Orville takes off for the first flight with Wilbur running beside

In 1904 they built the Wright Flyer 11 and began slowly withdrawing from their cycle business to concentrate on marketing a practical aeroplane, a brave decision owing to the fact that they were not rich by any means and had no government backing. For this reason, they became much more secretive about their work on the advice of their patent attorney Henry Toulmin.

After several crashes in Flyer 11, Wilbur finally made the first ever complete circular flight in history by a manned heavier-than-air powered machine, covering 4,080 feet (1,244 m) in about a minute and a half. Eventually they scrapped the now somewhat battered and bruised Flyer 11 but kept the engine and built a new craft, the Flyer 111, shown here.

The Wright Flyer 111

After Wilbur suffered a near fatal crash on 14th July 1905, they rebuilt the machine with the forward elevator and rear rudder both enlarged and placed several feet further away from the wings. They also installed a separate control for the rear rudder instead of linking it to the wing-warping cradle as before. Each of the three axes, pitch, roll and yaw, now had its own independent control and these modifications greatly improved stability and control, enabling a series of six long flights ranging from 17 to 38 minutes and 11 to 24 miles (39 km) around the three-quarter mile course over Huffman Prairie between September 26th and October 5th.

Wilbur made the last and longest flight, 24.5 miles (39.4 km) in 38 minutes and 3 seconds, ending with a safe landing when the fuel ran out. The flight was seen by a number of people, including several invited friends, their father Milton, and neighbouring farmers.

Despite these remarkable events, and possibly due to their own secrecy surrounding their test flights, there was a great deal of scepticism about their achievements in both the American press and in Europe.

The Wright brothers didn't make any flights at all in 1906 or 1907, instead spending their time trying to persuade the U.S. and European governments that they had indeed invented a successful flying machine and that they were prepared to negotiate a contract to sell such machines. They also experimented with a pontoon and engine setup on the Miami River (Ohio) in hopes of flying from the water but these experiments proved unsuccessful. Disappointed that the American government appeared unimpressed they turned their attention to France where there was great enthusiasm for aviation and also to Britain and Germany where they met aviation representatives who were impressed with the Model A Flyer that they had shipped over.

On returning to the U.S. they found that the U.S. Board of Ordnance in Washington had had a change of heart. Both America and France now wanted them to bid for contracts and both contracts required them to give public demonstrations and to carry a passenger. To comply with the contracts, they modified their 1905 Flyer by adding two seats and upright control levers.

After several tests with sandbags in the passenger seat, Charlie Furnas, a helper from Dayton, became the first fixed-wing aircraft passenger in a few short flights on 14th May 1908. For safety, and as a promise to their father, Wilbur and Orville never flew together but several newspaper reporters at the time mistakenly took Orville's flight with Furnas as both brothers flying together. Later that day, after flying solo for seven minutes, Wilbur suffered his worst ever crash when, still not well-acquainted with the two new control levers, he apparently moved one the wrong way and slammed the Flyer into the sand at between 40 and 50 miles per hour. Luckily, he emerged with only bruises and a cut nose, but the accident ended both the practice flights and that aeroplane's flying career.

On August 8th 1908, Wilbur Wright made his first flight in public at the Hunaudieres race course, five miles south of Le Mans, France and over the next several weeks he made headlines around the world with one stunning flight after another, demonstrating once and for all that the Wrights' claim to priority in the invention of the aeroplane was true and that their aeroplanes were capable of tight turns and a degree of control not possible with other machines.

Orville Wright joined his brother in the limelight on September 3rd 1908, when he made his first public flight at Fort Myer, Virginia. Tragedy struck however on September 17th when Orville crashed at Fort Myer while flying with Thomas Etholen Selfridge, a first lieutenant in the U. S. Army, as a passenger. Three or four minutes into the flight, a blade on one of the two wooden propellers split and caused the engine to shake violently.

Orville shut down the engine but was unable to control the aeroplane. The propeller had hit a bracing wire and pulled a rear rudder from its vertical position to a horizontal one causing the aeroplane to pitch nose-down and rendering control impossible.

The Wright Flyer hit the ground hard, and both men were injured. Orville suffered a fractured leg and several broken ribs but the unfortunate Thomas Selfridge suffered a fractured skull and a few hours later, he became the first person to die in a powered aeroplane crash. Orville recovered, but lived with the pain resulting from the accident for the rest of his life.

Lieutenant Thomas
Etholen Selfridge

Once Orville Wright was back on his feet, he and his sister Katharine joined their brother in Europe. The three Wrights were now the toast of the continent. Crowned heads, political leaders, captains of industry and ordinary folk travelled to witness the miracle of flight. Wilbur capped off this extraordinary year with a flight of more than 76 miles in 2 hours 18 minutes 33 seconds on December 31st which earned him the Michelin Cup and a 20,000-franc cash prize for the best flight of 1908.

In the Summer of 1909, the Wright brothers arrived home to find they had become celebrities in America as well as Europe. They were treated to an endless series of awards and honours, including a city-wide homecoming celebration in Dayton, Ohio. They spent what little spare time they could find building a new Military Flyer. In the summer they took their new aeroplane back to Fort Myer, Virginia and completed the trials that had been interrupted almost a year earlier and the U.S. Army purchased its first military aircraft for $30,000.

Engine development 1903 - 1910

In 1903 when Charlie Taylor built the engine for the Wright Flyer, Stephen Balzer was busy building a five-cylinder rotary engine for the Langley Aerodrome project but the engine failed to deliver enough power. The Blazer engine was then reworked by Langley's chief assistant, Charles Manly, who turned it into a non-rotating radial engine, after which it held the record for power-to-weight ratio for several years. His main concern had been finding a successful method of cooling the engine, a problem that he solved by welding a water filled jacket to each cylinder.

In 1906 Léon Levavasseur produced a successful water cooled V8 engine for aircraft use, shown here.

He was a French powerplant engineer, aircraft designer and inventor and his innovations included the V8 engine, direct fuel injection, and liquid engine cooling.

In the summer of 1902, Levavasseur suggested to industrialist Jules Gastambide that powerful, lightweight engines would be necessary for powered flight, and proposed the manufacture of such engines. He also proposed that the engines be named after Gastambide's daughter,

Levasseur's V-8 engne. Image courtesy of Pline.

Antoinette. Gastambide agreed to finance the venture and Levavasseur patented the V8 engine configuration that year. By 1904, most of the prize-winning speedboats in Europe were powered with Antoinette engines and during this time, he designed engines of various configurations of up to thirty-two cylinders.

The Antoinette company was incorporated in 1906, with Gastambide as president and Levavasseur as technical director. The vice-president was aviation pioneer Louis Blériot and the company's primary business was the sale of engines to aircraft manufacturers.

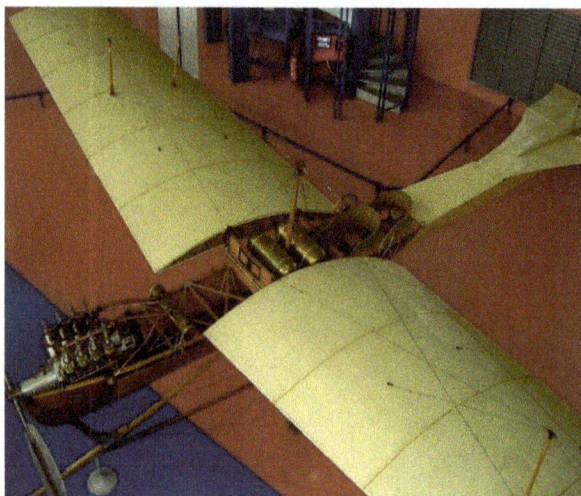

Antoinette two seat monoplane. Image courtesy of Deep silence.

In 1908, René Lorin (1877 – 1933,) a French aviation engineer, patented a design for a subsonic ramjet engine. He published the principles of his ramjet in articles in the journal L'Aérophile from 1908 to 1913, expressing the idea that the exhaust from internal combustion engines could be directed into nozzles to create jet propulsion, illustrated here. He couldn't build this invention because aircraft at that time were unable to travel fast enough for a ramjet to function.

A ramjet is a form of air-breathing jet engine that uses the engine's forward motion to compress incoming air without either an axial or centrifugal compressor. Because ramjets cannot produce thrust at zero airspeed, they cannot move an aircraft from a standstill. A ramjet-powered vehicle, therefore, requires an assisted take-off to accelerate to a speed where it begins to produce thrust.

Also in 1908, Louise Sequin designed the Gnome Omega, it was the first rotary engine to be produced in quantity. Its introduction revolutionized the aviation industry and it was used by many early aircraft manufacturers. It produced 50 horsepower (37 kW) from its capacity of 8 litres (488 cubic inches).

A Gnome Omega engine powers the 1912 Blackburn Monoplane, owned and operated by the Shuttleworth Collection, the oldest known airworthy British-designed aeroplane worldwide. A version of the same engine with two rows of pistons was also produced, known as the Gnome 14 Omega-Omega or Gnome 100 hp.

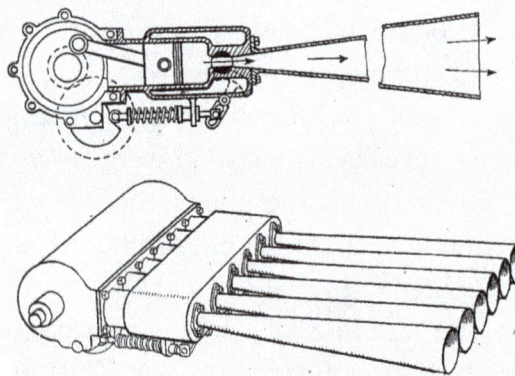

Re

The Gnome Omega 7 cylinder rotory engine. Courtesy
of Mimbus 227

Blackburn monoplane. Darren harbar Photography

Henri Coandă

Henri Coandă

The Coandă-1910, designed by Romanian inventor Henri Coandă was an unconventional sesquiplane aircraft powered by a ducted fan. Called the "turbo-propulsor" by Coandă himself, its engine consisted of a conventional piston engine driving a multi-bladed centrifugal blower which exhausted into a duct. The strange arrangement attracted a lot of attention at the Second International Aeronautical Exhibition in Paris in October 1910, presumably because it was the only exhibit without a propeller. The aeroplane does not appear to have been shown anywhere else but Coandă used a similar turbo-propulsion engine to drive a snow sledge, although he did abandon the idea for aircraft.

Impression of the Coanda tibo-propulsor 1910

He discovered the Coandă effect in fluid dynamics and invented a great number of devices, he also designed a "flying saucer" employing the Coandă effect.

Between 1911 and 1914, he worked as technical manager of the Bristol Aeroplane Company at Filton in the United Kingdom, where he designed several aeroplanes known as the Bristol-Coanda Monoplanes. In 1912 one of these aircraft won a prize in the British Military Aeroplane Competition.

One of the Bristol Coanda monoplanes 1912

More Pioneers

Chapter Three

More Pioneers

Samuel Franklin Cowdery (1868-1913)

Samuel Franklin Cowdery,
aka S. F. Cody

On October 16th 1908 the American Samuel Franklin Cowdery, aka S.F. Cody, made the first flight in Great Britain. Born in Davenport, Iowa, he was a showman and early pioneer of manned flight but is best remembered for his Cody War-kites that were used by the British in World War One for artillery spotting. A flamboyant showman he was often confused with Buffalo Bill Cody whose surname he took when young and from his picture shown here you can see why.

His flight of 16th October 1908 is recognised as the first official flight of a piloted heavier-than-air machine in Great Britain.

The machine was damaged at the end of the flight but after some repairs and extensive modifications, Cody flew it again early in 1909. The War Office then decided, in their infinite wisdom, to stop backing development of heavier-than-air aircraft, and Cody's contract with the Army ended in April 1909. Cody however, was fortunate enough to be given the aircraft, and he continued to work on it at Farnborough.

On 14th May 1909, he succeeded in flying his aircraft for over a mile, establishing the first official British distance and endurance records and by August he had completed the last of a long series of modifications to his aircraft. He carried passengers for the first time on 14th August 1909, first an old workmate and then Lela Cody.

On 29th December 1909, he became the first man to fly from Liverpool in an unsuccessful attempt to fly non-stop between Liverpool and Manchester. He set off from Aintree Racecourse at 12.16 p.m. but only nineteen minutes later he was forced to land at Valencia Farm near to Eccleston Hill, St. Helens because of thick fog.

The following year in 1910, Cody received Royal Aero Club certificate number 9 using a newly built aircraft and later the same year, he won the Michelin Cup for the longest flight made in England during 1910, with a flight of 4 hours 47 minutes on 31st December. In 1911, in a third aircraft, he piloted the only British machine to complete the Daily Mail's, Circuit of Great Britain air race, finishing fourth, for which achievement he was awarded the Silver Medal of the Royal Aero Club in 1912.

Cody flying his British Army Aeroplane No 1

Cody continued to work on aircraft using his own funds and on 7th August 1913, he was test flying his latest design, the Cody Floatplane, when it broke up at 200 feet and he and his passenger, the cricketer William Evans were killed.

The two men, who were not wearing harnesses of any kind, were thrown out of the aircraft and the Royal Aero Club accident investigation concluded that the accident was due to "inherent structural weakness," and suggested that the two might have survived the crash if they had been strapped in. Cody's body was buried with full military honours in the Aldershot Military Cemetery and the funeral procession drew an estimated crowd of 100,000 people, proving just what a popular figure he'd become.

Postcard showing Cody's funeral procession 11th
August 1913

Adjacent to Cody's own grave marker is a memorial to his only son, Samuel Franklin Leslie Cody, born Basel, Switzerland in 1895 and who joined the Royal Flying Corps and was killed in Belgium on 23rd January 1917 while serving with 41 Squadron.

Louis Charles Joseph Blériot (1872–1936,)

Louis Charles Joseph
Blériot (1872-1936)

It was also in 1909 that Louis Blériot, flying a small monoplane of his own design, crossed the English Channel on 25th July in his model X1, winning the prize of £1,000offered by the Daily Mail newspaper for a crossing of the English Channel. Although it was only a relatively short flight, Blériot had conquered an important physical and national boundary and all of a sudden, people begin to realize the importance of aviation and its ability to make distances shrink.

Blériot was a French aviator, inventor and engineer. He had developed the first practical headlamp for cars and established a profitable business manufacturing and selling them, but his main passion was aviation. He used the profits from his headlamp business to finance his attempts to build a successful aircraft and he was the first aviator to use a combination of hand operated joystick and foot pedal rudder control. Blériot was also the first to make a working, powered, piloted monoplane and was also the founder of a successful aircraft manufacturing company, "Blériot Aéronautique".

Blériot built several aircraft, the most successful of which was the X1, that benefited from having a reliable engine teamed with a laminated walnut propeller designed by Lucian Chauviere, a French aeronautical engineer, it was also the aircraft that established the tractor (engine in front) monoplane with a tail-dragger landing gear as the norm. It was also the aircraft that challenged the supremacy of the Wright's and Curtiss aircraft.

It had been Glenn Curtiss winning the first Gordon Bennett race, that was held in France, that had caused so much consternation in France, the French being embarrassed at losing to an American!

This was shortly followed by the Blériot X 11, a high-wing two-seater monoplane with a deep uncovered fuselage and first flown on 21st May 1909. For a while Blériot concentrated on flying this machine, flying it with a passenger on 2nd July, and on 12th July making the world's first flight with two passengers, one of whom was Santos Dumont, (1873-1932), the Brazilian inventor and aviation pioneer, one of the very few people to have contributed significantly to the development of both lighter-than-air and heavier-than-air aircraft. A few days later the crankshaft of the E.N.V. engine broke and Blériot resumed trials of the Type XI.

On 25th June he made a flight lasting 15 minutes and 30 seconds, his longest to date, and the following day increased this personal record to over 36 minutes. At the end of July he took part in an aviation meet at Douai, where he made a flight lasting over 47 minutes in the Type XII and on 3rd July and the following day he flew the Type XI for 50 minutes at another meet at Juvisy, and on 13th July, he made a cross-country flight of 41 km (25 mi) from Etampes to Orléans.

Blériot's X1 Darren Harbar Photography

Blériot X 11

Bleriot's determination is shown by the fact that during the flight at Douai, part of the asbestos insulation worked loose from the exhaust pipe after only 15 minutes in the air. After half an hour, one of his shoes had been burnt through and he was in considerable pain, but nevertheless, he continued his flight until engine failure ended it. Blériot suffered third-degree-burns and his injuries took over two months to heal.

Blériot, who intended to fly across the Channel in his Type X l monoplane, had three rivals for the prize, the most serious being Hubert Latham, a French national of English extraction flying an Antoinette IV monoplane who was favoured by both France and Britain to win, Charles de Lambert, a Russian aristocrat and Arthur Seymour an Englishman.

Wilbur Wright was also keen to go for the crossing and cabled his brother in America where he was recovering from injuries sustained in a crash. Orville implored his brother not to do anything until he could be there to assist and also pointed out that they had already amassed a great deal of prize money from distance and altitude flights and that they had valuable contracts for sales of the Wright Flyer in Britain, France, Germany and Italy, and that the prize of only one thousand pounds was a small reward for such a dangerous undertaking.

The event itself however was world news and attracted a large crowd both in Calais and Dover and the Marconi Company set up a special radio link for the occasion. The weather was windy and Latham didn't make his first attempt until 19th July, when, six miles out he developed engine trouble and was forced to make the world's first forced aircraft landing at sea before being rescued by the French destroyer "Haron."

Blériot, with his friend Alfred Leblanc and a couple of mechanics arrived on Wednesday the 21st July but it wasn't until Sunday 25th that the weather was suitable for an attempt at the crossing.

Blériot took off at 4:41, that morning after a short test flight, to attempt the crossing. Flying at approximately 45 mph (72 km/h) and at an altitude of about 250 ft (76 m), he set off across the Channel. He didn't have a compass with him, so took his course from the "Escopette," the accompanying French destroyer which was heading for Dover, but he soon overtook the ship. The visibility deteriorated, and he later said, *"for more than 10 minutes I was alone, isolated, lost in the midst of the immense sea, and I did not see anything on the horizon or a single ship"*.

Eventually the English coast came into view on his left, the wind having increased and blown him to the east of his intended course. Altering course, he followed the line of the coast about a mile offshore until he spotted Charles Fontaine, the correspondent from Le Matin waving a large Tricolour as a signal.

Unlike Latham, Blériot had not visited Dover to find a suitable spot to land, and the choice had been made by Fontaine, who had selected a patch of gently sloping land called Northfall Meadow, close to Dover Castle. Once over land, Blériot circled twice to lose height and cut his engine at an altitude of about 20 m (66 ft). The landing was a heavy one due to the gusty wind conditions and the undercarriage was damaged along with one blade of the propeller but Blériot himself was unhurt. The flight had taken 36 minutes and 30 seconds.

Although news of his departure had been sent by radio to Dover, it had been generally expected that he would attempt to land on the beach to the west of the town. The Daily Mail correspondent, however, realising that Blériot had landed near the castle, set off at speed in a motor car and took Blériot to the harbour, where he was reunited with his wife, who had been aboard the Escopette. The couple, surrounded by a cheering crowd and photographers, were then taken to the Lord Warden Hotel at the foot of the Admiralty Pier; Blériot had become a celebrity.

Alberto Santos-Dumont (1873-1932)

Alberto Santos-Dumont

Santos-Dumont was the heir of a wealthy Brazilian family of coffee producers. He emigrated to France and dedicated himself to aeronautical study and experimentation in Paris where he spent most of his adult life. In the early years he designed, built, and flew both hot air balloons and dirigibles, culminating in his winning the Deutsch de la Meurthe prize on 19th October 1901 for a flight that rounded the Eiffel Tower. He then turned to heavier-than-air machines, and on 23rd October 1906 his 14-bis aircraft made the first powered heavier-than-air flight in Europe to be certified by the Aero-Club de France and the Federation Aéronautique International. Dumont was something of a romantic and his conviction that aviation would usher in an era of worldwide peace and prosperity led him to freely publish his designs and forego patenting his various innovations.

Dumont's 14-bis in flight

Santos-Dumont's final design was for the Demoiselle monoplanes numbers 19 and 20.

The fuselage consisted of three specially reinforced bamboo booms, and the pilot sat in a seat between the main wheels of a tricycle landing gear. The Demoiselle was controlled in flight by a tail unit that functioned as both elevator and rudder with a system of wing warping for roll.

In 1908 Santos-Dumont started working with Adolphe Clément's Clément-Bayard company to mass-produce the Demoiselle No 19.

They planned a production run of 100 units, built 50 but sold only 15, at a price of 7,500 francs for each airframe. It was the world's first series production aircraft and by 1909 was being offered with a choice of three engines: the Clément 20 hp; the Wright 4-cyl 30 hp built under licence and the Clément-Bayard 40 hp designed by Pierre Clerget.

Demoiselle No 19 in flight

J. T. C. Moore-Brabazon

John Theodore Cuthbert
Moore-Brabazon
(1884–1964)

In 1909 The British Michelin cup was won by J. T. C. Moore-Brabazon who had learned to fly in 1908 in France in a Voisin biplane.

Moore-Brabazon became the first resident Englishman to make an officially recognized aeroplane flight in England on 2nd May 1909, at Shellbeach on the Isle of Sheppey, with flights of 450 ft, 600 ft, and 1500 ft. and on 4th May 1909, he was photographed outside the Royal Aero Club clubhouse, Mussel Manor, alongside the Wright brothers, the Short brothers, Charles Rolls and other notable figures in aviation.

On 30th October 1909, flying the Short Biplane No 2, he flew a circular mile and won a £1,000 prize offered by the Daily Mail newspaper and on 4th November that same year, as a joke to prove that pigs could fly, he put a small pig in a waste-paper basket and tied it to a wing-strut of his aeroplane, possibly making the first live cargo flight by aeroplane.

Moore-Brabazon outside Muswell Manor 1909

Back row: JDF Andrews, owner of Musell Manor, Oswald Short, Horace Short, Eustace Short, Francis McClean, Griffith Brewer, Frank Butler, WJS Lockyer, Warick Wright.
Front row: JTC Moore-Brabazon, Wilbur Wright, Orville Wright, Charles Rolls.

On 8th March 1910, Moore-Brabazon became the first person to qualify as a pilot in the United Kingdom and was awarded the Royal Aero Club's Aviator's Certificate No 1, his car also bore the number plate FLY 1. However, only four months later, his friend Charles Rolls was killed in a flying accident and his wife persuaded him to give up flying, which he did until the outbreak of war when he joined The Royal Flying Corps and rose from the rank of second lieutenant in 1914 to that of major in 1916.

He served on the Western Front and played a key role in the development of aerial photography and reconnaissance. When the Royal Flying Corps merged with the Royal Naval Air Service to form the Royal Air Force on 1st April 1918, Moore-Brabazon was appointed as a staff officer and made a temporary lieutenant-colonel. He was promoted to the full rank of lieutenant-colonel in the RAF on 1st January 1919 in recognition of his wartime services.

He was decorated with the Military Cross (MC) on 1st January 1917 and was also twice mentioned in dispatches, first on the 15th October 1915 and again on 13th November 1916 and was further decorated as a Knight of the legion d'honneur, (the highest French order of merit for excellent civil or military conduct), in February 1916.

In the summer of 1909 Glenn Curtiss, a motor cycling pioneer who in 1904 began making engines for airships, got together with Augustus Herring to create an aeroplane manufacturing company, the "Herring-Curtiss Company" and they sold their first aircraft to the Aeronautical Society of Long Island. The Wright brothers filed suit, claiming that Curtiss was infringing their patent. Later in the year both Curtiss and the Wright brothers were invited to fly for the Hudson-Fulton Celebration in New York. Unable to fly his underpowered aircraft in the heavy winds, Curtiss had to default, and Wilbur Wright showed him up by flying around the Statue of Liberty and then up the Hudson River to Grant's Tomb and back.

The British Michelin Cup

In 1909, Michelin instituted a United Kingdom award, offering an annual award for five years of a trophy and £500. The competition was limited to British subjects flying aircraft of British construction and it was run by the Aero Club of Great Britain. It was won by Moore-Brabazon

1910: The minimum qualifying distance was raised to 38 miles and it was won by Samuel Cody.

1911: Won again by Samuel Cody flying his Circuit of Britain biplane 261.5 miles.

1912: The rules were redefined for the 1912 competition with the No. 1 cup and cash prize of £5,000 purely for endurance. The No. 2 cup and prize of £600 was for distance covered over a cross-country course of about 186 miles of the competitor's choosing. The No. 1 cup was won by Harry Hawker, flying the Sopwith-Wright biplane. The flight, lasting 8 hours 23 minutes was made on 24 October 1912 at Brooklands. The No. 2 cup was won by Samuel Cody flying the Cody V with a flight of 186 miles in 3hr 26m.

1913: The Michelin Cup No. 1 was for the longest distance flight round the course Brooklands–Hendon–Farnborough with a minimum distance of 300 miles. Competitors had to make periodical stops of not less than five minutes with their engine stopped. The prize had not been won by the closing date of 31st October 1913, so the closing date was extended to 14 November 1913 and was eventually won by Reginald H. Carr, flying the Grahame White "Charabanc" with a flight of over 300 miles (480 km). The No. 2 cup, for the fastest time round a circuit, was not awarded. Although the prize was carried over to the next year, competition was terminated by the outbreak of War.

Harry George Hawker MBE (1889-1921)

Harry George Hawker MBE was a member of the Australian Flying Corps and an aviation pioneer. He was the chief test pilot for Sopwith and was also involved in the design of many of their aircraft. After World War One he co-founded Hawker Aircraft, the firm that would later be responsible for a long series of successful military aircraft.

He died on 12 July 1921 when piloting the aircraft he was to fly in the Aerial Derby, he crashed in a park at Burnt Oak Edgware, not far from Hendon Aerodrome.

Harry Geore Hawker MBE

John Bevins Moisant (1868 – 1910)

John Moisant was the first to conduct passenger flights over a city (Paris), as well as across the English Channel, from Paris to London. He also co-founded a prominent flying circus, the Moisant International Aviators and his sister Matilda was only the second American woman to gain a pilots' licence . He funded his aviation career with the proceeds from business ventures in El Salvador, where he had led two failed revolution and coup attempts against President Figueroa in 1907 and 1909.

John Moisant with his cat in 1910

He designed and built two aircraft between August 1909 and 1910, before he became an officially licensed pilot.

His first was the Moisant biplane which he had built in Paris, France. This experimental aircraft was constructed entirely from aluminium and steel by workers hired by Moisant and was the first all-metal aircraft in the world and was completed in February 1910. The Moisant biplane's inaugural flight, and Moisant's first flight, ultimately resulted in a crash after ascending only 90 feet with limited airtime. Only months after becoming a trained pilot, he died after being ejected from his aeroplane by a strong gust of wind over a field just west of New Orleans, Louisiana, where he was competing for the 1910 Michelin Cup.

Matilda Moisant

Howard and Warwick Wright

Known as The British Wright brothers, Howard Theophilus Wright was born in 1867 and his brother, Joseph Warwick Wright in 1876.

The three brothers, Howard, Warwick and their other brother Walter, ran a steam technology business named "Wright's Patent Heater and Condenser Company" with their father Joseph Wright. This business flourished for a while, building some huge water softeners and feed-water heaters. A feed-water heater is a component used to pre-heat water that is delivered to a steam generating boiler. The whole family moved to London, but Joseph died in 1893 and shortly after the company became bankrupt.

Soon after, Hiram Maxim put in an appearance. He was attempting to build steam powered aircraft at the time and that made him interested in the Wrights and their steam technology. He engaged Howard Wright as a Works Manager in the Maxim Electrical Engineering and Export Company, and involved him in aviation experiments while also the employing his brother Warwick at the works.

In 1901 Vickers Maxim ltd had taken over Wolseley cars, and it seems possible that this was Warwick Wright's introduction to the motor business, for which he is possibly more famous later on.

Far away in Naples, Federico Capone was Italy's own aviation pioneer. He had built an experimental pilotless helicopter in 1905 that apparently worked well and his next aim was to build a piloted helicopter. For this, he joined forces with Howard Wright who then built the first full sized Capone helicopter in 1908, followed by one or two more versions. After some successful tests in England, it was shipped to Italy in late 1908, and it is said that Howard Wright attended trials of the helicopter in Naples during 1909.

By now however, Howard and Warwick had concluded that winged flight was the real way forward and Warwick Wright went with Brabazon to Chalons in France in 1908 to learn to fly in a Voisin biplane and Howard Wright then embarked on the construction of a Voisin type biplane of his own design. He had acquired premises at Battersea next to the Short Brothers premises where they had been making balloons.

In December 1908, Howard Wright received a £1,200 order from Malcolm Seton Karr for a biplane, and this was built and exhibited at the first Olympia Aero Show in March 1909.

Howard Wright's 1909 biplane and it's 1910 successor were in many ways ahead of their opposition. They were of welded metal construction, using drawn steel tubing with oval sections to reduce wind resistance when most other constructors were still using wood or bamboo. Their design used ailerons instead of wing warping and contra-rotating coaxial propellers. They also paid meticulous attention to shaping and surface finish to reduce wind resistance and had a production system which would allow them to build a completed aircraft in two weeks.

Cigarette card depicting Howard Wright's biplane

For the next couple of years, Howard Wright was probably the leading British aeroplane manufacturer.

The business built numerous aircraft to several designs, some of which used the Metallurgique engine supplied by Warwick Wright. Others used the E-N-V engine, a British engine also supplied by Warwick Wright. Tom Sopwith was an important customer having both money and talent.

Other pioneers also possessed Howard Wright aircraft. People like, Claude Grahame-White (1879 – 1959), who was the first to make a night flight during the 1910 London to Manchester air race and flew to his own wedding reception in his Howard Wright aeroplane.

Now brother Warwick Wright was selling cars and driving fast but he was also closely involved with the aviation activities providing aero engines. He flew

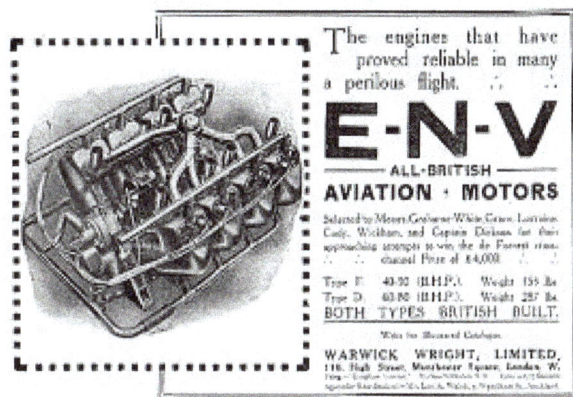
Advertisement for the E-N-V engine supplied by Warwick Wright

Howard Wright's aeroplanes, something which Howard himself had not yet learnt to do and he had the contacts with some wealthy people, such as Tom Sopwith.

It transpired that in late 1911 Howard and Warwick's business association came to an end, never to resume. We don't know what precipitated this turn of events, but they went their separate ways.   The Howard Wright business was taken over by Coventry Ordnance Works who wanted to get into aviation. Howard Wright teamed up with William Oke Manning briefly and led the new enterprise which designed a biplane for the 1912 War Office competition and Tom Sopwith was their test pilot.

This seems to have been a capable aeroplane but the team broke up prematurely. Howard Wright left Coventry Ordnance Works and Sopwith had his own competing business interests.

The first experimental seaplane had flown in 1910 and Samuel White who had a boatbuilding business on the Isle of Wight and was quick to see the potential, started an aviation business in November 1912 headed by Howard Wright. Because of the company's location on the Isle of Wight it was called the "Wight Aircraft Company." In January 1913 they exhibited a hydro-biplane at Olympia and that was soon followed by a Naval seaplane. The German Navy ordered some of these in 1914, but never received them because of the outbreak of World War One.

Next came some very large aeroplanes, some of the largest constructed at that time. One, the twin fuselage Wight 2 was designed as a torpedo carrier and was known as the "Wight Elephant".

The twin fuselage Wight 2

Quite a lot of naval aircraft were built to Howard Wright's and Wight's designs. Howard Wright himself had three patents in this period, one for the "Dual-profile aerofoil", another for a "Folding Wing", and one for "Engine valves".

His work on seaplane float design was very influential and he was also on the Committee of the Society of British Aircraft Constructors.

The last of the Samuel White aircraft was this quadruplane land aircraft, however the aircraft had several design deficiencies including a lack of yaw control and difficulty taking off due to shallow wing incidence. After some redesigns the final example was involved in a crash and further work on the aircraft was abandoned.

The quadruplane land aircraft

Robert Lorraine (1876 – 1935)

Robert Lorraine was a successful British born London and Broadway stage actor, actor-manager and soldier, who later enjoyed a side career as a pioneer aviator and who learnt to fly at the Bleriot school at Pau, France. He later switched to the easier to fly Farman biplane in which, in September 1910 he made what is credited as being the first aeroplane flight from England to Ireland, although he actually came down in the sea about 200 feet from the shore.

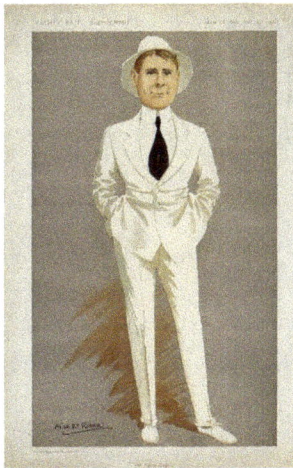

Caricature of Robert Lorraine from Vanity Fair 1912

The same month he piloted one of the two Bristol Boxkites, which took part in the British Army manoeuvres on Salisbury Plain, during which he sent the first radio signals to be sent from an aeroplane in Britain. His diary is cited by the Oxford English Dictionary as the first written example of the word *"joystick"* to describe an aircraft's stick controls.

Loraine served as a volunteer in the Boer War and flew with the Royal Flying Corps during the First World War when he was appointed Flight Commander with the rank of Captain in September 1915. He was awarded the Military Cross for his conspicuous gallantry and skill in shooting down an Albatross biplane on 26th October 1915 whilst flying a Vickers FB 5 Gunbus, the first aircraft to be designed from the outset as a fighter.

This incident is recorded in RFC Communiqué 16, which notes that he and his observer/gunner Lt. Lubbock, shot down an Albatross within British lines, killing the pilot (Unteroffizier Gereld) and wounding the observer. The 17-year-old observer, 2nd Lt. Buchholz of 33 FFA, was able to provide interesting background on his squadron and the German Air Force. The Communiqué lists various equipment found on the aircraft and the contents of a document. Unusually the next RFC Communiqué, No 17, was devoted to an interrogation report on Lt Buchholz, the contents of which clearly constituted a valuable intelligence report at the time.

Vickers FB Gunbus Courtesy of Ruth AS

In 1917 Loraine was awarded the DSO for distinguished service in the field and that same year was made Wing Commander with the rank of Lieutenant-Colonel. On 11th December 1918 he relinquished his commission in the Royal Air Force due to ill-health brought on by his wounds, and was granted the honorary rank of Major.

Sir Thomas Octave Murdoch Sopwith CBE

Thomas Sopwith CBE
(1888-1989)

Sir Thomas Octave Murdoch Sopwith CBE, (1888-1989), became interested in flying after seeing John Moisant flying the first cross channel passenger flight. He taught himself to fly on a Howard Wright Avis monoplane and took to the air on his own for the first time on 22nd October 1910. He crashed after travelling about 300 yards, but soon improved, and on 22nd November was awarded Royal Aero Club Aviation Certificate No. 31, flying a Howard Wright 1910 biplane.

On 18th December 1910, Sopwith won a £4000 prize for the longest flight from England to the Continent in a British-built aeroplane, flying 169 miles in 3 hours 40 minutes. He used the winnings to set up the Sopwith School of Flying at Brooklands.

In June 1912 Sopwith, along with Fred Sigrist and others, set up the Sopwith Aviation Company, initially at Brooklands. Sopwith Aviation got its first military aircraft order in November 1912, and in December moved to larger premises in Kingston upon Thames. The company produced more than 18,000 World War One aircraft for the allied forces, including 5747 Sopwith Camel single-seat fighters. Sopwith was awarded the CBE in 1918 and lived to be 101.

Sir George White

Sir george White

When George White first heard of the Wright brothers' achievement, he decided to turn his interest in aviation into a commercial business. He was well versed in the transportation business, running several businesses, although not an engineer himself. At the Annual General Meeting of one of his companies, the "Bristol Tramways & Carriage Company" in 1910 he announced that he had registered the names of four new companies, Bristol Aeroplane Company Limited, British & Colonial Aeroplane Company Limited, Bristol Aviation Company Limited and British & Colonial Aviation Company Limited.

Choosing to operate initially as the British & Colonial Aeroplane Company rather than use the name Bristol, in case it proved difficult to register as a trade mark, he set up the head office in Clair Street House, Bristol, which was also home to some of his other companies, George White & Co, Stockbrokers, the Western Wagon & Property Company Limited, Bristol Tramways & Carriage Company Limited and Imperial Tramways Company Limited. The manufacturing workshops were based initially in two sheds leased from the Tramways company at their depot in Filton, just north of Bristol.

Most aeroplane companies at that time were being set up by designers and engineers who struggled to get funding, George White on the other hand was a wealthy businessman, willing to invest heavily in his new venture and by February 1913 the share capital of the business had risen to £250,000, enough to cover the expansion of the Filton site.

White's initial intention had been to build existing aircraft under licence rather than develop new designs and it was agreed that they would assemble six Zodiac biplanes, designed by Gabriel Voisin. One aircraft was sent to Brooklands airfield in Surrey where the company was leasing a shed for test flights. The actual test flight took place on the 28th May 1910 and was so disappointing that the other five aircraft were scrapped and the company sued for compensation. The company then dropped the Zodiac trademark that had been on their paperwork and adopted the now famous Bristol scroll that become a well-known and trusted trade mark.

The Bristol Scroll

Sir George was advised to acquire rights to build copies of the successful Farman biplane but this proved impossible since George Holt Thomas was already negotiating rights with the Farman company. George Challenger however, the chief engineer at the Bristol factory in Filton, believed that he could produce a satisfactory copy of the aircraft, since full details of the Farman machine had been published in "Flight." This controversial idea was authorized by Sir George, and Challenger set to work on drawings for a new aircraft. The first example, that employed elements of both the Farman and Zodiac aircraft, was constructed in a matter of just weeks, and was delivered to the company's flying school at Larkhill on Salisbury Plain, where it was first flown on 30th July 1910, piloted by Maurice Edmond.

Farman sued Bristol for patent infringement but the company's lawyers claimed substantial design improvements in matters of constructional detail, and the lawsuit was subsequently dropped.

Between 11th and 16th November a series of demonstration flights of the new Bristol Boxkite were made in Bristol. Temporary hangars were built for the aircraft on Durham Down, Bristol, and although flying was limited by the weather conditions a crowd of almost 10,000 saw Maurice Tetard make a fifteen-minute flight on the Saturday.

Bristol Boxkite : Darren Harbar Photography

That first flight was later eclipsed by some spectacular flights that were made the following Tuesday, when around ten flights were made between 7 and 9 o'clock, including a fifteen-minute flight by Tetard, during which he flew over Clifton Suspension Bridge, and made a circuit over the Bristol suburbs of Redland and Westbury.

Bristol Boxkite on Durdham Down with Sir George White. Courtesy of Bristol and Colonial Aerospace Co Ltd

On 14th March 1911, the British War Office ordered four Bristol Boxkites for the planned Air Battalion Royal Engineers, the first production contract for military aircraft for Britain's armed forces.

The first Boxkite, powered by a 50 hp Gnome engine, was delivered to Larkhill on 18th May that year. An order for a further four Boxkites was placed later that year, for use mainly as a trainer.

Because it was used as a trainer at Bristol, Larkhill and Brooklands, many early British aviators would have learned to fly in a Bristol Boxkite. Four were purchased in

1911 by the War Office and examples were sold to Russia and Australia. It continued to be used for training purposes until after the outbreak of the First World War.

The first Boxkites to be built had upper and lower wings of equal span, although most of the aircraft eventually produced had an extended upper wing and were known as the Military Version. The examples of this type sold to the Russian government and the first aircraft sold to the British Army were fitted with a third rudder, hinged to the centre leading-edge interplane strut of the tailplane, but this was not made standard.

Tetard flying over Clifton Suspention Bridge

Two modified Boxkites were produced for competition purposes. The first, No. 44, was a single-seater built to compete in the 1911 Circuit of Europe air race and had reduced wingspan and a semi-enclosed housing or cockpit for the pilot, similar to the Bristol Type T. The second, No.69, was a redesign by Gabriel Voisin, who was being employed as a consultant by Bristol. This had no front elevator, monoplane tail with a single rudder, and a reduced gap between the wings. It was tested at Larkhill in February 1912, but was evidently unsuccessful since it was soon rebuilt as a standard Boxkite and was to crash in November 1912.

Production continued until 1914 with a total of 78 being built, 60 of which were the extended Military Version, one racer (No. 44) and the Voisin variant (No. 69); all but the last six aircraft were built at Filton but the remaining six were built at Brislington by the Tramway Company.

The majority of the aircraft produced were employed at the Bristol flying schools at Brooklands and Larkhill. These schools were responsible for training nearly half the pilots who gained licences in Britain before the First World War, and many distinguished pilots gained their licence in a Boxkite, including Brigadier-General Henderson the first commander of the Royal Flying Corps who gained his licence after less than a week of instruction.

Some more pre-war aircraft

Voisin Biplane 1907

Voisin biplane 1907

After assisting Ernest Archdeacon with his gliding experiments in 1904 Gabriel Voisin briefly entered a partnership with Louis Blériot in 1905. After the failure of their second aircraft, the Blériot 1V, the partnership was dissolved in November 1906 and after parting from Blériot, Gabriel Voisin set up his own aircraft construction company, Les Frères Voisin, in partnership with his brother Charles. The first powered aircraft designed by the Voisin brothers was built for Henry Kapferer. It was completed in March 1907 but never flew. Kapferer had insisted on a Buchet gasoline engine which developed only 20 horsepower, which was inadequate to achieve flight.

The Voisin brothers and their draughtsman Maurice Colliex were building a similar aircraft, this time powered by a 50 hp V8 Antoinette engine, which had been ordered by the sculptor Léon Delagrange. This became known as the Delagrange l, since the Voisin brothers had decided that the aircraft they built would bear the name of their owner prominently placed on the tail surfaces, "Voisin Frères" appearing underneath in much smaller lettering. This was done because Voisin believed that people would be more ready to buy aircraft if the glory of flying them went to the pilots rather than the builder. This practice is a source of confusion to historians and was also to lead to considerable resentment on Gabriel Voisin's part, since the focus of attention was indeed generally on the pilots rather than on those who were responsible for the design and construction of the aircraft.

The successful flights made in 1907 and 1908 by léon Delagrange and Henri Farman in their Voisin aircraft put the Voisin brothers at the forefront of European aviation development.

Powered by the Antoinette engine, it was a two-bay biplane with a wingspan of 10 m (33 ft). There was no provision for direct lateral control because before Wilbur Wright's flying demonstrations in France in August 1908 the importance of roll control to make controlled turns was not appreciated by European experimenters, who concentrated on attempting to produce inherently stable aircraft.

Fokker Spin 1910

Fokker Spin 1910

The Fokker Spin was the first aeroplane built by Dutch aviation pioneer Anthony Fokker. The many bracing wires used to strengthen the aircraft made it resemble a giant spider, hence its name, Spin (Dutch for "spider").

The fuselage simply consists of two wooden beams with cross members on which the pilot is seated and on which an Argus four-cylinder water-cooled engine is mounted in the front with radiators placed on the side of the fuselage. The wings and tail consist of two steel tubes with bamboo ribs. The landing gear is also constructed of steel tubing and the whole structure is held together with steel wire. Later versions have a more streamlined fuselage.

Shorts S27 1910

The Short S.27 and its derivative the Short, improved S.27, were a series of early British aircraft built by the Short Brothers. They were used by the Admiralty and Naval Wing of the Royal Flying Corps for training the Royal Navy's first pilots as well as for early naval aviation experiments.

The Shorts S.27

In 1911, Lieutenant Longmore and Oswald Short installed streamlined air bags on the undercarriage struts and under the tail of an Improved S.27 No. 38, to enable the aircraft to land on water and on 1st December 1911, Longmore used the aircraft to become the first person in the United Kingdom to take off from land and make a successful water landing when he landed in the river Medway off Sheerness, after which No.38 was brought ashore and flown back to Eastchurch. A flying-off platform was then constructed over the foredeck and forward 12-inch gun turret of the battleship HMS Africa and on 10th January 1912, C R Samson, piloting No.38, used the platform while HMS Africa was anchored off Sheerness to make the United Kingdom's first successful aeroplane take-off from a ship. The platform was later transferred to the battleship HMS Hibernia, from where Samson made the first successful take-off from a moving ship, on 9th May 1912, shown here.

First take-off from a moving ship 1912

Avro Triplane 1V 1910

Avro Triplane : Darren Harbar Photography

The Avro IV Triplane was an early British aircraft designed by Alliot Verdon Roe, hence the name AVRO, and built by A.V. Roe and Company. It was first flown in September 1910.

The wings were connected by four unequally-spaced pairs of interplane struts on either side, the innermost pair on each side being just outboard of the upper longerons and the outer pair connecting only the upper pair of wings due to the shorter span of the lower wing. Although the ailerons fitted to the previous design had been satisfactory, Roe returned to wing warping for lateral control. The lifting triplane tailplanes of the earlier design were replaced by a non-lifting single triangular tailplane with a divided elevator and a small unbalanced rudder. The undercarriage consisted of a pair of skids extending forward of the propeller, with a pair of wheels mounted on each skid, and a sprung tailskid. It was powered by a 35 horsepower (26 kW) Green water-cooled four-cylinder inline engine.

Deperdussin Type A 1910

Deperdussin Type A 1910 : Darren Harbar Photography

Aéroplanes Deperdussin was established in 1909 by the silk broker, Armand Deperdussin with Louis Béchereau acting as the technical director.

The first aircraft they produced at Laon was a canard configuration design, which was unsuccessful but the later 1910 monoplane, shown here, was a success. The prototype, which was first flown by George Busson at Issy-les-Moulineaux in October 1910, was probably powered by a water-cooled inline 4-cylinder Clerget engine. The 1910 Deperdussin monoplane was a tractor configuration mid-wing monoplane, with a very slender fuselage formed by a shallow fabric covered wire-braced wooden box-girder, the longerons curving in to a vertical knife-edge at the back. The depth of the front section of the fuselage was increased by a shallow shell of wood veneer built over curved formers. Due to the extremely shallow fuselage, the pilot was almost completely exposed, sitting on, rather than in the fuselage.

1911 saw the first flight of the Deperdussin *Monocoque* which introduced the stressed-skin shell structure to aircraft design, which later became a global design standard, first in wood and then in metal. Monocoque is a structural system where loads are supported through an object's external skin, similar to an egg shell. The word *monocoque* is a French term for "single shell". First used in boats, a true monocoque carries both tensile and compressive forces within the skin and can be recognised by the absence of a load-carrying internal frame. This shapely machine also launched the streamlining revolution that continues to the present day. The Deperdussin *Monocoque* racer blended the Blériot-style monoplane approach with a much more refined form, giving it an appearance more typical of racers at the end of the 1920s rather than 1911. The aircraft underwent a series of design modifications. In September 1912, a more powerful and even smoother formed Deperdussin won the Gordon-Bennett Trophy Race in Chicago, becoming the first airplane to exceed 100 mph. It also introduced the powerful rotary engine to aircraft design.

Deperdussin's firm later collapsed amid charges of fraud and embezzlement, and he was sent to jail. Blériot reorganized the firm, and Béchéreau remained its chief engineer, working with André Herbemont to design the wartime SPAD fighter, an aircraft that, featuring lots of struts and wires, hardly resembled the streamlined design of its predecessor. But others did bear the resemblance, most notably the German Albatros, whose distinctive shark-like shape reflected more of Béchéreau's pre-war design.

Wallbro monoplane 1910

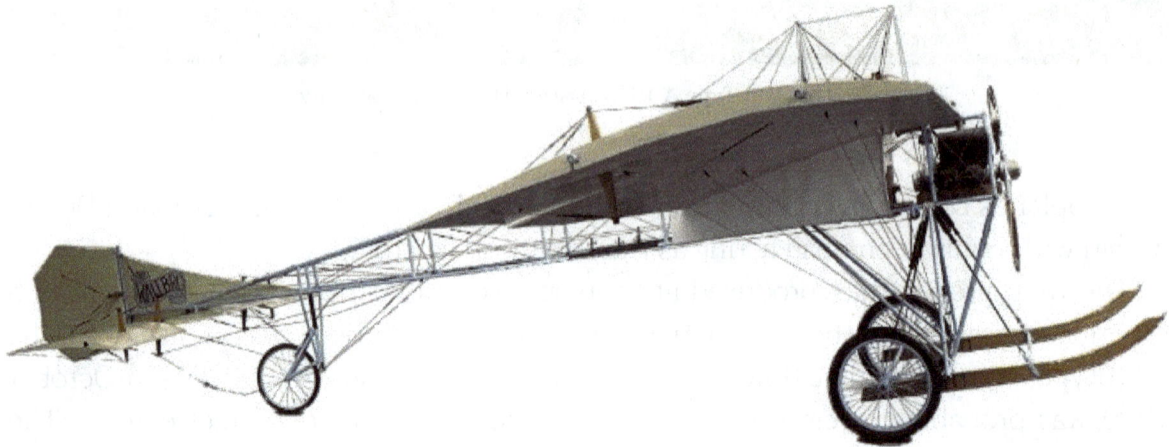

Wallbro monoplane 1910

Built by the motorcycle racing Wallis brothers who were strong believers in the strength of steel tubing, the fuselage of this aircraft used mainly one-inch diameter tube of 20 gauge, arranged on the girder principle, strongly braced with steel wire. The cross tubing was double bolted onto steel lugs similar to those used in motor cycle construction and the wire stays were attached to eyebolts passing through these lugs.

Tightening of the wires was accomplished by means of bronze tensioning screws, which have right and left-hand screw threads. These ideas together with a multitude of others succeeded in producing a machine which was both light and very strong. The fuselage was twenty-five feet long with a wing span of thirty feet. The undercarriage was also of tubular design but used heavier gauge tubing.

Events of 1910

First United States Air show
JTC Moore-Brabazon is first Royal Aero Club's certificated pilot
Baroness de Laroche in France is world's first qualified female pilot
Claude Grahame-White makes Europe' first night flight
Louis Paulhan wins Daily Mail London-Manchester challenge
Charles Rolls makes first double crossing of English Channel
Rolls killed at Bournemouth air show
First flight over Swiss Alps
First flight over 100km an hour
Grahame-White wins Gordon Bennett International Air Race
First mid-air collision
First take-off from deck of a ship
First float-plane flight

Events of 1911

First flight of Curtiss float plane
First London Paris non-stop flight
First wartime use of aeroplane

Events of 1912

First enclosed cabin aeroplane
First parachute drop from aeroplane
Wilbur Wright dies
Monocoque (single shell) construction introduced
First recorded recovery from a spin

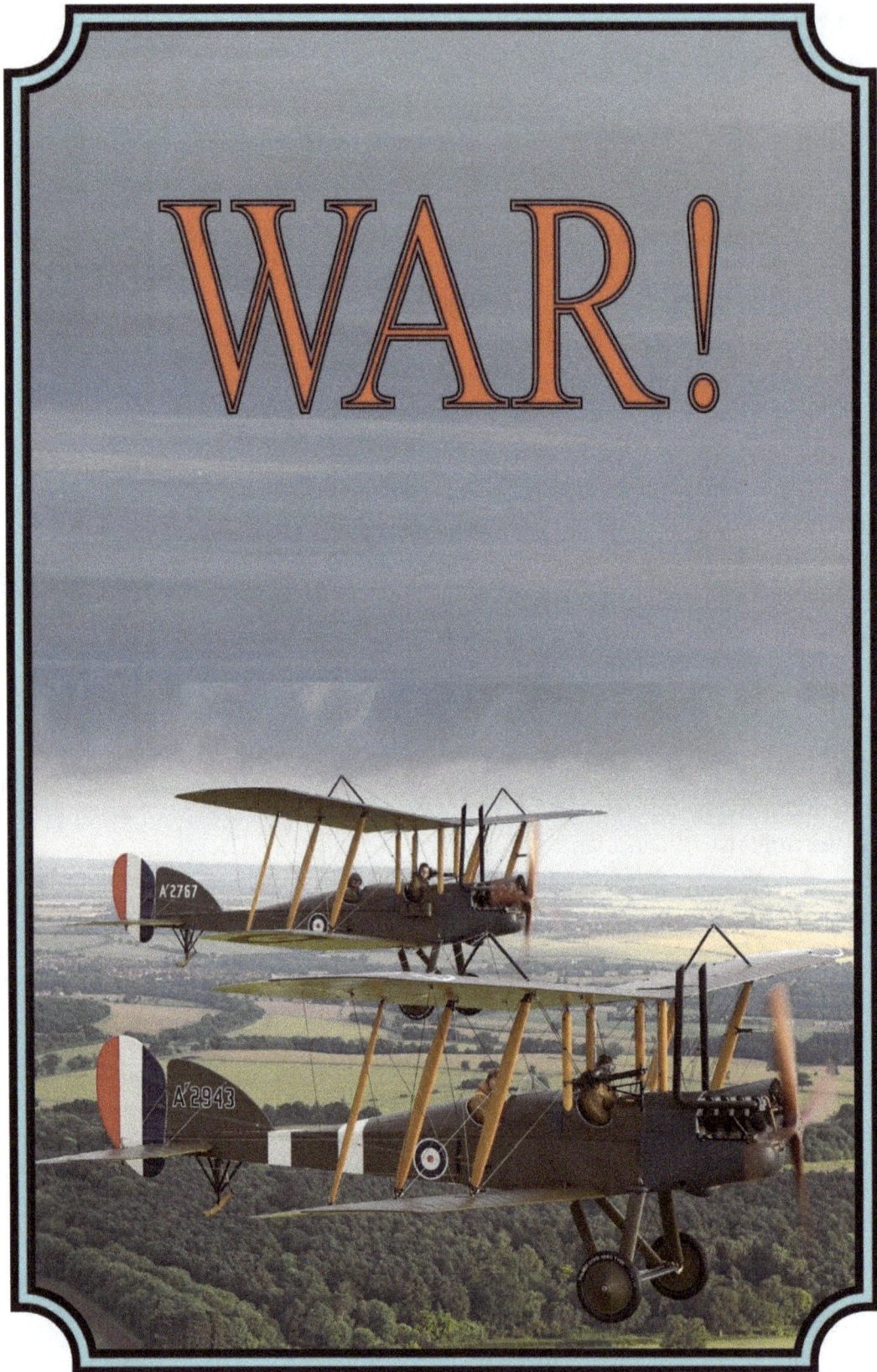

Chapter Four

War!

On the 28th June 1914, Gavrilo Princip, a Bosnian Serb nationalist, assassinated the Austro-Hungarian heir, Archduke Franz Ferdinand in Sarajevo and the world went to war. In Britain, thousands of young men enlisted, keen to do their patriotic and heroic duty, little suspecting the butchery and carnage that awaited them.

In some ways it was an old fashioned war, fought with old fashioned tactics, at least at first, but it was to be fought with some very modern weapons, not least of which was the machine gun, a weapon that inspired a future Prime Minister, Sir Winston Churchill, to write in a later memoir, *"War, that used to be cruel and magnificent, has now become cruel and squalid."*

The new flying machines of course played their part and this itself brought about a great many changes, aircraft were now being flown every day with much more powerful engines and they needed to be constantly maintained and repaired.

Actually, the first use of aeroplanes in war was carried out by the Italian Air Force during the war between Italy and Turkey in 1911-1912, when on the 23rd October 1911, an Italian pilot, Capt. Carlo Piazza, flew over the Turkish lines in Libya to conduct possibly the world's first aerial reconnaissance mission and on 1st November 1911, the first ever aerial bomb was dropped on the Turkish troops in Libya by the Italia Air Corps flying Blérot X1 and Nieuport monoplanes.

In the First Balkan War of 1912, the Bulgarian Air Force bombed Turkish positions at Adrianople.

Aeroplanes were also used by the United States Army against Pancho Villa in 1916. By the end of the first decade of the twentieth century the United States Army had begun to appreciate what the use of military aircraft could achieve and this realization led to the establishment of an aviation section in San Antonio, Texas, and the use of the unit stationed there to support a military expedition against Pancho Villa in 1916.

It had been in December 1909 that Lieutenant Benjamin Foulois was directed to take the only aircraft owned by the United States Army, a Wright Flyer Model B, along with nine enlisted men to Fort Sam Houston, in San Antonio, Texas, with instructions to teach himself to fly. The group arrived with a crated airplane in southwest Texas in February 1910 and set to work. Since he did not then know how, Foulois corresponded with the Wright Brothers for instructions on how to fly their machine, and used their written comments to teach himself. He first went aloft on March 2nd, 1910, flying over San Antonio four times that day.

Bulgarian aircrew preparing to bomb Turkish positions

During the rest of 1910 and 1911 the fledgling Army air arm built up from its base in Texas, a body of knowledge about aircraft and flight that proved invaluable in coming years. Foulois also proved, at least to his immediate superiors in Texas, that aircraft had an important role to play. When skirmishes broke out along the Mexican border in 1911 he took his Wright Flyer up and set a cross-country distance record of 106 miles on March 3rd while on a reconnaissance flight in support of American ground forces.

The first real test of the Army's aviation capability came on 13th April 1915, when Foulois with two pilots, took eight ground crew and one aircraft to Brownsville, Texas, to assist ground troops in patrolling the Mexican border. They flew for only one week before crashing the airplane and being forced to end air support. It was a rather inauspicious beginning.

Later that same year, the 1st Aero Squadron was assigned to San Antonio, Texas. It was from San Antonio that the 1st Aero Squadron participated in the Pershing Punitive Expedition against Pancho Villa. On March 9th, 1916, Villa's forces crossed the border and raided Columbus, New Mexico, killing 17 Americans.

The next day Brigadier General John J. Pershing, commanding American forces in the region, organized a 15,000 man force to punish Villa. The 1st Aero Squadron left San Antonio with eight aircraft on March 13th and its aircraft began flying reconnaissance missions on March 16th but once again, the contribution of aviation was limited. The difficulty of operating at relatively high altitudes with primitive equipment over the mountainous terrain of northern Mexico proved to be too demanding for the unit.

At the start of World War One, aircraft were still used mostly for reconnaissance and artillery spotting, roles for which they were ideally suited, they could report back to the Generals about troop movements and gun emplacements, useful information that was unfortunately sometimes mistrusted and ignored by those in charge. Accidents were frequent, sometimes due to the fragility of the aircraft itself but mostly from the necessity of flying every day, no matter how low the cloud cover or changeable the weather. Pilots were expected to draw maps of the area they were flying over, no easy task when trying to control the aeroplane at the same time as navigate your way over unfamiliar terrain and pilots frequently got lost.

Although pilots were sometime required to carry out strategic bombing, their roll was still mostly reconnaissance and aircraft started to have an observer as well as a pilot. The observes were now supplied with box cameras to take photographs of enemy positions rather than having to draw maps, but the cameras were difficult to manage with cold fingers so they were later attached to the side of the aircraft.

The use of aerial photography rapidly matured during the First World War. Frederick Charles Victor Laws had started experiments in aerial photography in 1912 using the British dirigible "Beta." He discovered that vertical photographs taken with a 60% overlap could be used to create a "stereoscopic" effect when viewed in a stereoscope, thus creating a perception of depth that could aid in cartography and in intelligence derived from aerial images. A stereoscope, shown here, is a device for viewing a pair of separate images, depicting left-eye and right-eye views of the same scene, as a single three-dimensional image.

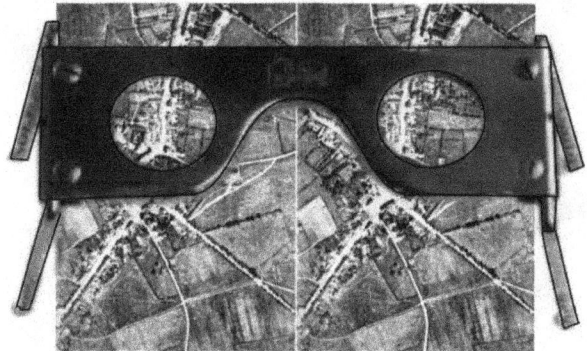

A stereoscope

Laws formed the first aerial reconnaissance unit of fixed-wing aircraft, and this became No 3 Squadron R.F.C .

The Royal Flying Corps reconnaissance pilots began to use cameras for recording their observations in 1914 and by the Battle of Neuve Chapelle in 1915, the entire system of German trenches was being photographed. The first purpose-built and practical aerial camera was invented by Captain John Moore-Brabazon in 1915 with the help of the Thornton-Pickard company, greatly enhancing the efficiency of aerial photography. Moore-Brabazon also pioneered the incorporation of stereoscopic techniques, as just described, into aerial photography, allowing the height of objects on the landscape to be discerned by comparing photographs taken at different angles.

Still, in 1914, the British entered into aerial reconnaissance in World War One with no credible heavier-than-air capability, the shortages being in optics and cameras as well as aircraft and pilots.

Laws and his collaborators first created the A-camera, then later the L-camera (the L being for Laws), which became the standard British airborne camera, usually fixed on the side of the fuselage pointing down, and with Lieutenant John Moore-Brabazon, Laws built the L/B camera for special situations, introduced late in the war.

Reconnaissance camera fitted to the side of the aircraft

The Russians in the East only possessed a few aircraft and didn't use them to any real advantage, whereas the Germans made great use of their "Taube" (Dove), to great advantage and at the battle of Tannenberg, where they were able to concentrate their numerically smaller forces in the right places and pull off a great victory, thanks to aerial reconnaissance.

In the West, German forces were on the advance, Paris was threatened and by the first week of September, the Germans had come to within thirty kilometres of the Cathedral of Notre-Dame.

Replica of a German Taube : Courtesy of the Combat Air Museum, Kansas, USA

The French and British armies were engaged in fierce fighting with the Germans in the first battle of the Marne. When one of the German armies turned southeast to attack the French army on the flank, it opened a gap between the German armies which was spotted by French reconnaissance pilots and the French forces, led by Marechal Joffe, took the opportunity to attack them on their own flank. The Germans were taken completely by surprise and were pushed back by the French and British armies.

By the end of the war, aerial cameras had dramatically increased in size and focal power and were used increasingly frequently as they proved their pivotal military worth; by 1918 both sides were photographing the entire front twice a day and had taken over half a million photographs since the beginning of the conflict.

It was inevitable that sooner or later enemy reconnaissance pilots would start shooting at one another with pistols and trying to drop stones and even bombs onto them from above and it wasn't long before aircraft were fitted with their very own machine guns and the fighter plane was born.

Pilots and observers, when shooting at enemy aircraft, had to be careful not to hit their own aircraft, especially when machine guns were fitted. A French pilot by the name of Roland Garros, along with designer Raymond Saulnier fitted deflector plates to the back of the propellers on his Monane-Saulnier monoplane in 1915 so that he could shoot through them and it wasn't long after that, Anthony Fokker developed a successful method of synchronizing the firing of the gun to the rotation of the propeller, enabling the machine gun to fire through them without fear of damage. German pilot Leutnant Kurt Wintgens was the first pilot to shoot down an enemy plane using a synchronised machine gun on his Fokker Eindecker on the 1st July 1915. The Allies quickly developed their own synchronization gears, leading to the birth of aerial combat between planes, more commonly known as dogfighting.

Oswald Boelcke

Tactics for dogfighting evolved by trial and error but the German ace Oswald Boelcke created eight essential rules of dogfighting, the Dicta Boelcke.

Air combat tactical manuals based on the Dicta Boelcke have become more elaborate over time, and have become a mainstay for NATO's air combat training of American, German, Dutch, Norwegian, Turkish, Italian, and Greek fighter pilots.

The synchronised machine gun.

The problems involved in designing a system synchronising the firing of a machine gun with the rotation of a propeller were plentiful, mostly because the firing of the machine gun in those days was not always that precise for various reasons and the fact that the speed of rotation of the propeller was dependent on the throttle setting and therefore variable, also there was the high speed at which both operated.

The success of the Eindecker however, led to numerous gun synchronization devices being designed, culminating in the more reliable hydraulic British Constantinesco gear of 1917 invented by the Romanian scientist and inventor George Constantinesco, and by the end of the war, German engineers were well on the way to perfecting a gear using an electrical rather than a mechanical or hydraulic link between the engine and the gun, with the gun itself being triggered by a solenoid rather than by a mechanical trigger.

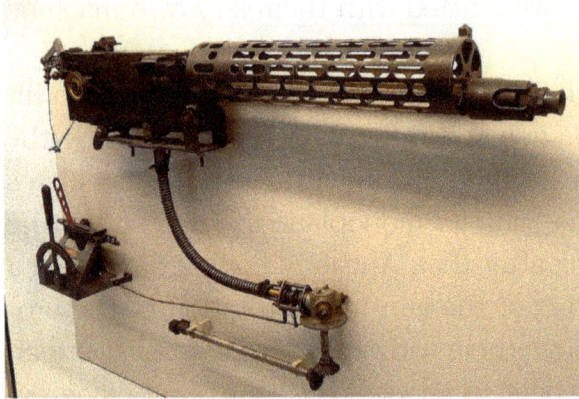

Synchonised 7.92mm Spandau machine gun : Courtesy of WerWill.

From 1918 to the mid-1930s the standard armament for a fighter aircraft remained two synchronized rifle-calibre machine guns, firing forward through the propeller, however, during the late 1930s, the main role of the fighter was increasingly seen as that of the destruction of large, all-metal bombers, for which the traditional light armament was inadequate.

It was impractical to fit more than one or two extra guns in front of a single-engine aircraft's fuselage so an increasing proportion of the armaments being mounted were fitted in the wings, firing outside the arc of the propeller. There were in fact some advantages in dispensing with centrally mounted guns altogether, however, the final end of synchronized guns did not finally come until the introduction of jet propulsion and the absence of a propeller for guns to be synchronized with.

Both sides now made use of aircraft for reconnaissance, bombing, strafing and anti-submarine warfare and aeroplanes had become specialised into fighters, bombers and reconnaissance aircraft.

Engine development 1914 – 1918.

Perhaps now is a good time to explain the difference between the distinctive types of engine in use at the time so that everyone is familiar with the different terms used to describe them.

Normally the term **inline engine** would refer only to an engine with a single row of pistons but in aviation parlance it also covers V-configurations, where the pistons are in two, in line banks, typically angled at some 60-90 degrees from each other and driving a common crankshaft, and opposing engines where the cylinders work in opposite directions. None of these engines need to be limited to just a single row of pistons. All these engines are referred to as in-line in order to differentiate them from radial and rotary engines. An Inline engine has the advantage of a typically low frontal area to minimise drag. Some inline aviation engines are inverted, that's to say that the crankshaft is situated above the cylinders, allowing the propeller to be mounted high up, giving greater ground clearance and allowing for shorter landing gear. Inline engines can be liquid or air cooled but liquid cooling was far more prevalent because of the difficulty of getting good airflow over the rear cylinders, however for military aircraft, consideration has to be given to the fact that radiators are vulnerable to battle damage. These types of engine were common on the very early aircraft but were soon abandoned in favour of the radial type.

A **radial engine** has one or two rows of cylinders arranged around a central crankshaft and each row generally has an odd number of cylinders to provide a smooth operation. Because so much of the heat radiating surfaces are exposed, they tend to be air cooled and because of the piston configuration, many of the reciprocating forces of an in-line engine are cancelled out.

A **rotary engine** also has the cylinders arranged in rows around the crankshaft but in this case the crankshaft is anchored to the airframe and the engine block and cylinders rotate around it, the propeller being bolted to the face of the engine block.

Gnome Omega 7 cylinder rotory engine

The first practical rotary engine was the Gnome Omega shown here. Designed and built by the Seguin brothers in 1909. It was a very reliable engine and was responsible for many speed records before the First World War and was used in many aircraft types during it.

Although successful, the rotary engine had many disadvantages as well. The heavy gyroscopic effects of a heavy rotating engine produced handling problems and the total loss lubrication system used huge amounts of oil that was mixed with the fuel and ejected with the exhaust gasses. Most rotary engines consumed about five or six quarts of oil or more per hour, so you can imagine how much was needed to keep a whole squadron in the air. Castor oil was used as the lubricant because it is not soluble in petrol and the resulting fumes were a problem. Although the engines were installed in nacelles which collected the exhaust gases and ducted them under the fuselage, pilots in open cockpits were still exposed to some extent and this caused frequent stomach problems and diarrhoea for the pilots breathing them in.

The LeRhone C-9. 1915

A dependable French 9 cylinder rotary engine, that was initially rated at 80 hp, and was later increased to 130 hp. (The Oberursel engine made in Germany was almost an exact reproduction of the 110-hp LeRhone.) The air-cooled engine powered military planes in the first part of World War One. By the end of the war, it had been surpassed in terms of power and was then used mostly for trainers but it was also licensed for manufacturing in the U.S. by Union Switch and Signal in Pennsylvania.

LeRhone C-9 Courtesy of Paul Richter

Liberty 12-A

1918 saw the introduction of the in-line twelve cylinder Liberty 12-A, designed and built by Dayton-Wright Airplane Company. Sometime said to be America's best technological contribution to the First World War it was also manufactured by Packard, Lincoln, Ford, General Motors, Nordyke, and Marmon and primarily used in U.S. built De Havilland DH-4s, the only U.S.-built plane to see combat in the first world war.

Liberty 12-A Courtesy of Stahlkocher

The United States possessed no combat-worthy aircraft upon entry into World War I in 1917. Several European aircraft were considered and the British DH-4 was selected because of its comparatively simple construction and its apparent adaptability to mass production. It was also well-suited to the new American 400-horsepower Liberty V-12 engine. American-built DH-4s were sometimes dubbed the "Liberty Plane".

Over 20,000 Liberty 12-A were made during the war, after which, they powered the NC-4 in its series of flights across the Atlantic, a Fokker T-2 in the first transcontinental flight across the U.S., and the Martin planes that formed the U.S. Army's first bomber fleet.

The water cooled engine uses a coil ignition system, similar to those used in cars, because American companies could not build enough high-quality magnetos. The angle between cylinder banks was 45˚ rather than the more conventional 60˚ and this made the engine narrower, giving it a smaller cross section, and easier to fit into airframes. The engine produced 410hp, making it far more powerful than other mass-produced engines of the time, designers eventually turbocharged it, giving it 443 hp and more power and efficiency at higher altitudes.

Some World War One aircraft

Fokker Eindecker

Fokker Eindecker : Darren Harbar Photography

The Fokker E.IV was the final variant of the Eindecker fighter aircraft that was operated by Germany during World War One. Given the Fokker designation of M.15, the E.IV it was essentially a lengthened Fokker E.III powered by the 119 kW (160 hp) Oberursel U.III two-row, 14-cylinder rotary engine, a copy of the Gnome Double Lambda.

The more powerful engine was intended to enable the Eindecker to carry two or three 7.92 mm (.312 in) machine guns, thereby increasing its firepower and providing backup if one gun jammed, a common occurrence at the time. However, the E.IV was a troubled design that never achieved the success of its predecessor and was soon outclassed by French and British fighters.

The prototype E.IV was accepted for testing by the German 'Inspektion der Fliegertruppen' in September 1915. It was fitted with three forward-firing 7.92 mm (.312 in) lMG 08 "Spandau" machine guns, mounted to fire upwards at 15°.

Anthony Fokker demonstrated the E.IV at Essen but the complicated triple-synchronization gear failed and the propeller was damaged. The removal of the left-side gun is believed to have been pioneered on Oswald Boelcke's E.IV, with a simpler double-synchronization system used on the retained centre-line and right side MG 08 Spandau guns.

The fitment of dual MG 08 "Spandau" forward-firing, synchronized machine guns became the standard armament for production E.IVs, and indeed for all subsequent German D-type biplane fighters, however the angling of the guns was abandoned. The modified prototype underwent combat evaluation on the Western Front by Oberleutnant Otto Parschau in October 1915, making it the first twin-gun fighter in service.

Airco de Havilland 2

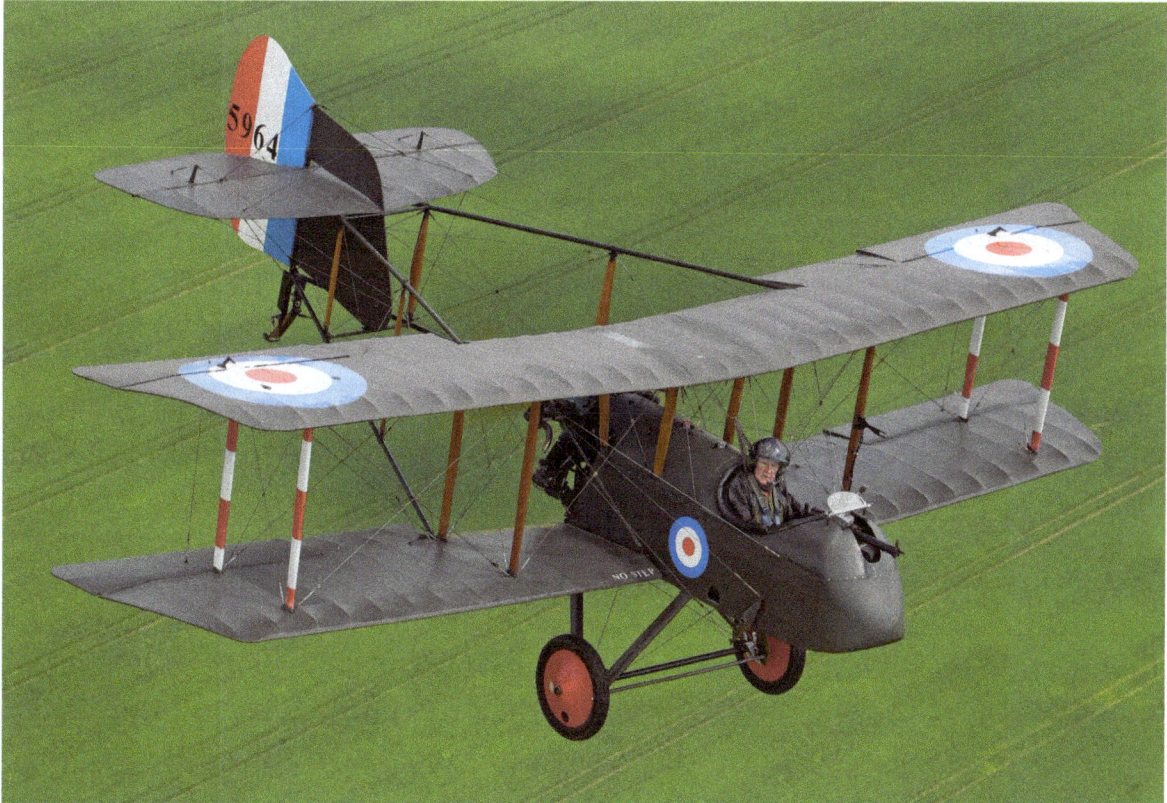

Airco de Havilland 2 : Darren Harbar Photography

Developed in 1915, the DH-2 biplane was one of the first effective British fighters of World War One. The DH-2 was the second design by Geoffrey de Havilland for the Aircraft Manufacturing Company of Great Britain. In its short life span the DH-2 was the best pusher configuration scout of the war and one of the best fighting aircraft. This highly successful aircraft had good manoeuvrability with an excellent rate of climb.

Mounting the engine to the rear of the fuselage permitted the use of a fixed, forward-firing machine gun. The DH-2 was designed before the Fokker, with its synchronized gun, became a menace and thus, for a short period, the DH-2 proved superior to the older model Fokker Eindecker of early 1916.

Major Lanoe George Hawker (V.C. DSO) commanded the first DH-2 squadron (24 RFC) which landed in France on February 7th 1916. It was the first squadron composed of all single-seat fighters. Hawker became the first widely known British ace with seven credited victories. The DH-2 used the 100 HP Gnome rotary engine, climbed to 6,500 feet in 12 minutes and did 86 mph at that level. Its ceiling was 14,000 feet, but few pilots flew that high as it took over an hour to get to that level.

Major Hawker was flying his DH-2 (Serial No. 5964) at 10,000 feet on November 23rd, 1916, with two members of his squadron, when he saw three Albatross D.IIs below. The German D.II, a product of late 1916 with synchronized Spandau machine guns, was in every way superior to the British DH-2. The DH-2 pilots, however, did not hesitate to attack with altitude in their favour. Hawker's opponent was the 'Red Baron', Manfred Von Richthofen. The resulting duel was probably one of the most spectacular man-to-man aerial battles in history.

Hawker and Richthofen became separated from the rest and fought for nearly 45 minutes. They began circling each other at 9,000 feet and fought down to the tree tops. Richthofen apparently fired about 900 rounds during the running battle. The wind, blowing toward the German lines, tipped the scales against Hawker as the two ships gradually lost altitude.

Almost down to ground level and running short on fuel, Hawker had only two choices; land in German territory or risk being killed in an attempt to break off combat and head for Allied lines.Von Richthofen's guns jammed 50 yards from the lines, but a bullet from his last burst struck Hawker in the back of his head, killing him instantly.

German soldiers reported burying Major Hawker 250 yards east of Luisenhof Farm, just south of Bapaume on the Flers Road, along the roadside. Richthofen claimed Hawker's Lewis gun from the wreck as a trophy and hung it above the door of his quarters. Major Lanoe George Hawker is listed on the Arras Flying Services Memorial for airmen lost with no known grave.

There were over 200 DH-2s in France during mid-1916, a big factor in the early British air dominance during the Somme Offensive but it was gradually replaced by the French Nieuports during 1917, however, although well past its prime and almost two years after its introduction, some squadrons of the Royal Flying Corps were still equipped with DH-2s in 1918.

Nieuport 27

Nieuport 27 : Darren Harbar Photography

Nieuport originally formed as Nieuport-Duplex in 1902 but it went through several changes of name and management until Gustave Delage's appointment as Nieuport's chief designer in January 1914. This was followed by a series of sesquiplane designs. Nieuport had been famous for wire-braced monoplanes, however they had been developed as far as possible and Nieuport had been looking at other ideas.

The sesquiplane configuration shown here was adopted by Delage as a compromise between the low drag of a monoplane and the greater strength of a biplane configuration. The first of Delage's sesquiplanes was the two seat Nieuport 10 of 1914, which was followed the next year by the smaller single seat Nieuport 11, this was in turn supplemented by the Nieuport 16 and the Nieuport 17 shown above, which was slightly larger with longer wings and fuselage, improved aerodynamic form and better balance. It was initially fitted with the 110 hp (82 kW) Le Rhône 9J engine, though later examples used 120 hp (89 kW) engines and It was armed with a synchronised Vickers gun. The first major break from this design was the Nieuport 28, this was the first Nieuport fighter with two spars to both upper and lower wings, but by the time it was ready for service the French had already chosen the SPAD S.XIII as their primary fighter.

Fokker Albatros DVa 1916

Fokker Albatros DVa 1916 : Darren Harbar Photography

In 1916, Albatros Werke produced the remarkably advanced Albatros D.I. It featured a streamlined fully covered fuselage, with an almost fully-enclosed 160-horsepower in-line Mercedes engine. A sesquiplane version with narrow-chord lower wings, designated the D-III, was introduced early in 1917, and served with great success, despite the narrow lower wing being susceptible to frequent failure in prolonged dives.

The Albatros D.V model, shown here, was fitted with a more powerful 180-horsepower engine. It was however plagued by upper-wing failures so the wings were strengthened, resulting in a re-designation, the D.Va. Unfortunately, the necessary strengthening increased the weight and negated the performance advantage of the new engine.

The D.V and D.Va also continued to experience the same lower wing failure problems in a dive similar to the earlier D.III. A small auxiliary strut was added at the bottom of the outer wing struts to address the issue, but was not entirely successful.

Curtiss JN-4D-2

A Curtiss Jenny : Courtesy of the Combat Air Mseum, Kansas, USA

The Curtiss JN-4 or "Jenny" was one of a series of "JN" biplanes built by the Curtiss Aeroplane Company of Hammondsport, New York, later the Curtiss Aeroplane and Motor Company

Although the Curtiss JN series was originally produced as a training aircraft for the U.S. Army, the "Jenny" continued after World War One as a civil aircraft and became the mainstay of American post-war civil aviation.

Thousands of surplus Jennys were sold at bargain prices to private owners in the years after the war, helping to issue in the barnstorming era of the 1920s. Many former World War One pilots flew the planes trying to make a living as barnstormers, giving aeroplane rides to aviation enthusiasts and flying in aerobatic displays. Charles A. Lindbergh was among them, going on a barnstorming tour of the Midwest with his $500

JN-4 purchased in 1923. It was in this role that the Jenny gained its greatest fame. Flying Circuses were born and entertained crowds with death defying stunts.

In a more docile but sometimes equally dangerous role, the Jenny served as a mail plane in the first continuous airmail service between Washington D.C. and New York City and in other airmail routes. A number of planes and pilots were lost due to weather and mechanical problems during the inaugural Air-Mail service flights.

Sopwith Pup

Sopwith Pup : Darren Harbar Photography

Designed by Herbert Smith, the Sopwith Pup was a British single-seater biplane fighter. It entered service with the Royal Flying Corps and the Royal Naval Air Service in the autumn of 1916. With pleasant flying characteristics and good manoeuvrability, the aircraft was a favourite with pilots. The Pup was eventually outclassed by newer

German fighters, but it was not completely replaced on the Western Front until the end of 1917 with remaining Pups relegated to Home Defence and training units. The Pup's docile flying characteristics also made it ideal for use in aircraft carrier deck landing and take-off experiments.

In May 1916, the Royal Navy Air Service received its first Pups for operational trials with "A" Naval Squadron and the first Pups reached the Western Front in October 1916 with No 8 Squadron RNAS and proved successful, with the squadron's Pups claiming 20 enemy machines destroyed in operations over the Somme battlefield by the end of the year. The first RFC Squadron to re-equip with the Pup was No. 54 Squadron, which arrived in France in December and quickly proved its superiority over the early Fokker Halberstadt and Albartros biplanes. After encountering the Pup in combat, Manfred von Richthofen remarked, *"We saw at once that the enemy aeroplane was superior to ours."*

Sopwith Camel

Sopwith Camel : Darren Harbar Photography

Although some reports state that the Camel was difficult to fly, it nevertheless accounted for a great many enemy losses and was powered by a 130 hp Clerget air cooled rotary engine.

The main variant of the Camel was designated as the F1 but several other dedicated variants were built for a variety of roles, including the 2F.1 Ship's Camel, which was used for operating from the flight decks of aircraft carriers. On the night fighter variant known as the "Comic," the Camels Vickers guns were replaced by Lewis guns mounted over the wings, as the flash from the Vickers tended to dazzle the pilot when they were fired, and synchronised guns were considered unsafe for firing incendiary ammunition. The T.F.1 variant, a dedicated trench fighter, was armoured for the purpose of conducting ground attacks upon heavily defended enemy lines. Further modification led to the cockpit being moved rearwards and the Camel also saw use as a two-seat trainer aircraft introduced. In January 1920, the last aircraft of the type were withdrawn from RAF service.

SPAD SV11 1916

SPAD SV-11 : Courtesy of Bergfalke2

The SPAD S.VII was the first of a series of highly successful biplane fighters produced by, Société Pour L'Aviation et ses Dérivés (SPAD) during the war. Like its 1918 successor the SPAD X111, the S.V11 was known as a sturdy and rugged aircraft with good climbing and flying characteristics and also as a stable gun platform, although pilots that were used to the more manoeuvrable Nieuport fighters found it heavy on the controls. It was flown by a number of the famous aces, such as France's Georges Guynemer (1894-1917) with 54 victories, Italy's Francesco Baracca (1888-1918) with 34 victories and Australia's Alexander Pentland D.S.O. with over 10, Who later saw service in World War Two and died in 1983.

Pfaiz D.111 1917

The Pfalz D.111 : Courtesy of Oren Rozen

The Pfalz D.III was a fighter aircraft used by the Luftstreitkräfte (Imperial German Air Service) during the war. The D.III was the first major original design from Pfalz Flugzeugwerke and although generally considered inferior to the contemporary Albatros and Fokker fighters, the D.III was widely used by the Jagdstaffein from late 1917 to mid-1918 and it continued to serve as a training aircraft until the end of the war.

Deliveries to operational units began in August 1917 with *Jasta* 10 being the first recipient followed by *Jasta* 4.   German pilots variously criticized the Pfalz's heavy controls, low speed, lack of power, or low rate of climb compared to the Albatros. The D.III slipped in turns, leading to crashes when unwary pilots turned at very low altitudes and moreover, the Pfalz also stalled sharply and spun readily. The Pfalz's main advantage was its strength and sturdiness and it could safely dive at high speeds due to its twin-spar lower wing. For this reason, the Pfalz was well-suited to diving attacks on observation balloons which were usually heavily defended by antiaircraft guns trained to the balloon's altitude.

Bristol Fighter

A Bristol Fighter F.2 : Darren Harbar Photography

The Bristol F.2 Fighter was a British two-seat biplane fighter and reconnaissance aircraft developed by Frank Barnwell at the Bristol Aeroplane Company in Filton Bristol. Although initially intended as a replacement for the pre-war Royal Aircraft Factory B.E.2c reconnaissance aircraft, the newly-available Rolls-Royce Falcon V12 engine gave it the performance of a two-seat fighter.

The later F.2B version proved to be an agile aircraft that was able to hold its own against opposing single-seat fighters and its robust design ensured that it remained in military service with many countries into the 1930s with over 5,000 aircraft being built . Some surplus military aircraft were later registered for civilian use, and dedicated civilian versions also proved popular.

Upon America's entry into the First World War they lacked any competitive combat aircraft and so on 1st August 1917, General John J. Pershing, the commander of the American Expeditionary Forces on the Western Front, issued his personal recommendation for the Bristol Fighter to be manufactured in the United States, leading to plans being drawn up for the development and production of an American version of the Fighter by the United States Army Engineering Division.

Original proposals for the American production had the 200 hp (149 kW) Hispano-Suiza engine.

On 5th September 1917, a single F.2B Fighter was delivered to the Smithsonian Institution in Washington. However, efforts to commence production in the United States floundered due to the decision by Colonel V.E. Clark of the Bolling Commission to re-design the Fighter to be powered with the 400 hp (298 kW) Liberty L-12 engine. The Liberty was a totally unsuitable engine for the Bristol, as it was far too heavy and bulky, and the resulting aircraft had a nose-heavy attitude during flight.

Fokker Dr.1 Triplane

The Fokker Dr.1 Triplane : Darren Harbar Photography

Reinhold Platz designed the Fokker Dr.1 Triplane in Germany during the First World War and the first production model, designated as the model Fokker V.5, came off the production line in August 1917. The German ace, Manfred von Richthofen tested the design in September of that year, declaring the model superior to the recently commissioned British Sopwith Triplane design. The Dr.1 saw widespread frontline service in the spring of 1918, becoming famous in a red livery as the aircraft in which von Richthofen achieved the last 19 of his 80 wartime air combat victories, and the plane in which he was killed on 21st April 1918.

The Dr.1's twin, synchronized 7.92mm Spandau machine guns were standard firepower for the era.

The manoeuvrability of the plane was deemed to be exceptional and, despite some minor design aileron and other structural shortcomings and poor quality control and workmanship at the Fokker plant, von Richthofen wanted quick delivery of the model to his Jasta squadrons to counter the British Sopwith aircraft.

Fokker delivered over 300 Dr.1s up to mid-1918, when the updated and vastly superior model Fokker D V11 superseded the triplane. Later tests on the Dr.1 showed that the lower wing carried a much lower lift capability than the upper wing, an imbalance which proved to be a critical negative at higher airspeeds.

Fokker D.V11

Fokker D.V.11

Fokker produced around 3,300 D.V11 aircraft in the second half of 1918 and in service with the Luftsteitkräfte, the D.VII quickly proved itself to be a formidable aircraft.

The Armistice ending the war specifically required, as the fourth clause of the "Clauses Relating to the Western Front", that Germany was required to surrender all D.V11s to the Allies and surviving aircraft saw plenty of service with many other countries in the years after World War One.

Royal Aircraft Factory SE 5

Developed by a team consisting of Henry Folland, John Kenworthy and Major Frank Gooden, the SE5 was one of the fastest aircraft of the war, while being both stable and relatively manoeuvrable. In most respects the S.E.5 had superior performance to the rival Sopwith Camel despite it being less immediately responsive to the controls.

Problems with its engine however, meant that there was a chronic shortage of the type until well into 1918, so while the first examples had reached the Western Front before the Camel, there were fewer squadrons equipped with the S.E.5 than with the Sopwith machine.

Royal Aircraft Factory S.E.5 : Darren Harbar Photography

The Camel and the SE5 together, allowed the RFC to gain air superiority after 1917 and the S.E.5s remained in RAF service for some time following the end of the war with some being transferred to various overseas military operators, while a number were also adopted by civilian operators.

The Bomber

Aircraft design had moved on quickly from the start of the war and machines were now more efficient and had more powerful engines, they could be made bigger and heavier and carry larger payloads, and larger payloads during wartime meant one thing.....bombs!

When the war started, bombing consisted mainly of hand-held devices thrown over the side of the aircraft but by the end of the war, long-range bombers equipped with complex mechanical bombing aids were being built.

I've already mentioned the First Balkan War, when bombs were first dropped from aircraft but these planes were not specialised in any way, they were still basically reconnaissance aircraft. The first truly, purpose built bombers were the Italian Caproni Ca 30s and the British, Coanda Bristol T.B.8. both of which date from 1913.

Bristol T.B.8

Bristol T.B.8

The Bristol T.B.8 was a single engine biplane built by the Bristol Aeroplane Company in Filton, Bristol and powered by either a Gnome or a Le Rhône engine. They were fitted with a prismatic bombsight in the front cockpit and a cylindrical bomb carrier in the lower forward fuselage capable of carrying twelve 10 lb (4.5 kg) bombs, which could be dropped singly or as a salvo as required. Just 56 were built and mostly used for training by the Royal Naval Air Service.

Caproni Ca 30

Italian Caproni Ca 30 : Courtesy of the National Museum of the United States Air Force

The Caproni Ca 30 was built by Gianni Caproni in Italy and was a twin-boom biplane with three 67 kW (80 hp) Gnome rotary engines. It first flew in October 1914. Test flights revealed power to be insufficient and the engine layout unworkable, and Caproni soon adopted a more conventional approach installing three 81 kW (110 hp) Fiat A. 10s. The improved design was bought by the Italian Army and it was delivered in quantity from August 1915.

Avro 504

Avro 504 : Darren Harbar Photography

While mainly used as a trainer, the Avro 504 was also briefly used as a bomber at the start of the war by the Royal Naval Air Service to bomb German airship sheds.

Bréguet 14

The Breguet 14 was a French biplane bomber and reconnaissance aircraft was one of the most important bombers used in World War One and was built in very large numbers both during and after the war.

Apart from its widespread usage, the Bréguet 14 is known for being the first mass-produced aircraft to use large amounts of metal, rather than wood, in its structure. The metal airframe was lighter than a wooden one, making it a fast, agile aircraft, ideal for combat situations. The Bréguet 14's strong construction also allowed it to sustain considerable damage in addition to being easy to handle and possessing favourable performance. The type has often been considered to have been one of the best aircraft of the war.

Breguet 14

Airco de Havilland DH-4

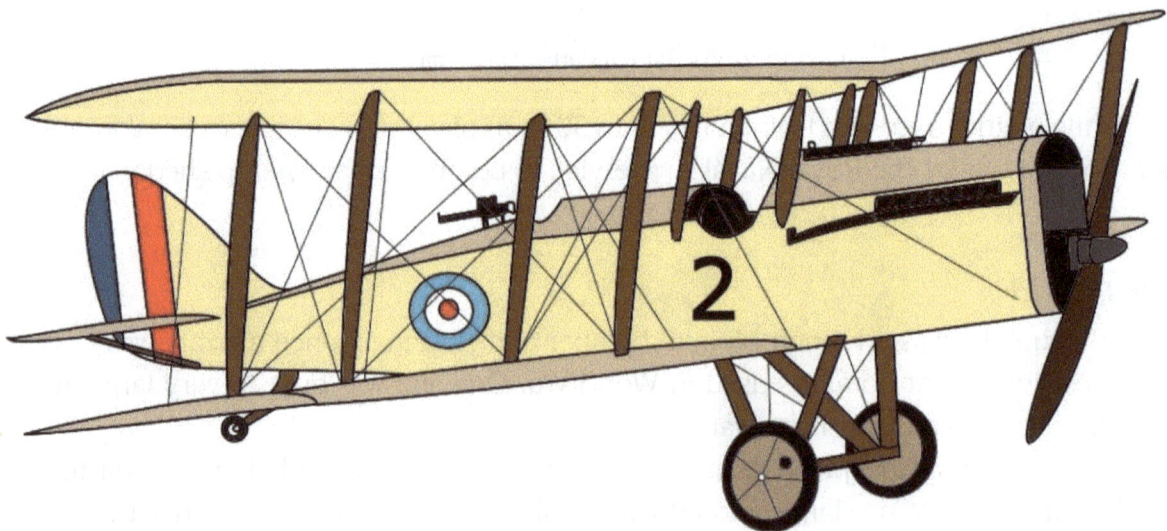

Impression of an Arco de Havelland DH-14

The Airco DH.4 was a British two-seat biplane day bomber. It was designed by Geoffrey de Havilland (hence "DH") for Airco, and was the first British two-seater, light, day-bomber to have an effective defensive armament.

Airco was a British aircraft manufacturer operating from 1912 to 1920. It produced thousands of aircraft for the British military during the First World War, most of which were designed by their chief designer, Geoffrey de Havilland. Advertised in 1918 as the largest aircraft company in the world, Airco also established the first airline in the United Kingdom, "Aircraft Transport and Travel International".

The DH.4 was intended to perform both aerial reconnaissance and day bombing missions. One of the early aims of the design was for it to be powered by the newly developed Beardmore Halford Pullinger engine that was capable of generating up to 160 hp. but actually during its first years of flight, it was tried with several different engines, perhaps the best of which was the 375 hp (280 kW) Rolls-Royce Eagle engine. Armament and ordnance for the aircraft consisted of one 0.303 in (7.7 mm) Vickers machine gun for the pilot and one 0.303 in (7.7 mm) Lewis gun mounted on a Scarff ring for the observer.

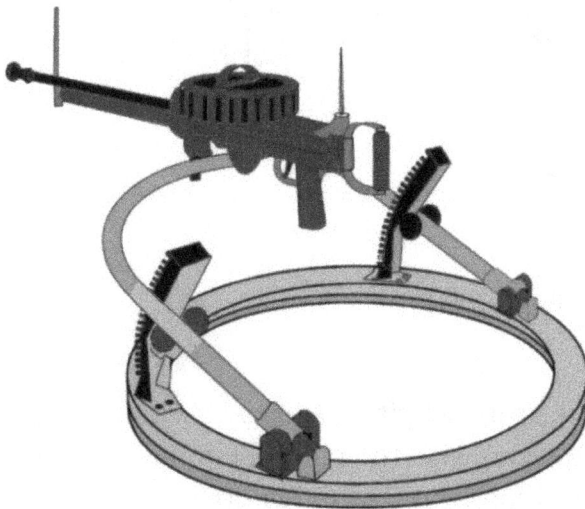

Observer's scarff ring

The Scarff ring was a type of machine gun mounting specifically developed for use on two-seater aircraft. The mount incorporated bungee cord suspension in elevation to compensate for the weight of the gun and allowed a gunner in an open cockpit to swivel and elevate his weapon quickly and fire easily in any direction. In addition to the guns, the aircraft carried either a pair of 230 lb (100 kg) bombs or a maximum payload of four 112 lb (51 kg) bombs.

The DH.4 entered operational service in France on 6th March 1917 with No 55 Squadron of the Royal Flying Corps but the majority of DH.4s were actually manufactured as general purpose two-seaters in the United States and intended to be used in service with the American expeditionary forces being deployed to fight in France. Those built in America were fitted with Liberty 12-A engines.

Following the signing of the Armistice of 11th November 1918 many surplus aircraft, along with many of their counterparts, were sold to civil operators.

Shortly after the conflict, the U.S. Army issued contracts to several companies to re-manufacture many of their DH.4s to the improved DH.4B standard; and continued to operate them into the early 1930s.

German Albatros C.111

The Albatros C.111 was used in a wide variety of roles, including observation, photo-reconnaissance and light bombing and the first twelve aircraft went to the front in December 1915. The largest number were available on the front in August 1916 but they were mostly withdrawn from frontline service by mid-1917. Production continued however and the aircraft was used for training with a total of 2200 aircraft being built. The Polish Air Force also operated the Albatros C.111 in 1918-1920 during the Polish-Soviet War.

Impression of an Albatros C.111

The observer, who occupied the rear cockpit, was armed with a single 7.92 mm (0.312 in) Parabellum MG14 machine gun with the pilot operating a forward facing synchronised 7.92 mm LMG 08/15 machine gun. The C.111 could also carry a bomb load of up to 90 kg (200 lb) in four vertical tubes either in the fuselage or in external racks.

The Russian Sikorsky Ilya Muromets

The Sikorsky Ilya Muromets, Sikorsky S-22, S-23, S-24, S-25, S-26 and S-27 were a class of Russian pre-World War One, large four-engine commercial airliners and military heavy bombers used during the War by the Russian Empire. The aircraft series was named after Ilya Muromets, a hero from Slavic mythology.

Sikorsky Ilaya Muromets

The series was based on the Russian Vityaz or Le Grand, the world's first four-engine aircraft, designed by Igor Sikorsky. The Ilya Muromets aircraft, as it appeared in 1913, was a revolutionary design originally intended for commercial service with its spacious fuselage incorporating a passenger saloon and washroom on board and it was the world's first multi-engine aircraft to go into production.

During World War One, it became the first four-engine bomber to equip a dedicated strategic bombing unit and no other power had a machine to rival it until later in the war.

Shorts 184 Seaplane

Shorts 184 Seaplane

The Shorts Admiralty Type 184, often called the Shorts 225 after the power rating of the first engine fitted, was a British two-seat reconnaissance, bombing and torpedo carrying folding-wing seaplane, designed by Horace Short of the Short brothers. It was first flown in 1915 and remained in service until after the end of the war.

Torpedo-dropping trials had been undertaken using a 160 hp (120 kW) Gnome powered Short Admiralty Type 166 but this had proved insufficiently powerful, and so in

September 1914, arrangement were made for an aircraft to be powered by the 225 hp (168 kW) Sunbeam Mohawk engine which was currently being developed.

Sunbeam Mohawk engine

Design proposals were invited from several companies but Murray Sueter, the director of the naval air department, was impressed by Horace Short's response and on the strength of that alone, two prototypes were ordered.

This aircraft has the distinction of being the first to sink a ship using a torpedo.

Similar in basic design to earlier Short floatplanes built for the Navy, the Type 184 was an equal-span three bay tractor configuration biplane with the fuselage conventionally constructed with a wire-braced wooden box-girder.

The lower wings had a parallel-chord along their full length, while the upper wings increased in chord from the centre section to the wingtips.

The two prototype aircraft had ailerons on the upper wing only. These were single-acting, relying on the airflow to maintain them in a neutral position unless pulled downwards by using the flight controls.

The wings folded for ease of lifting and storing on carriers and could be swung out from the pilot's position by means of a hand-winch in the cockpit, locking being accomplished by means of a spigot in the forward spar locked and unlocked by a quarter-turn.

In the folded position the wings were supported by a transverse shaft mounted in front of the tailplane: this was rotated by a lever in the cockpit so that its upturned ends engaged with slots on the interplane struts in order to lock the wings in the folded position.

Shorts 184 with wings folded

The two main floats were carried by two struts attached to the front cross-tube and two pairs of struts attached to the rear cross-tube, both cross-tubes being arched in the middle to accommodate the torpedo clamps. The wooden tail float incorporated a small water-rudder actuated by torque tubes connected to the main rudder, and cylindrical air-bags were fitted beneath the lower wing-tips.

Initial trials revealed a lack of longitudinal control, and the single-acting ailerons caused problems when taxying downwind, so after trying various other options, ailerons were added to the lower wings as well, these being fitted to all the aircraft built apart from the two prototypes.

The aircraft was also fitted with a radio transmitter and receiver, which was powered by a wind-driven generator mounted on a hinged arm, so that it could be folded back when not being used and a basket of carrier pigeons was also carried, to be used as a back-up for the radio in the event of forced landings.

Some events of 1917

First London blitz by aeroplane
    Russian Revolution begins
    British Royal Family renounces its German name and adopts the name Windsor
    German Großadmiral Alfred von Tirpitz announces unlimited submarine war
    Train at Ciurea station in Romania catches fire and explodes, between 800-1,000 die, making it the third worst rail accident in history

Gotha GV 1917

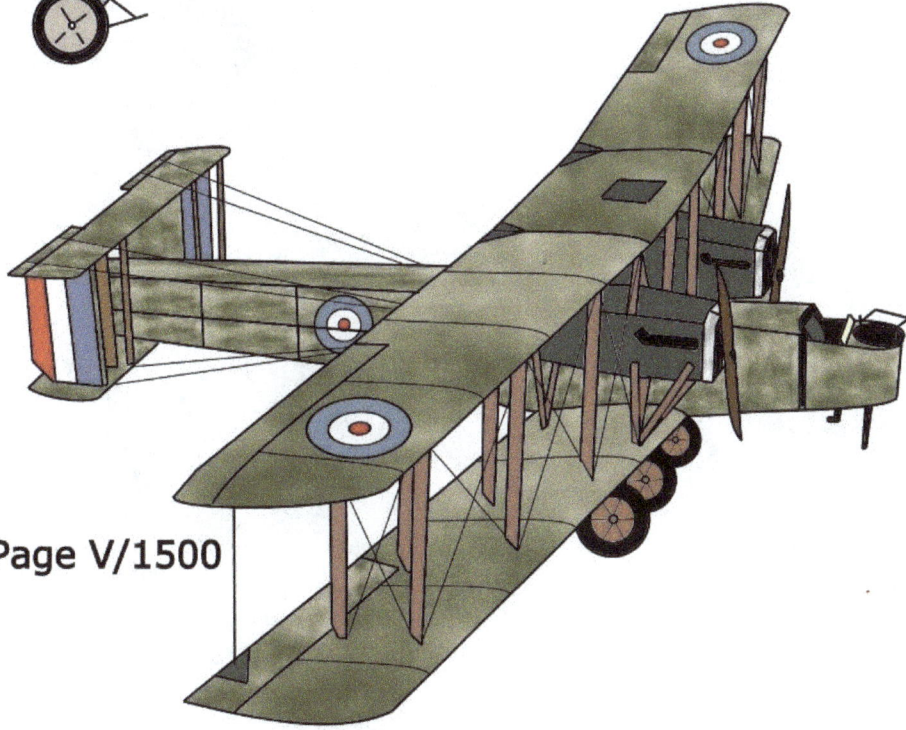

Hadley Page V/1500

Zeppelin Staaken R. V1 1917

Three more World War One bombers

Between the Wars

Chapter Five

Between the Wars

After the end of the war, demand for military aircraft naturally dropped off but interest in aviation among the general public had never been greater and a lot of surplus military aircraft were being sold off to private buyers. Farmers in America and elsewhere employed pilots, with specially adapted planes, to dust their crops with pesticide, businessmen saw the potential of getting to meetings and conferences further afield and much quicker than they ever could before and the public were being enthralled by flying circuses and aerobatic displays. The race was also on among the more competitive aviators for new speed and distance records.

The challenge of the Atlantic

It was inevitable, that once the true potential of the aeroplane had been fully realised and the first regular airmail and passenger services established in 1919, attention should focus on intercontinental travel and 1919 was the year that witnessed the first transatlantic crossing in an aeroplane.

During the 14th and 15th June 1919, the British aviators Alcock and Brown made the first non-stop transatlantic flight. It had been during the War that John Alcock, who had been a regular competitor in aircraft competitions at Hendon before the war, had resolved to fly the Atlantic, and after the war he approached the Vickers engineering and aviation firm at Weybridge in Surrey. Vickers had already considered entering its Vickers Vimy twin-engined bomber in the Daily Mail's transatlantic competition but had not yet found a pilot. Alcock's enthusiasm and previous experience impressed the Vickers' team, and he was quickly appointed as their pilot. Work soon began on converting the Vimy for the long flight, by replacing its bomb racks with extra fuel tanks andshortly afterwards, Arthur Brown, who was still unemployed after being a prisoner of war, approached Vickers seeking a post and it was his knowledge of long distance navigation that convinced them to take him on as Alcock's navigator.

The Vickers's team quickly assembled its plane and at around 16.45 on 14th June, while their main rival, the Handley Page team, was conducting yet another test. The Vickers Vimy, powered by two Rolls Royce Eagle 360 hp engines and carrying 865 imperial gallons of fuel, took off from Lester's Field, in St. John's, Newfoundland.

During the flight at around 17:20, the wind-driven electrical generator failed, depriving the intrepid duo of radio contact, as well as their intercom and more crucially, their heating. As if that wasn't enough, an exhaust pipe burst shortly afterwards, causing a loud noise which subsequently made conversation between them practically impossible.

A replica Vickers Vimy : Darren Harbar Photography

Later they had to fly through a thick fog that prevented Brown from using his sextant to navigate. Blind flying in fog or cloud should only ever be undertaken with gyroscopic instruments, which they didn't have and Alcock twice became disoriented, lost control of the aircraft and nearly hit the sea after a spiral dive. He also had to deal with a broken trim control that caused the plane to become increasingly nose-heavy as fuel was consumed.

At a little after midnight, Brown got a brief glimpse of the stars and was able to fleetingly use his sextant and thankfully verify that they were still on course. Then, at 3:00

a.m. they flew into a large snowstorm and their instruments iced up, the plane itself was also in danger of icing and becoming unflyable.

Eventually, due to a combination of skill, dogged determination and good luck, they made landfall on 15th June 1919, not far from their intended landing place, in Clifden, County Galway at 8:15 a.m. after a slightly less than sixteen-hour flight.

The aircraft was damaged on finally setting down because they had landed on what appeared from the air to be a suitable green field, but which in fact turned out to be Derrygilmlagh Bog, and this caused the aircraft to nose-over, but thankfully neither of the brave airmen were hurt. Brown later said that if the weather had been kinder to them, they could have pressed on to London.

The Secretary of state for Air, Winston Churchill, presented Alcock and Brown with the Daily Mail prize for the first crossing of the Atlantic Ocean in less than 72 consecutive hours. They had carried a small amount of mail on the flight with them making it also the first transatlantic airmail flight.

The two aviators were awarded the honour of Knight Commander of the Most Excellent Order of the British Empire (KBE) by King George V at Windsor Castle, one week later.

The South Atlantic

In 1922 the first aerial crossing of the South Atlantic was made by the Portuguese naval aviators Gago Coutinho and Sacadura Cabral. They flew from Lisbon, Portugal, to Rio de Janeiro, Brazil in stages, using three different Fairey 111 biplanes, and they covered a distance of 8,383 kilometres (5,209 mi) between 30th March and 17th June.

The first stage of their journey ended in the Canary Islands but resumed again on the 5th April. They had to make repairs to their plane on reaching Sao Vincent Island, Cape Verde but then flew on to Santiago Island and then the Saint Peter and Saint Paul Archipelago where they had to ditch in rough seas just off the coast. Their aircraft lost one of its floats and sank but the two aviators were rescued by the Portuguese cruisier NRP República that had been sent to support the aerial crossing.

The loss of the plane seemed at first to have put an end to their intrepid venture, but support for the flight from both the Brazilian and Portuguese public, led the Portuguese government to send another Fairey 111 seaplane to complete the flight, however an engine problem with the new aircraft forced them to ditch once again, this time in the middle of the ocean, where they drifted for nine hours before being rescued by the British cargo ship, Paris City.

A third Fairey 111 was sent out, carried by the Cruisier NRP Carvaiho Araújo and put in the waters off Fernando Noronha, from where the intrepid aviators were able to complete their most eventful of journeys.

Coutinho and Cabral's flight remains notable as a milestone in aviation, not just as the first crossing of the South Atlantic but also for its use of new technologies such as the artificial horizon, invented by Lawrence Burst Sperry (1892–1923), Sperry also invented the first autopilot which he demonstrated to great effect in France in 1914

Claude Dornier

The first night-time crossing of the Atlantic was accomplished during 16th and 17th April 1927 by the Portuguese aviators Sarmento de Beires, Jorge de Castilho and Manuel Gouveia, flying from the Bijagos Archipelago, Portuguese Guinea to Fernando de Noronha, Brazil, in the "*Argos,*" a Dornier Wal flying boat.

Claude Honoré Désiré Dornier (born in Kempten in Allgäu (1884–1969) was a prominent German aeroplane designer. His notable designs include the 12-engine Dornier Do X flying boat that as first flown in 1929 and for decades the world's largest and most powerful aeroplane.

Claude Dornier pictured before a Dornier Do K-3 in 1931

The Do X was a semi-cantilever monoplane that had an all duralumin hull with wings composed of a steel reinforced duralumin framework covered in heavy linen fabric, finished with aluminium paint.

Dornier Wal flying-boat

It was initially powered by twelve 391 kW (524 hp) Siemens built, Bristol Jupiter radial engines in tandem mountings with six tractor propellers and six pushers mounted in six strut-mounted nacelles above the wing.

The nacelles were joined by an auxiliary wing whose purpose was to stabilise the mountings. The air-cooled Jupiter engines were prone to overheating however and could barely lift the Do X to an altitude of 425 m (1,400 ft). After completing 103 flights in 1930, the Do X was refitted with 455 kW (610 hp) Curtiss V-1570 Conqueror liquid-cooled V-12 engines, after which it was able to reach the altitude of 500 m (1,650 ft) necessary to cross the Atlantic.

Dornier Do X flying-boat

The engines were supervised during flight by a flight engineer, who also controlled the 12 throttles and monitored the 12 sets of engine gauges. The pilot would ask the engineer to adjust the power setting, in a manner similar to the system used on ships via a speaking tube, indeed, many aspects of the aircraft echoed nautical arrangements of the time, including the flight deck that was said to resemble a ships bridge.

Dornier designed the flying boat to carry 66 passengers on long-distance flights or 100 passengers on short flights. The luxurious passenger accommodation approached the standards of transatlantic liners. There were three decks. On the main deck was a smoking room, a dining salon, and seating for the 66 passengers which could also be converted to sleeping berths for night flights. Aft of the passenger spaces was an all-electric galley, toilets and cargo hold. The cockpit, navigational office, engine control and radio rooms were on the upper deck. The lower deck held fuel tanks and nine watertight compartments, only seven of which were needed to provide full flotation. Similar to the later Boeing 314, the Do-X lacked conventional wing floats, instead using fuselage mounted "stub wings" to stabilise the craft in the water, which also doubled as an embarkation platform for passengers.

Charles Lindbergh

Lindbergh and the Spirit of St. Louis

The first solo crossing of the Atlantic was made on the 20th and 21st May 1927 by Charles Lindbergh in the Spirit of St Louis, a single engine monoplane designed by Donald Albert Hall (no relation to the building). Lindbergh took off from Roosevelt Field, Mineola, New York and landed at Le Bourget Airport near Paris, a flight of some thirty-three and a half hours, during which he flew over Cape Cod and Nova Scotia, reaching the ocean as the sun set.

Fog thickened in the night sky, and ice formed on his plane when he attempted to pass through the clouds. He also struggled with drowsiness, fighting to stay awake as he sometimes flew only 10 feet above the ocean.

A tiny fishing boat provided the first sign that he had reached Europe, which must have been a huge relief and within an hour of that sighting he had reached land. He flew about 1,500 feet (460 meters) over Ireland and England, before heading toward France as the weather cleared. Darkness fell again as he passed over the coast of his target country.

The engine that powered the Spirit of St Louis was the Wright J-5 Whirlwind, air-cooled radial. The J-5 was a follow-on engine to the J-4 and sported a redesigned head and widely spaced valves. This allowed engineers to use larger valves with more cooling fins and better airflow between the ports. Valves were machined from tungsten and their hollow stems filled with sodium and potassium salts for cooling.

Rocker arms and push rods were fully enclosed, a first for U.S. air-cooled engines, and a new three-barrel carburettor solved the mixture and distribution problems of previous models, (The original J-1 used three carburettors, each serving three cylinders), As a result, the J-5 Whirl-

Wright J-5 Whirlwing engine

wind was the most reliable radial of its time and said to be everything a simple air-cooled engine can be, by simple, we mean one without super or turbocharging, fuel injection, or reduction gearing for the prop. Its performance, power-to-weight ratio and reliability made it the engine of choice for many world explorers.

Tragedy famously struck the Lindbergh family in 1932 when the couple's first child was kidnapped from their home. The crime made headlines around the world and although the Lindberghs paid the $50,000 ransom, sadly, the boy's body was found in nearby woods some weeks later. A carpenter, Bruno Hauptmann, was arrested and charged with murder, found guilty and executed in 1936. The Lindberghs later had five more children.

Amelia Earhart (1897-1937)

Amelia developed a passion for flying as a teenager and in 1928 she was the first woman passenger to cross the Atlantic in a Fokker F.V11 Tri-Motor piloted by Wilmer Stultz and Louis Gordon. The intrepid three crossed from Newfoundland to South Wales in twenty hours and forty minutes.

Although Earhart had gained fame for her transatlantic flight, she endeavoured to set a record of her own. Shortly after her return, piloting an Avro Avian 7083, she set off on her first long solo flight and by making the trip in August 1928, became the first woman to fly solo across the North American continent and back.

Her piloting skills and experience were growing all the time and General Leigh Wade, who flew with Earhart in 1929 said *"She was a born flier, with a delicate touch on the stick."*

On the morning of May 20th 1932, the 34-year-old Amelia Earhart set off from Harbour Grace in Newfoundland in a Lockheed Vega 5B with the intention of flying to Paris. After a flight lasting 14 hours, 56 minutes, during which she contended with strong northerly winds, icy conditions and mechanical problems, Earhart landed in a pasture at Culmore, Northern Ireland. The landing was witnessed by locals, Cecil King and T. Sawyer and when a farm hand asked her, "Have you flown far?" "From America" Earhart replied, at that moment becoming the first woman to fly solo across the Atlantic.

Early in 1936, Earhart started planning a round-the-world flight. Although others had flown around the world, her flight would be the longest at 29,000 miles (47,000 km) because it followed a roughly equatorial route. With financing from Purdue University, in July 1936, a Lockheed Electra 10E was built by the Lockheed Aircraft Company to her specifications, which included extensive modifications to the fuselage to incorporate many additional fuel tanks.

Earhart chose Captain Harry Manning as her navigator; he had been the captain of the President Roosevelt, the ship that had brought Earhart back from Europe in 1928. Manning was not only a navigator, but he was also a pilot and a skilled radio operator who knew Morse code. However, a second navigator, Fred Noonan was chosen to navigate from Hawaii to Howland Island, a particularly difficult portion of the flight; then Manning would continue with Earhart to Australia and she would proceed on her own for the remainder of the project.

The first attempt on 17th March ended in failure due to an accident on take-off and Manning walked away from the project while the aircraft was being repaired, leaving just Amelia and Noonan, neither of whom were skilled radio operators. While the Electra was being repaired, Earhart and her husband George Putnam secured additional funds and prepared for a second attempt. This time flying west to east, the second attempt began with an unpublicised flight from Oakland to Miami, Florida, and after arriving there, Earhart publicly announced her plans to circumnavigate the globe.

The decision to fly in the opposite direction was partly the result of changes in global wind and weather patterns along the planned route. On this second flight, Fred Noonan was Earhart's only crew member and the pair departed Miami on June 1st. After numerous stops in South America, Africa, the Indian subcontinent and South-east Asia, they arrived at Lae, New Guinea Lae, on June 29th 1937. At this stage, about 22,000 miles (35,000 km) of the journey had been completed. The remaining 7,000 miles (11,000 km) would be over the Pacific.

Earhart and Noonan departed from Lae on the 2nd July 1937 at midnight GMT. Bound for Howard Island some 2,600 miles distant. Two brightly lit ships were stationed to mark the route and Earhart was in intermittent contact with a U.S. Coast-guard ship, the Itasca, that was near Howard Island. One of the last communications from Earhart said that they were running out of fuel. The plane was believed to have gone down some 100 miles from the island, and an extensive search was undertaken to find Earhart and Noonan. However, on July 19th 1937, the operation was called off, and the pair were declared lost at sea.

The first east to west non-stop transatlantic crossing by an aeroplane was made in 1928 by the Bremen, a German Junkers W33 type aircraft, from Baldonnel Airfield in County Dublin, Ireland. On board were the owner, Ehrenfried von Hünefield, pilot Hermann Köhl and Irish navigator Major James Fitzmaurice.

On 18th August 1932, Jim Mollison made the first east to west solo trans-Atlantic flight; flying from Portmarnock in Ireland to Pennfield, New Brunswick, Canada, in a de Havilland Puss Moth.

de Havilland Puss Moth

The first transpolar transatlantic crossing was the non-stop flight piloted by Valery Chkalov and covering some 8,811 kilometres (5,475 mi) over 63 hours from St. Petersburg, Russia to Vancouver, Washington, between the 18th and the 20th June 1937 flying in a Tupolev ANT-25.

Britain to Australia

In 1919 the Australian government offered a prize of £10,000 for the first flight from Great Britain to Australia. Of the six entries that started the race, the winners were the Vickers Vimy team.

Vickers Vimy team

Vickers entered the converted Vimy bomber, (G-EAOU), the registration being whimsically said to stand for "God 'elp all of us", crewed by Captain Ross Macpherson with his brother Lieutenant Keith Macpherson Smith as co-pilot and mechanics Sergeant W.H. (Wally) Shiers and J.M. (Jim) Bennett.

The Vimy left Hounslow Heath at 8am on 12th November 1919 and flew via Lyon, Rome, Cairo, Damascus, Basra, Karachi, Delhi, Calcutta, Akyab, Rangoon, Singora in Siam (Thailand,) Singapore, Batavia, and Surabaya, reaching Darwin at 4.10pm on 10th December 1919. The flight distance was estimated as 17,911 kilometres (11,123 mi) and total flying time was 135 hours 55 minutes (131.8 km/h or 81.9 mph). The prize money was shared between the Smith brothers and the two mechanics.

The Smith brothers each received a knighthood for this exploit, and the company presented their aircraft to the Australian government and it is now displayed at Adelaide Airport.

Sopwith Wallaby team

Impression of a Sopwith Wallaby

At 11.44 a.m. on 21st October 1919, Captain George Campbell Matthews AFC as pilot, and Sergeant Thomas D. Kay as mechanic, took off from Hounslow Heath Aerodrome in a Sopwith Wallaby (G-EAKS). Bad weather caused delays at Cologne and Vienna and then they were imprisoned as suspected Bolsheviks in Yugoslavia with further delays due to snow at Belgrade. A cracked engine cylinder at Constantinople and bad weather at Aleppo caused even more delays until finally, on 17th April 1920, the Wallaby crashed on landing at Grokgak, on Bali. Matthews was slightly injured.

Alliance P.2 team

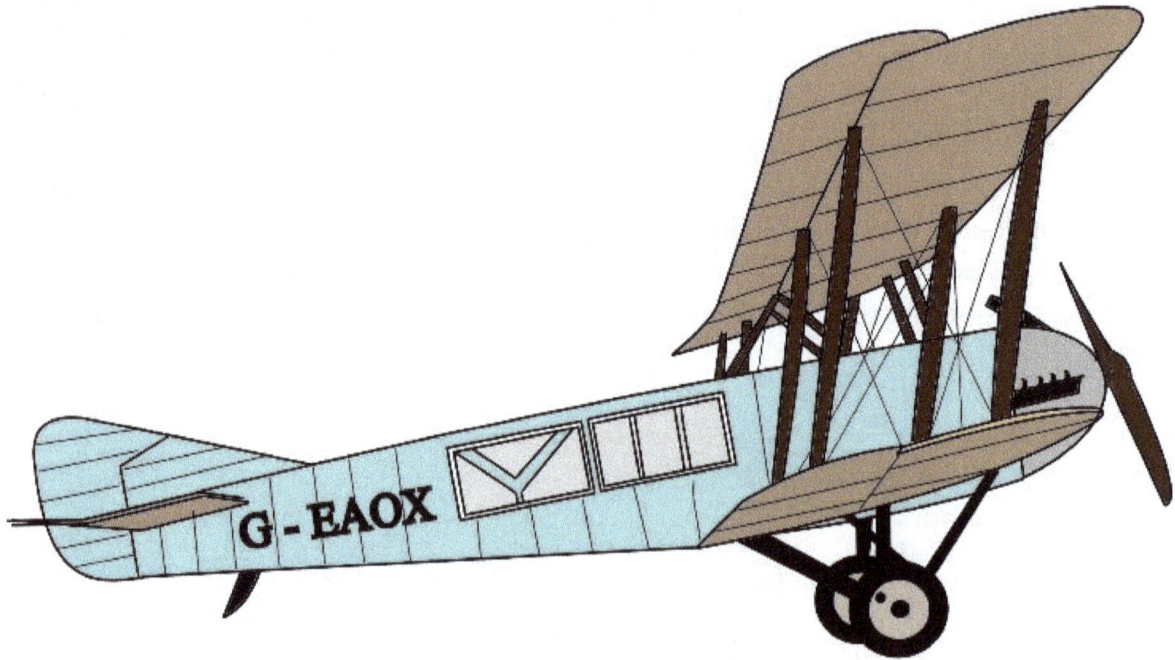

impression of an Alliance P.2 Seabird

On 13th November 1919, Lieutenant Roger M. Douglas, MC DCM and Lieutenant J.S.L. Ross took off from Hounslow Heath in an Alliance P. 2 Seabird (G-EAOX) named 'Endeavour'.

The aircraft unfortunately crashed in an orchard in Surbiton, killing Lieutenant Ross outright. Roger Douglas died soon after of his injuries and it is tragic events such as those, that go to show the enormity of the risks they were taking and just how brave these pioneers of flight really were.

Blackburn Kangaroo team

Impression of a Blackburn Kanaroo

A team consisting of Lieutenant V. Rendle, Captain Wilkins, Lieutenant D.R. Williams and Lieutenant Garnsey St. C. Potts as crew and flying a Blackburn Kangaroo (G-EAOW), had selected an Australian aviator, Charles Kingford Smith, to be their navigator but Smith withdrew from the contest and Captain Hubert Wilkins MC and bar, took his place.

On 21st November 1919, the Kangaroo took off from Hounslow Heath. Problems were experienced with the engines and the plane was forced down over France. Repairs were made and the flight continued, although still with engine problems. On 8th December 1919, the aircraft crash-landed at Suba Bay, Crete, ending up against the fence of a mental hospital. Fortunately, the crew escaped without injury.

Martinsyde Type A team

Martinsyde Type A

On 5th December 1919, Captain Cedric E. Howell and Lieutenant George Henry Fraser, left London in a Martinsyde Type A Mk. 1 (G-EAMR) aircraft. On 9th December, the aircraft disappeared near Corfu, the wreckage and Howell's body were found off-shore, but Fraser's body was never recovered.

Airco DH.9 team

Wartime Airco DH.9 : Darren Harbar Photography

On 8th January 1920, an Airco DH.9 (G-EAQM), piloted by Lieutenant Ray Parer with co-pilot Lieutenant John C. McIntosh, took off from Hounslow Heath. The aircraft completed the flight, the first by a single-engine machine, in an epic 206 days later on 2 August 1920, earning Parer the nickname "Battling Ray". Although outside the time limit, the crew were awarded a consolation prize of £1,000, second only to the Vimy.

Retractable Undercarriage

In 1920 a Dayton-Wright RB-1, also known as the Dayton-Wright Racer was entered in the Gordon Bennett Cup air race.

Advanced for its day, it incorporated a mechanism designed by Charles Hampson Grant to vary its camber in flight by moving the leading edge and trailing edge.

The aircraft also featured a retractable undercarriage operated by a hand-crank, making it one of the first instances of undercarriage retraction for aerodynamic benefit alone. The propeller shaft was mounted through a large oval radiator, depriving the pilot of any forward view, although he was provided with flexible celluloid side windows. Cockpit access was through a hatch in the top of the fuselage.

Dayton-Wright RB-1

Other events of the twenties

Pullman airliner shown at Olympia, 1920
First test sinking of a battleship by aerial bombardment, 1921
First flights of Bristol Bulldog 1927
First flight Dornier Do X flying boat 1929

Amy Johnson (1903-1941)

Amy Johnson achieved worldwide recognition when, in 1930, she became the first woman to fly solo from England to Australia in a Tiger Moth, G-AAAH *"Jason"*. She left Croyden, Surrey, on 5th May and landed at Darwin, Northern Territory on 24th May, a flight of some 11,000 miles (18,000 km), for which she received the Harmon Trophy as well as a CBE in George Vs 1930 Birthday Honours in recognition of her achievement, and was also honoured with the No. 1 civil pilot's licence under Australia's 1921 Air Navigation Regulations.

Johnson next obtained a de Havilland DH 80 Puss Moth G-AAZV which she named *"Jason II"* and in July 1931, she and co-pilot Jack Humphreys became the first people to fly from London to Moscow in one day, completing the 1,760 miles (2,830 km) journey in approximately 21 hours. From there, they continued across Siberia and on to Tokyo, setting a record time for Britain to Japan.

She married Scottish pilot Jim Mollison in 1932, after he had apparently proposed to her during a flight together some eight hours after they had first met. In July 1932, Johnson set a solo record for the flight from London to Cape Town, South Africa, in Puss Moth G-ACAB, named *"Desert Cloud"*, breaking her new husband's record. After several more record breaking flights, including a record time from Britain to India in 1934 and regaining her Britain to South Africa record in 1936, she was awarded the Gold Medal of the Royal Aero Club.

On 5th January 1941, whilst delivering an Airspeed Oxford from Prestwick, via Blackpool to RAF Kidlington near Oxford, for the Air Transport Auxiliary, she was blown off course and ran out of fuel. She bailed out of her aircraft, which crashed into the Thames Estuary near Herne Bay. A convoy of wartime vessels in the Thames Estuary spotted Johnson's parachute coming down and saw her alive in the water, calling for help. Conditions were poor, there was a heavy sea and a strong tide, snow was falling and it was intensely cold. Lt Commander Walter Fletcher, the Captain of HMS Haslemere, navigated his ship to attempt a rescue. The crew of the vessel threw ropes out to Johnson but she was unable to reach them and was lost under the ship. She was thirty-seven at the time. Various rumours have surrounded her death, including one that she was shot down by friendly fire when failing to give the correct call sign and some say that there was a cover-up by the Navy and that her would-be recue ship reversed causing her to be dragged underneath. Some attempts have been made to find the wreckage of her plane but we may never know the exact circumstances of her death.

Tiger Moth similar to the one flown by Amy Johnson : Darren Harbar Photography

Bristol Bulldog

Bristol Bulldog

1932 saw the Perseus sleeve-valve engine cleared for flight in a Bristol Bulldog fighter. The Bristol Bulldog was a British Royal Air Force single-seat biplane fighter designed during the 1920s by the Bristol Aeroplane Company. More than 400 Bulldogs were produced for the RAF and overseas customers, and it was one of the most famous aircraft used by the RAF during the inter-war period. The Bulldog never saw combat with the RAF, although during the Abyssinian Crisis of 1935–36, Bristol Bulldogs were sent to the Sudan to reinforce Middle East Command. Douglas Bader, better known for his Second World War actions, lost both of his legs when his Bristol Bulldog crashed while he was performing unauthorised aerobatics at Woodley airfield near Reading.

The Bulldog was withdrawn from RAF fighter command in July 1937, being primarily replaced by the Gloster Gauntlet.

Bristol Gauntlet

The Bristol Gauntlet was another British single-seat biplane fighter, designed and built by Gloster Aircraft in the 1930s

The Gloster aircraft company was formerly The Gloucestershire Aircraft Company but foreigners found it difficult to pronounce so it shortened to simply Gloster, later it became part of the Hawker Siddeley group and the Gloster name disappeared in 1963.

Bristol Gauntlet

The Gloster was the last RAF fighter to have an open cockpit and the penultimate biplane fighter in service. The Bulldog's RAF career was not over though, for the type continued to serve for a few years with Service Flying Training Schools and was exported to foreign air forces, seeing service with Australia, Denmark, Estonia, Finland, Japan, Siam and Sweden.

The Sleeve Valve

Until the introduction of the sleeve-valve, aero-engines had poppet valves that moved up and down to open and close the inlet and exhaust ports, the same as on a car engine. In a sleeve-valve piston engine, a sleeve is fitted between the piston and the cylinder wall and rotates or slides back and forth. The sleeve has holes in it that line up with the ports at the appropriate stage of the cycle to let air in or expel exhaust gases.

poppet valves

sleeve valve

ports

pistons

driving pin

cylinder block

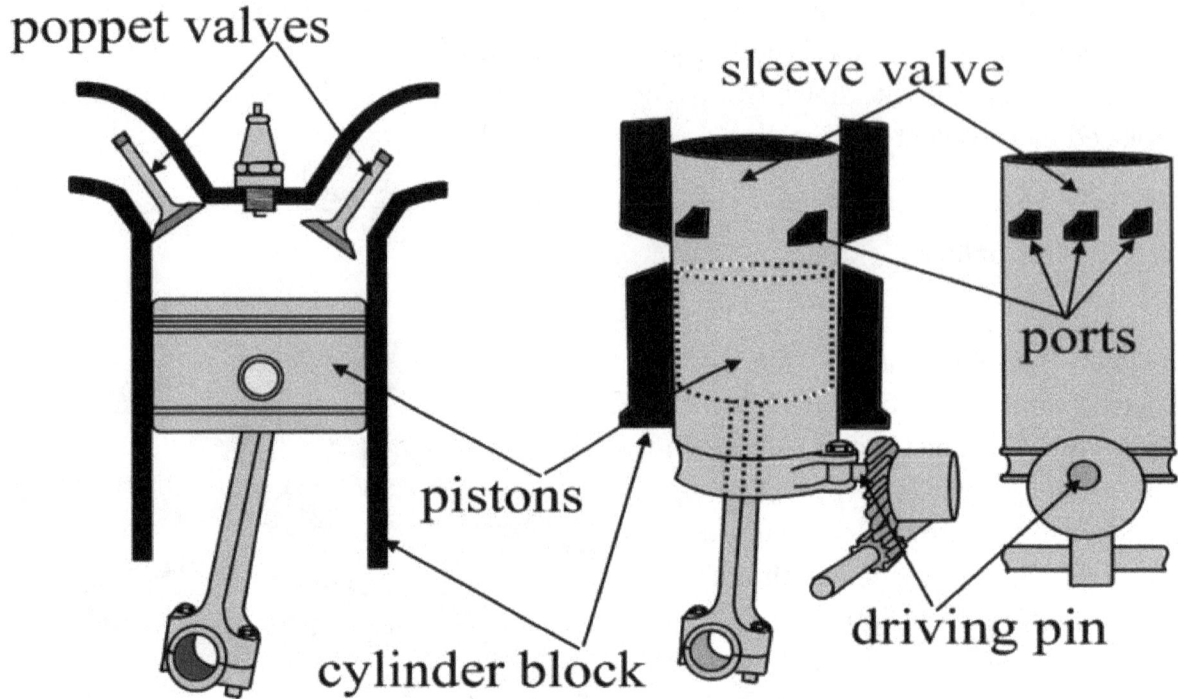

The difference between poppet and sleeve valves

The advantage of a sleeve valve is that it is subject to less wear as well as having fewer moving parts, meaning it can remain serviceable for longer periods between servicing.

As previously mentioned, the first aircraft to benefit from a Perseus nine-cylinder sleeve-valve engine was the Bristol Bulldog in 1933. In 1936, the Hercules 14-cylinder radial sleeve-valve engine was built with over 50,000 being produced before production ended 1966, making it the most successful sleeve-valve engine in the world. It developed from 1,270hp to 2,00hp.

Later in 1938, the Centaurus, an 18-cylinder two row sleeve valve radial had its first run beginning at 2,000hp and eventually reaching 3.200hp.

First Monoplane Airliners

Ford tri-motor

Nicknamed the "Tin Goose" production of the Ford Tri-motor started in 1925 and ended in 1933. Although designed for the civilian market it also saw some military use and was similar in design and appearance to the Fokker F.V11, except for being of all metal construction, a feature that led Henry Ford to describe it as "the safest airliner around".

Ford Tri-Motor : Courtesy of Alexf

Its fuselage and wings followed a design pioneered by Junkers during World War One along with the Junkers J.1 and used post-war in a series of airliners, starting with the Junkers F.13 low-wing monoplane of 1920, of which a number were exported to the US, the Junkers K 16 high-wing airliner of 1921, and the Junkers G 24 trimotor of 1924. All of these were constructed of aluminium alloy, which was corrugated for added stiffness, although the resulting drag reduced its overall performance. So similar were the designs that Junkers sued and won when Ford attempted to export an aircraft to Europe. In 1930, Ford countersued in Prague but was decisively defeated a second time, with the court finding that Ford had infringed upon Junkers' patents.

The original commercial production 4-AT had three air-cooled Wright radial engines and carried a crew of three, a pilot, a co-pilot, and a stewardess, as well as eight or nine passengers. The later 5-AT was fitted with the more powerful Pratt & Whitney engines. All the models had an aluminium corrugated sheet-metal body and wings. Unlike many aircraft of this era, its control surfaces were not fabric-covered, but were also made of corrugated metal and as was common at the time, its rudder and elevators were operated by metal cables that were strung along the external surface of the aircraft. Engine gauges were also mounted externally, on the engines, to be read by the pilot while looking through the aircraft windshield.

Boeing 247

Boeing 247 : Courtesy of United Airlines

1933 saw the flight of the first truly modern looking monoplane airliner, considered the first such aircraft to fully incorporate advances such as all-metal anodized aluminium semi-monocoque construction and a fully cantilevered wing and retractable landing gear.

Other advanced features included control surface trim tabs, an autopilot and de-icing boots for the wings and tailplane. A de-icing boot consists of a thick rubber membrane that is installed over the surface to be de-iced. As atmospheric icing occurs, a pneumatic system inflates the boot with compressed air. This expansion in size cracks any ice that has accumulated, and this ice is blown away into the airflow. The boots are then deflated to return the wing or surface to its optimal shape.

The 247 was also the first twin-engine passenger transport that was able to fly on just one engine. The cockpit windshield was at first angled forward, instead of having the conventional aft sweep. This was the design solution to the problem of lit control panel instruments reflecting off the windshield at night, but it turned out that the forward-sloping windshield would reflect ground lights instead, especially during landings as well as increasing drag slightly. By the introduction of the 247D, the windshield was sloped aft in the usual way, and the night-glare problem was resolved by installing an extension or screen over the control panel itself.

Ordered straight off the drawing board, the 247 first flew on February 8th 1933 and entered service later that year. Although subsequent development in airliner design saw both engines and airframes becoming larger and four-engine designs emerging, no significant changes to this basic design appeared until cabin pressurization and high-altitude cruise were introduced in 1940.DC-3

C47 a military version of the DC-3 : Darren Harbar Photography

By the mid 1930s, the gold standard of airliner construction was achieved: the DC-3 was a full aluminium aircraft with monocoque construction and a cantilever wing. It was developed as a larger, improved 14-bed sleeper version of the Douglas DC-2.

It was a low-wing metal monoplane with a tailwheel landing gear and was powered by two 1,200 hp (890 kW) Pratt & Whitney Twin Wasp radial piston engines. It had a cruise speed of 207 mph (333 km/h) and the capacity to carry 21 to 32 passengers or 6,000 lbs (2,700 kg) of cargo, a range of 1,500 miles (2,400 km), and could operate from short runways.

Before World War Two, it pioneered a lot of new air travel routes, as it was capable of crossing America and made worldwide flights possible, it carried passengers in greater comfort than they were used to, and was reliable and easy to maintain. It is considered the first airliner that could profitably carry passengers alone.

Following the war, the airliner market was flooded with surplus military transport aircraft, and the DC-3 could not be upgraded by Douglas because of the cost involved. It was then made obsolete on main routes by more advanced aircraft such as the Douglas DC-6 and the Lockheed Constellation.

Civil DC-3 production ended in 1942 at 607 aircraft. Military versions, including the C-47 Skytrain shown above, as well as Soviet and Japanese-built versions, brought total production to over 16,000. Many continued to see service in a variety of niche roles and as many as 2,000 DC-3s and military derivatives were estimated to be still flying as late as 2013.

A Quick look at a helicopter

Louis Charles Breguet

Louis Charles Breguet is especially known for his development of reconnaissance aircraft used by the French in World War One, like the Bréguet 14, shown in chapter 10, and after the war he was one of the pioneers in the construction of metal aircraft.

1934 saw the first flight of his Gyroplane Laboratoire, an early helicopter. Bréguet had already experimented with rotor aircraft in 1909, however, he chose to concentrate on aeroplanes until the end of the 1920s, then in 1929 he announced a set of patents which addressed the flight stabilization of roto aircraft, and in 1931, Bréguet created the "Syndicate for Gyroplane Studies," together with Rene Dorand as technical director. Their goal was the development of an experimental helicopter, the Gyroplane Laboratoire shown here.

Working with a limited budget, Dorand built the craft using as many salvaged bits and pieces as he could, including a Bréguet 19 airplane fuselage for the craft's body and a surplus aircraft engine to power it.

The craft consisted of a thin metallic frame with a tail and three wheels, one on either side mounted on outriggers and a smaller one at the front of the aircraft. The engine was located forward, and the pilot sat behind it in an open cage. Two twin-bladed rotors, each nearly 54 feet (16.5 meters) long, were stacked on top of each other, and rotated in opposite directions, thereby cancelling out their torque. The rotor blades were attached to the shaft with a hinge mechanism (they were "articulated"), and the pitch of the rotor could be increased or decreased on each revolution (cyclic pitch control), thereby controlling lift. If the propellers were angled so they pushed the air down more, lift would increase, and the craft would rise.

Bréguet had confidence in his machine despite warnings from his mechanics that the controls were not yet perfected and in November 1933, he scheduled a demonstration flight for his investors. A former French Army pilot named Maurice Claisse reluctantly agreed to make the test.

He climbed into the craft and started the engine as three men stood by on the ground to hold the machine. As the rotors turned the craft immediately tilted to the right and several bystanders as well as ground-staff had to run for cover as the rotor blades hit the ground and shattered. Fortunately, no one was hurt, but the aircraft was badly damaged, postponing any further tests.

Throughout 1934 and 1935, Bréguet extensively modified his craft and performed ground tests. His most important addition was a new system for controlling the direction of flight. By tilting the axle on which the rotors turned, pitching the rotor disk, the helicopter could be made to move forward, sideways, or even backward. He added a system for controlling the yaw of the aircraft by allowing the two rotors to each have a different pitch (differential collective pitch).

On June 26, 1935, test pilot Maurice Claisse piloted the craft for a second time. This time he was able to lift it off the ground without crashing and he then made several flights at speeds of 18 to 30 miles per hour.

The French Air Ministry was so impressed it gave Bréguet a contract that covered the cost of flight trials and provided a million-franc-bonus if all performance goals were achieved.

By December 1935, Bréguet began another series of test flights. He then proceeded to push his aircraft far beyond the limits of any previous rotary aircraft.

The craft achieved a record speed of 75 miles per hour (121 kilometres per hour) and climbed to a record altitude of 518 feet (158 meters), remaining in the air for more than an hour. It stayed in a hover over one spot for ten minutes which was also a record. Bréguet completed his initial tests in late 1936 and received the one-million-franc bonus.

Bréguet received another Air Ministry contract for further development but made little progress over the next several years. The big concern about helicopters was what would happen if the engine failed in flight. An airplane could glide to the ground, but a helicopter needed to descend while "autorotating," essentially using the rotor as a parachute.

Bréguet's aircraft was badly damaged during an autorotation test in 1939 and with war imminent, Bréguet put his craft in storage and turned his attention to the full-scale production of bombers. His helicopter was ultimately destroyed in 1943 during the Allied bombing of the Villacoublay Airfield.

Other events of the Thirties

1931 Empire State Building opens in US.

1932 First female solo transatlantic flight (Amelia Earhart)
Franklin Roosevelt elected president of US

1933 A Westland Wapitis, flown by Flt Lt David F. McIntyre and powered by a Pegasus engine is the first aeroplane to fly over Mt. Everest.
First solo flight around the world.
US Prohibition ends

1936 First helicopter flight of over an hour

1937 Hindenburg disaster shatters public confidence in airships.

1938 First flight of pressurised transport aeroplane.
Germany occupies Austria

1939 World War Two begins
BOAC formed

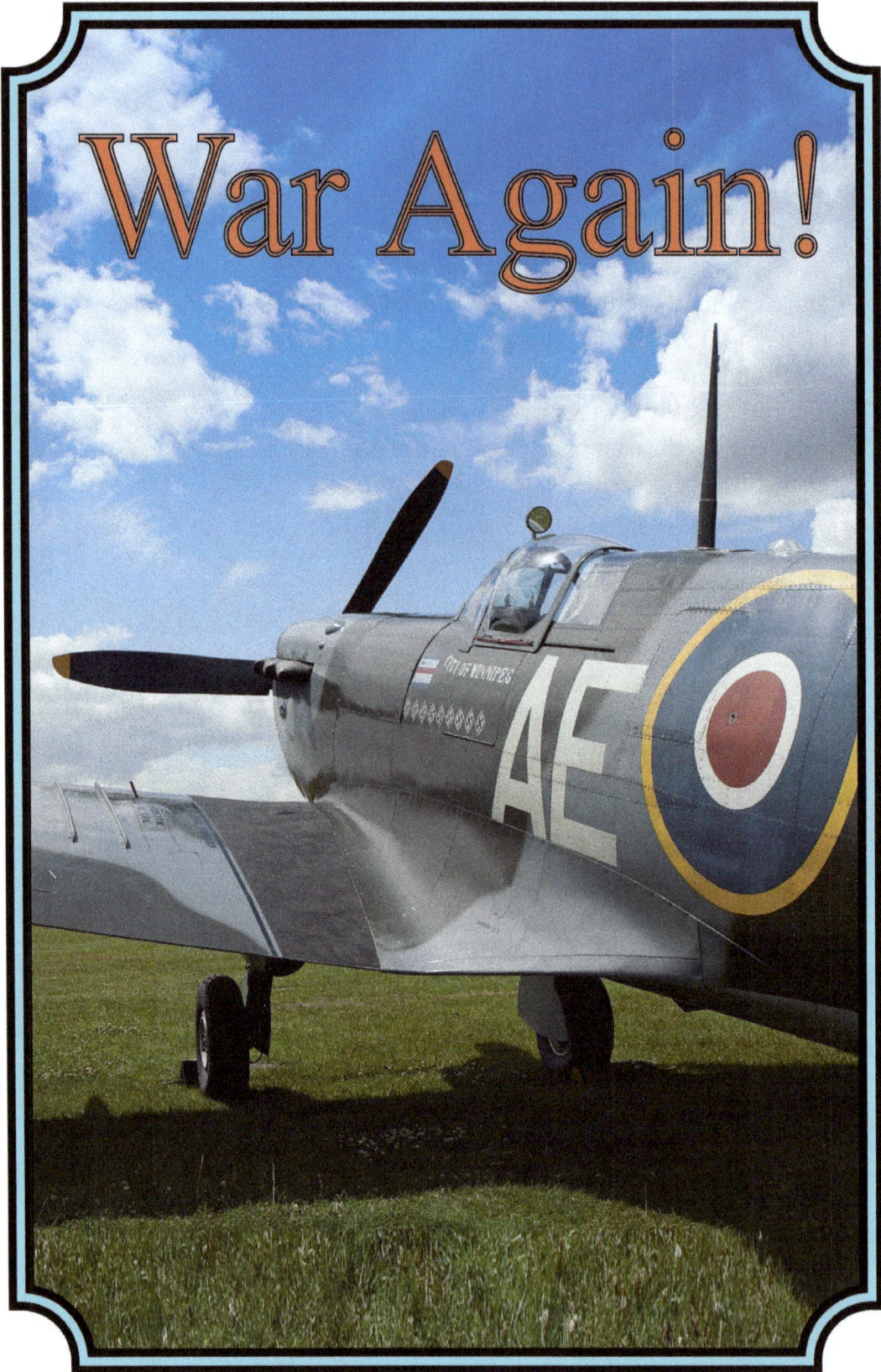

War Again!

Chapter Six

War Again!

The Great War of 1914-18 was supposed to be the war to end all wars but although man is capable of great ingenuity and of producing wonderful technological advances as well as beautiful works of art, he seems incapable of getting along with his fellow man and as a result, the world went to war again in 1939.

This time, the weapons available were capable of even greater destruction than before and the German war machine also employed an entirely new tactic. Blitzkrieg or lightning war, is a method of warfare whereby an army, spearheaded by fast moving, armoured and motorised infantry, break through defence lines with short powerful attacks and using speed and surprise, encircle and cut off elements of the enemy. This new type of warfare depends for its success on support from the air, in fact, in the Second World War, aircraft were to play a much more significant role in all theatres of war, both over land and sea.

The Dive Bomber

The dive bomber played a large role in the new tactic of lightning war, but if we are to look at the development of the dive bomber, we have to take a step back to World War One.

In the early years of World War One, pilots were urged by their commanding officers to drop their bombs from an altitude of around 500ft or 150m so that they could be more accurate, but as the pilots in these machines were pretty much unprotected against fire from the ground, it is unlikely that a great many complied with their officers wishes. Some pilots would have gone in at high level and then dived towards their intended target, thus reducing the amount of forward travel of their bomb after release; the dive angle would not have been very great back then however, as the early biplanes could not have taken the strain of pulling out of a steep sustained dive.

It is recorded that the Royal Navy Air Service used dive bombing tactics when attacking Zeppelin sheds in Germany and occupied Belgium but the angle of dive was never recorded and could not have been very steep.

On March 14th 1918, Second Lieutenant William Henry Brown, a Canadian from British Columbia, serving with the RFC and flying a Royal Aircraft Factory S.E.5a, is recorded as having made the first dive bombing attack on a vessel, destroying an ammunition barge on a canal at Bernot near St Quentin, diving to 500 ft (150 m) to release his bombs. He was awarded the Military Cross for this and other unspecified exploits. Brown's technique was emulated by pilots in other British squadrons but the heavy casualty rates sustained by unprotected pilots cast a pall over the results and influenced RAF thinking for the next twenty years.

In June 1918 the Royal Air Force took delivery of two Sopwith TF Salamanders. This was a single seat biplane and the TF stood for "Trench Fighter", it was armed with Vickers .303 machine guns and 25lb bombs, but the war ended before they saw action.

Sopwith TF Salamander

Whether the Salamander should be considered as a fighter bomber or as a dive bomber depends on the definition of "dive". It had armoured protection for the pilot and fuel system, enabling it to attack at low level, but it lacked dive brakes for a sustained vertical dive.

Colonel, later General, Billy Mitchell, arrived in France with the first US Army and Air Force units soon after 6th April 1917 and began to organize the US Army Air Force. Mitchell became a strong advocate of dive bombers after witnessing British and French aerial attacks and he was now assistant chief of the Air Service.

The United States Army arranged for tests to be carried out using captured German and obsolete US ships in June and July 1921 and these tests were repeated over the next two years using Royal Aircraft Factory S.E.5s as dive bombers and the Handley Page 0/400s and Martin NBS-1s as level bombers carrying bombs of different weights up to 2,000 lb (910 kg). The SMS Ostffriesland, USS Alabama and the USS New Jersey were all sunk during the tests.

As aircraft grew more powerful, dive bombing became a favoured tactic, particularly against small targets such as trains and ships and dive bombing had already been used during the United States occupation of Nicaragua from 1912 to 1934.

The Curtiss F8C Falcon biplane was deployed on carriers from 1925, while the Marine Corps operated them from land bases as the Helldiver, a name later reused by Curtiss for other dive bombers.

Heavy casualties resulting from air-to-ground attack on trenches however, had set the minds of senior officers in the newly-formed RAF against the tactic of dive bombing, so it wasn't until 1934 that the Air Ministry issued specifications for both land based and aircraft carrier based dive bombers.

Fairey, Gloster and Hawker, all attempted to fulfil this need and competition was tight to attain the highest performance possible. As the aircraft required only a modest bomb load and with performance being paramount, the Hawker design team chose to focus its efforts on developing an aircraft similar in size to their Hurricane fighter, that was in the advanced design stage. There would be economies of scale if some assemblies were common to both aircraft and this resulted in the Henley, as it was to become known, sharing identical outer wing panel and tailplane jigs with the Hurricane fighter. Both were equipped with the Rolls Royce Merlin engine as it offered the best power-weight ratio, as well as a minimal frontal area. The Henley's cantilever fabric-covered monoplane wing was mid-set and space was provided for both a pilot and an observer/gunner, which differed from the Hurricane's single-seat cockpit.

Although construction of a Henley prototype began as early as mid-1935, priority was given to Hurricane development, so it wasn't until 10th March 1937 that, powered by a Merlin "F" engine, the Henley was first flown at Brooklands, shortly after the competing Fairey P.4/34. Subsequently, the aircraft was refitted with light alloy stressed-skin wings and a Merlin I engine (production version of the F) and further test flights confirmed the excellence of its performance, showing that it could reach a top speed of 300 mph.

However, the Air Ministry had by this point decided that it no longer required a light bomber, probably because this role was felt to be adequately filled by the Fairey Battle.

Accordingly, the Henley, which in line with RAF policy had not been fitted with dive brakes, bomb crutches or specialised bomb sights and thus limited to attack angles of no greater than 70°, was relegated to target-towing duty, hence the second prototype was fitted with a winch to haul in a drogue cable after air-to-air firing sorties. This was first flown on 26th May 1938.

After the RAF relegated the Henley from dive bomber to target tug, the Fleet Air Arm's Blackburn Skua was expected to do double duty, performing as a fighter when out of reach of land-based fighter support, and as a dive bomber. The Skua had dive brakes that enabled it to recover from steep dives and that also doubled as flaps for carrier landings.

Curtiss F8C Falcon

Hawker Henley

Both the American and Japanese navies, as well as the Luftwaffe, opted for vertical dive bombers whose relatively low speeds had dire consequences when they encountered modern fighters.

In Japan, the Imperial Japanese Navy ordered the Heinkel He 50 in 1931 as a floatplane and carrier-based dive bomber and in 1935 deployed some of the later Heinkel He 66 models on their new carriers before going on to develop the Aichi D1A from the Heinkel He 66.

Navies increasingly operated carriers, despite the fact that they had a limited number of aircraft available for attack, each with only a small bomb load. However, targets were often likely to be small or fast-moving and the need for accuracy made dive bombers by far the best option.

Heinkel He 66

Ernst Udet (1896-1941), the highest scoring German fighter pilot to survive World War One, and the second-highest scoring after Manfred von Richthofen, was a strong advocate of dive-bombing tactics. He flew in one of the aerobatic displays at the 1936 Berlin Olympics and because of his connections to the Nazi party, he was appointed as, Director of the Ministry of Aviation's development department.

After his appointment, It wasn't long before the Luftwaffe issued a contract for its own dive bomber design and this resulted in the development of the Junkers K 47, that after extensive trials became the Junkers Ju 87, probably better known as the "Stuka", a contraction of *Sturzkampfflugzeug*, literally "diving combat aeroplane".

Designed by Hermann Pohlmann and

Aichi D1A

first flown in September 1935, several early Junkers Ju 87 dive bombers were shipped secretly from Germany to Spain, in order to assist General Franco's nationalist rebels in the Spanish Civil War. It was here that it first saw action with the Luftwaffe's Condor Legion before going on to serve the Axis forces in World War Two.

The aircraft was easily recognisable by its inverted gull wings and fixed undercarriage. On the leading edges of its faired main gear legs was mounted the "Jericho trumpet" a wailing siren that made the distinctive howling sound that become a symbol of German air power and the blitzkrieg victories of 1939–1942.

Junkers Ju 87 (Stukas) : Courtesy of Bundesarchi, Bild 183-J16050 CC-By-SA

The Stuka's design incorporated several innovations, including automatic pull-up dive brakes under both wings to ensure that the aircraft recovered from its attack dive, even if the pilot blacked out from the high G-forces. The Stuka led air assaults in the invasion of Poland in September 1939 and they were vital to the rapid conquest of Norway, the Netherlands, Belgium and France in 1940. Sturdy, accurate, and very effective against ground targets, the Stuka was nevertheless, like many other dive bombers of the period, vulnerable to attack by fighter aircraft. During the Battle of Britain its lack of manoeuvrability, speed and defensive armament meant that it required a heavy fighter escort to operate effectively.

After the Battle of Britain, the Stuka was used in the Balkans, Africa, the Mediterranean and on the Eastern Front, where it was used as a specialised anti-tank aircraft as well as being deployed in an anti-shipping role. Once the Luftwaffe lost its air superiority however, the Stuka became an easy target for enemy fighter aircraft on all fronts. It stayed in production until 1944 simply because of a lack of a suitable replacement but after 1944 the ground-attack versions of the Focke-Wulf Fw 190 took over and largely replaced it, but Stukas remained in service until the end of the war.

Some more World War Two Aircraft

The Focke-Wulf Fw 190 Würger:

Focke-Wulf Fw 109 : Darren Harbar Photography

A German single-seat, single-engine fighter aircraft designed by Kurt Tank in the late 1930s and widely used during the war.

Along with its well-known counterpart, the Messerschmitt Bf 109, the Fw 190 became the backbone of the Luftwaffe's fighter force. The twin-row BMW 801 radial engine that powered most operational versions enabled the Fw 190 to lift larger loads than the Bf 109, allowing its use as a day fighter, fighter bomber ground attack aircraft and night fighter.

The Fw 190A started flying operationally over France in August 1941, and quickly proved superior in all but turn radius to the Royal Air Force's main front-line fighter, the Spitfire Mk.V, particularly at low and medium altitudes. The 190 maintained superiority over Allied fighters until the introduction of the improved Spitfire Mk1X.

The Fw 190A series' performance decreased at high altitudes (usually 6,000 m (20,000 ft) and above), which reduced its effectiveness as a high-altitude interceptor. From the Fw 190's inception, there had been ongoing efforts to address this with a turbo-super-charged BMW 801 engine in the B model. Problems with the turbocharger in the B and C models meant that only the D model entered service, but too late to affect the outcome of the war.

The Messerschmitt Bf 109:

Messerschmitt Bf 109

A German fighter aircraft that first saw operational service in 1937 during the Spanish Civil War and was still in service at the dawn of the jet age at the end of World War Two in 1945. It was one of the most advanced fighters of the era, including such features as all-metal monocoque construction, (an aircraft structure in which the chassis is integral with the body,) a closed canopy, and retractable landing gear. It was powered by a liquid-cooled, inverted-V12 engine and was commonly called the Me 109, most often by Allied aircrew and among the German aces, even though this was not the official German designation.

Conceived originally as an interceptor it actually fulfilled multiple roles. It was supplied to several states during World War Two, and served with several countries for many years after the war, becoming the most produced fighter aircraft in history, with a total of nearly 33,000 airframes produced from 1936 to April 1945.

The Fairey Swordfish:

fairey Swordfish : Darren Harbar Photography

The Fairey Swordfish was a torpedo bomber designed by Fairey Aviation in the early 1930s. The Swordfish, nicknamed "Stringbag", was operated by the Fleet Air Arm of the Royal Navy in addition to the Royal Air Force, alongside multiple overseas operators, including the Royal Canadian Air Force and the Royal Netherlands Navy. Powered by a Bristol Pegasus 11M radial engine it was primarily a fleet attack aircraft and during its later years, the Swordfish became increasingly used as an anti-submarine and training aircraft. The type was in frontline service throughout the Second World War, despite already being considered obsolete at the outbreak of the conflict in 1939.

Nonetheless, the Swordfish achieved some spectacular successes during the war. Notable events included sinking one Italian battleship and damaging two others during the battle of Taranto, and the famous attack on the German Battleship "Bismarck" which contributed to her eventual demise. By the end of the war, the Swordfish held the distinction of having caused the destruction of a greater tonnage of Axis shipping than any other Allied aircraft. The Swordfish remained in front-line service until V-E Day, having outlived multiple aircraft that had been intended to replace it in service.

Hawker Hurricane:

The Hawker Hurricane is a low-wing cantilever monoplane with retractable undercarriage and an enclosed cockpit for the pilot. A clean, single-seat fighter, it was developed to compete against the latest fighter designs that were emerging amongst the air services of other powers.

Initially armed with an arrangement of eight remotely-operated wing-mounted Browning machine guns, the Hurricane was equipped with both navigation and landing lights together with instruments for blind-flying and a two-way radio.

Hawker had decided to employ its traditional construction techniques instead of radical measures such as the adoption of a stressed-skin metal exterior and the majority of the external surfaces were linen, except for a section between the cockpit and the engine cowling that used lightweight metal panels instead, similarly, a simple steel tube structure in the nose of the fuselage was used to support the engine and detachable panels across the cowling provided access to most of the engine's areas for inspection or adjustment.

Initially, the structure of the Hurricane's cantilever wing consisted of two steel spars, which possessed considerable strength and stiffness. The wing was mostly fabric covered as were the hydraulically actuated trailing edge flaps and the Frise type ailerons. An all-metal, stressed-skin wing of duraluminium was introduced in April 1939 and was used for all of the later models which allowed a diving speed that was 80 mph higher than the fabric-covered ones. The new wings were interchangeable with the old, allowing older models to be updated and changing the wings required only three hours work per aircraft.

Two separate hydraulic systems, one being power-operated and the other hand operated could be used for the deployment and retraction of the undercarriage and in the event of both failing, pilots can release the retaining catches holding the undercarriage in place, deploying the wheels to the "down" position using weight alone

The prototype and early production Hurricanes were fitted with a Watts two bladed fixed-pitch wooden propeller that was found to be inefficient at low airspeeds and meant that the aircraft required a long ground run to get airborne. After April 1939 however they were fitted with a De Havilland variable pitch propeller which considerably reduced the take-off run required and this was later replaced by a constant speed Rotol propeller that came into service in time for The Battle of Britain.

Hawker Hurricane
Darren Harbar Photography

The de Havilland DH.98 Mosquito

de Havelland Mosquito

Originally conceived as an unarmed fast bomber, the Mosquito's use evolved during the war to encompass many roles. The crew of two, pilot and navigator, sat side by side with the pilot on the left with the navigator to the right and a single passenger could ride in the aircraft's bomb bay if necessary. Entry/exit to the aircraft was through a hatch along the navigator's right.

The Mosquito FBVI was often flown in special raids, such as "Operation Jericho" an attack on Amiens Prison in early 1944, and precision attacks against military intelligence, security, and police facilities (such as Gestapo headquarters). On 30th January 1943, the 10th anniversary of the Nazis' seizure of power, a morning Mosquito attack knocked out the main Berlin broadcasting station while Hermann Göring was speaking, taking his speech off the air.

The cockpit was relatively well organized with throttle and engine gauges set along the left-hand side within easy reach. Basic dials were spread about the uncluttered instrument panel which pilots regarded as good to excellent. A small passageway along the right of the instrument panel allowed crew access to the nose which, in non-solid-nosed versions, featured a clear plastic windscreen for bombing. The cockpit was heated for high-altitude flying and generally regarded as more comfortable than the Bristol Beaufighter it replaced. The Beaufighter was however brought back for use in India and the Far East when it was discovered that the construction wood of the Mosquitos was under attack by insects weakening the structure. Other production versions introduced cockpit pressurization for extreme high-altitude work.

The use of wood as the main construction material was key to the success of the Mosquito, especially concerning its war time production. Metals were a sought-after resource as were those specialists that could work with such metals to form the hulls of ships and submarines as well as the airframes of aircraft. The Mosquito on the other hand, would rely on the readily available supplies of wood throughout the British Empire and crucially, required the skilled services of woodworkers who were not as critical to the primary British war effort. Such a revolutionary, forward-thinking approach greatly contributed to the successes of the Mosquito design.

The nose of the mosquito could either be clear Perspex for bombers or solid in the case of fighters and fitted with 4 x 7.7mm Browning machine guns in the nose with 4 x 20mm Hispano cannons under the cockpit floor. Some versions did away with the machine guns altogether, while other forms replaced the 4 x cannons with a single 57mm cannon. The bomb bay could hold up to 500lb of ordnance in the original versions and this later increased and bombs could also be added to hardpoints under each wing - initially 2 x 250lb types then 2 x 500lb types. Later Mosquitos were tested and cleared to fire underwing rockets and the navy versions were outfitted with a single torpedo under the fuselage.

Bristol Blenheim

Bristol Blenheim : Darren Harbar Photography

1935 saw the first flight of the Blenheim built in Bristol by the Bristol Aeroplane Company, formerly the British and Colonial Aeroplane Company. The Blenheim was a light bomber aircraft design and was used throughout the Second World War, especially in the first two years. The aircraft was developed as *Type 142*, a civil airliner, in response to a challenge from Lord Rothermere, to produce the fastest commercial aircraft in Europe. The *Type 142* first flew in April 1935, and the Air Ministry, impressed by its performance, ordered a modified design as the *Type 142M* for the Royal Air Force as a bomber. Deliveries of the newly named Blenheim to RAF squadrons commenced on 10th March 1937.

It was a twin-engine high-performance all-metal bomber, powered by a pair of Bristol Mercury V111 air cooled radial engines, each capable of delivering 860 hp. Each engine drove a three bladed controllable-pitch propeller and were equipped with both hand-based and electric engine starters. To ease maintenance, the engine mountings were designed with a split segment to facilitate rapid engine removal without disturbing the carburettors. Fuel tanks, each containing up to 140 gallons, were housed within the wing sections.

The Blenheim typically carried a crew of three – pilot, navigator/bombardier and wireless operator/air gunner. The pilot's quarters on the left side of the nose were so cramped that the control yoke obscured a lot of the instruments and the instruments themselves interfered with the pilots forward view when landing. Most secondary instruments were arranged along the left side of the cockpit, essential items such as the propeller pitch control were actually placed behind the pilot where they had to be operated by feel alone. The navigator/bombardier was seated alongside the pilot on a sliding seat so that he could perform both his duties. Dual flight controls could be installed. The wireless operator, who was situated aft of the wings also acted as gunner from the aircraft's semi-retracting Bristol Type B Mk1 dorsal gun turret, using a Lewis gun. There was also a forward firing 7.7mm Browning machine gun.

From 1939 onwards, the Lewis gun was replaced by the more modern .303 in (7.7 mm) Vickers VGO machine gun of the same calibre. A 1,000 lb (450 kg) bomb load could be carried in the internal bomb bay set into the centre section of the fuselage and like most contemporary British aircraft, the bomb bay doors were kept closed with bungee cords and opened under the weight of the released bombs. Other onboard equipment included a radio, cameras, navigation systems, electric lighting, oxygen apparatus, and there was stowage space for parachutes and clothing.

In early 1939, the first batch of Blenheim Mk IVs were accepted into service; these lacked outer fuel tanks but were accepted due to the urgent demand for the type. Early Blenheim Mk IVs were also equipped with the Mercury VIII engine, but later ones were fitted with the more powerful Mercury XV or Mercury 25 models.

The first Allied bombs of the war were dropped on 4th September by a Blenheim 1V (N6204) piloted by Flight Lieutenant Kenneth Doran and on the same day Sergeant George Booth became the first British prisoner of war, when his Blenheim was shot down in action. The first flight decorations of World War Two were awarded on 10th October 1939 to Blenheim pilots, Flight Lieutenant Doran (110 Squadron) and Flight Officer McPhearson (139 Squadron.) The Bristol Blenheim was also built under licence by Fairchild-Canada as a maritime patrol aircraft and was named as the Bolingbroke, an example of which is currently being restored at Bristol Aerospace Museum.

Bristol Beaufighter:

Bristol Beaufighter

The Bristol Beaufighter, nicknamed "Whispering Death" by the Japanese, was a versatile long-range fighter devised for both offensive and defensive roles.

In October 1938 at an Air Ministry meeting, Roy Fedden, a design engineer at Bristol Aircraft Company and Leslie Frise, the designer of the "Frise aileron" stated that the design of the Beaufort Bomber could be converted into a fighter and argued that it would make sense to concentrate on that rather than building more Beauforts, due to the lack of long range, cannon armed fighters and after some persuasion the Air Ministry agreed and the Beaufighter was born.

First flown in July 1939 it retained the Beaufort's wings, undercarriage and tail but had a smaller fuselage and more powerful Hercules engines. After disappointing initial kill rates the later Beaufighters had airborne interception radar fitted and were armed with four cannon and six Browning machine guns, significantly improving results. Four bombs were added to its arsenal in 1941.

During World War II, the Beaufighter played a significant role in the Battle of Britain, protecting the skies over the south of England. Flying at night, all-black painted Beaufighters acted as "Night Interceptors" in the hands of skilled pilots such as Grp Captain John 'Cats-Eyes' Cunningham who was credited with the highest number of 'Night Kills'.

Nicknamed "Cats' Eyes," a sobriquet that Cunningham never liked, his exceptional skill on the nocturnal battlefield was put down to eating carrots to improve his night vision.

This rather romantic explanation for his success was promoted by the government in an attempt to hide the fact that British scientists had secretly developed a sophisticated and formidable airborne radar system. The new system allowed pilots to home in on Luftwaffe bomber formations, often with devastating consequences.

UK production was split between Bristol Aeroplane Company (4,804, including the Weston-super-Mare Shadow Factory), Fairey Aviation Company at Stockport (500) and Rootes at Speke (260). Outside of the UK, the Mk.21 was built in Australia at the Government Aircraft Factory where some 364 aircraft were constructed.

The Kawasaki Ki 61

The Kawasaki Ki 61

The Ki-61 looked so different to the usual radial-engined Japanese fighters, that the Allies at first believed it to be of German or Italian origin, possibly a license-built Messerschmitt. In early reports, when it was thought to have been a German fighter, the Ki-61 had been code-named "Mike." The final, and better known code name adopted was "Tony", because the Ki-61 looked like an Italian aircraft.

The new Ki-61 *Hien* fighters entered service with a special training unit, the 23rd *Chutai*, and entered combat for the first time in early 1943, during the New Guinea campaign. Because the Ki-61 was so new, and had been rushed into service, it inevitably suffered from teething problems. Almost all of the modern Japanese aircraft engines, especially the Ki-61's liquid-cooled engines, suffered a disastrous series of failures and ongoing problems which resulted in the obsolete Ki-43 still forming the bulk of the JAAF's fighter capability.

The new Japanese fighter caused some consternation among Allied pilots, particularly when they found out the hard way that they could no longer go into a dive and escape as they had from lighter Japanese fighters, however, the increasing numerical strength of Allied bomber units, along with inadequate anti-aircraft systems, imposed crippling losses on Japanese forces.

Supermarine Spitfire:

One of the most instantly recognisable and beautiful looking aircraft ever built, the Spitfire was a single seat fighter used by the Royal Air Force and several allied countries during the war. Many variants of the Spitfire were built, using several wing configurations, and it was produced in greater numbers than any other British aircraft. It was also the only British fighter produced continuously throughout the war.

The Spitfire was designed as a short-range, high-performance interceptor aircraft by R. J. Mitchell, the chief designer for Supermarine Aviation Works, a subsidiary of Vickers-Armstrong from 1928. Mitchell had under him a man called Beverley Shenstone who had worked at the Junker factory in Germany in 1929 and was familiar with many advanced German designs. At an air show in Paris, he had run his hands over the wing of a new Heinkel and marvelled at its smoothness. He wrote to the firm's boss, Ernst Heinkel, and asked how this had been achieved. Heinkel revealed to him that they had used a technique to sink the rivets flush with the wing's skin, instead of what was then the common practice of leaving rivet heads sticking out and so Shenstone set about designing his own sunken rivets for use on the Spitfire.

Captain Hill a scientific officer in the Air Ministry who was trying to make the case for the new generation of fighter planes to be armed with eight rather than the four originally planned and to this end he enlisted the help of his thirteen year old daughter Hazel, a maths prodigy. Between them they managed to come up with calculations that proved to the powers that be that the aircraft needed eight machine guns instead of four and so in the end, a thirteen year old girl contributed, in no small way, to the success of one of the worlds most iconic aircraft.

Mitchell continued to refine the Spitfire's design until his death in 1937, whereupon his colleague, Joseph Smith, took over as chief designer, overseeing the Spitfire's development through its multitude of variants. During the Battle of Britain from July to October 1940, the public perceived the Spitfire to be the main RAF fighter, even though the more numerous Hurricane shouldered a greater proportion of the burden against the Luftwaffe. However, Spitfire units had a lower attrition rate and a higher victory-to-loss ratio than those flying Hurricanes because of the Spitfire's higher performance. After the Battle of Britain, the Spitfire superseded the Hurricane to become the backbone of Fighter Command and saw action in all theatres. Popular with its pilots, the Spitfire served in several roles, including interceptor, photo-reconnaissance, fighter-bomber, and trainer well into the 1950s alongside its carrier based, "Seafire" adaptation. Although originally powered by a Rolls-Royce Merlin engine producing 1,030hp (768 kW), the airframe was strong enough and adaptable enough to use increasingly more powerful Merlin engines with power climbing to 1420hp and with high octane fuel imported from America it could achieve 2,050hp. Later models powered with the Rolls-Royce Griffon produced up to 2,340 hp again improving its performance.

Supermarine Spitfire
Darren Harbar Photography

North American Aviation P-51 Mustang:

P-51 Mustang : Darren Haebar Photography

An American long-range, single-seat fighter and fighter-bomber used during World War Two and the Korean War among other conflicts.

The Mustang was designed in 1940 by North American Aviation in response to a requirement of the British Purchasing Commission who approached North American Aviation to build Curtiss P-40 fighters under license for the Royal Air Force.

Rather than build an old design from another company, North American Aviation proposed the design and production of a more modern fighter. The prototype NA-73X airframe was rolled out on 9th September 1940, 102 days after the contract was signed, and first flew on 26th October.

The Mustang was designed to use the Allison V-1710 engine but this proved to have limited high-altitude performance in its earlier models.

The aircraft was first flown operationally by the Royal Air Force as a reconnaissance and fighter/bomber.

Eventually the engine was replaced by a Rolls-Royce Merlin in the Mustang Mk111, transforming the aircraft's performance at altitudes above 15,000 ft without sacrificing range. This modification allowed it to compete with the latest Luftwaffe aircraft.

The definitive version, the P-51D, was powered by the Packard V-1650 licence-built version of the two-speed two-stage supercharged Merlin 66 and was armed with six 50 calibre Browning machine guns.

At the start of the Korean War, the Mustang, by then re-designated F-51, was the main fighter of the United Nations until jet fighters took over, although the Mustang remained in service with some air forces until the 1980s.

Vickers Wellington:

The Vickers Wellington was a British twin-engine, long-range bomber. It was designed during the mid-1930s at Brooklands, Surrey by Vickers-Armstrong's chief designer Rex Pierson. A key feature of the aircraft was its geodetic fuselage structure. principally designed by Barnes Wallis of bouncing bomb fame.

Vickers Wellington

Wallis' geodetic, sometimes called geodesic frame, consisted of the fuselage being built up from a number of duralumin alloy channel-beams that were formed into a large criss-cross framework. Wooden battens were screwed onto the metal, to which the doped linen skin of the aircraft was fixed.

During the development process, performance requirements, such as for the tare or unladen weight, changed substantially and the engine used was not the one originally intended.

The geodesic fuselage : Darren Harbar Photography

Vickers studied and compared the performance of various air and liquid engines to power the bomber, including the Bristol Pegasus IS2, The Pegasus 11S2, The Armstrong Siddeley Tiger and the Rolls-Royce Goshawk.

The Pegasus was selected as the engine for air-cooled versions of the bomber, while the Goshawk engine was chosen for the liquid-cooled engine variant. On 28th February 1933, two versions of the aircraft, one with each of the selected powerplants, were submitted to the tender and in September 1933, the Air Ministry issued an initial contract for the Goshawk-powered version.

In August 1934, Vickers proposed to use either the Pegasus or Bristol Perseus engines instead of the Goshawk, which promised improvements in speed, climb rate, ceiling, and single-engine flight capabilities without any major increase in overall weight and the Air Ministry accepted the proposed changes.

The Wellington was used as Bomber Command's principal bomber until it started to be superseded by larger four-engine bombers such as the Avro Lancaster.

The Wellington continued to serve throughout the war in other duties however, particularly as an anti-submarine aircraft and it still holds the distinction of having been the only British bomber produced for the duration of the war, and of having been produced in a greater quantity than any other British-built bomber.

One disadvantage of the geodesic fuselage structure was its insufficient lengthwise stiffness and when fitted with attachments for towing cargo gliders, its structure "gave" and would stretch slightly. So, while the airframe continued to be structurally sound, the forces in the long control runs of cables and push-pull rods to the empennage grew considerably, affecting controllability of the aeroplane. This is the reported reason why Wellingtons, nor Warwicks for that matter, were never used as glider tugs.

The Boeing B-17 Flying Fortress:

A four-engine heavy bomber developed in the 1930s for the United States Army Air Corps. Competing against Douglas and Martin for a contract to build 200 bombers, the Boeing entry (prototype Model 299/XB-17) outperformed both competitors and exceeded the air corps' performance specifications.

Unfortunately for Boeing, their prototype crashed and the contract went to the Douglas B-18 Bolo. Despite the crash the corps ordered 13 B-17s for further evaluation and from its introduction in 1938, the B-17 Flying Fortress underwent numerous design changes and has become, along with the Liberator, one of the most produced bombers of all time.

The B-17C changed from three bulged, oval-shaped gun blisters to two flush, oval-shaped gun windows and on the lower fuselage, a single "bathtub" gun gondola housing.

The B-17E was an extensive revision of the Model 299 design with the fuselage being extended by 10 ft, and a rear gunner position was added in a newly designed tail. The nose, especially the bombardier's well-framed, 10-panel nose glazing, remained relatively the same as the earlier B through D versions but a "Sperry" electrically powered, manned gun turret was added just behind the cockpit as well as a manned ball turret just aft of the bomb bay underneath, replacing the earlier remotely operated turret.

The B-17's turbocharged Wright R-1820 Cyclone engines were upgraded to increasingly more powerful versions of the same powerplants in order to compensate for the 20% increase in weight. The aircraft served in every World War Two combat zone, and by the time production ended in May 1945, 12,731 aircraft had been built by Boeing, Douglas and Vega, a subsidiary of Lockheed.

B-17 Flying Fortress
Darren Harbar Photography

Handley Page Halifax Bomber:

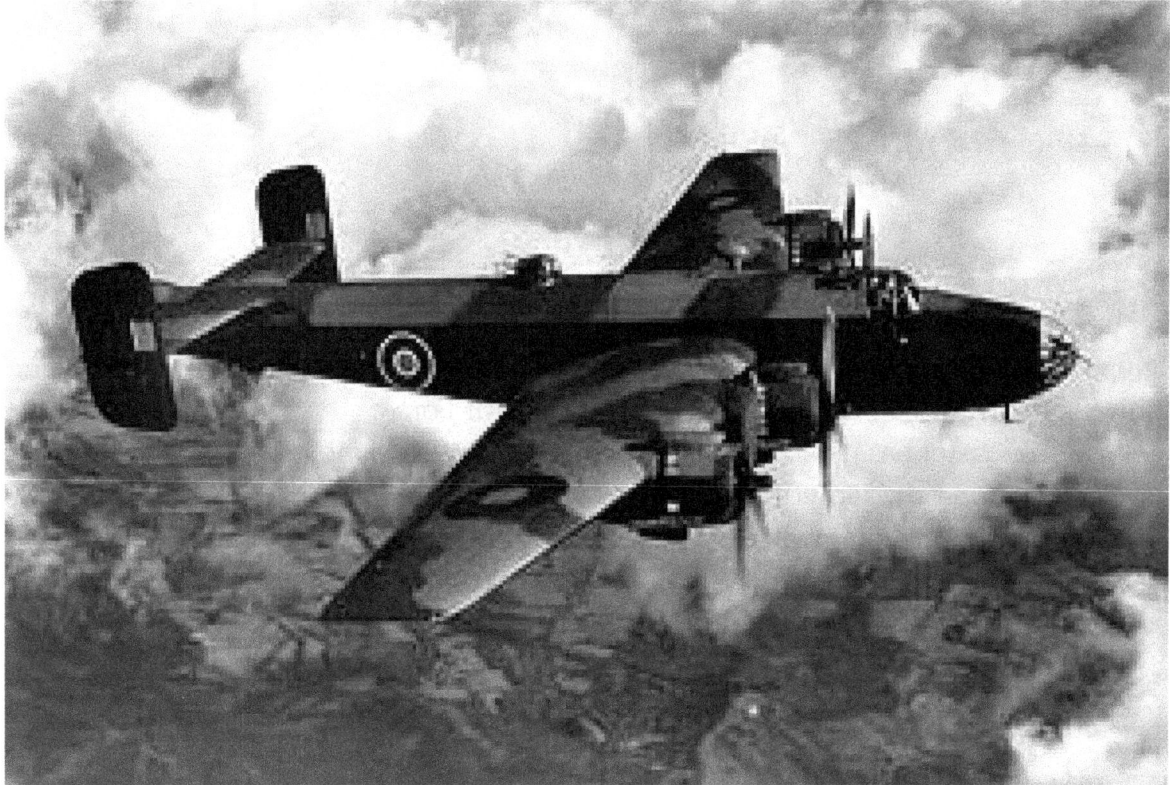

Halifax Bomber

The Halifax was developed in response to the Air Ministry's request for a medium bomber. It was powered by four Rolls-Royce Merlin engines and was one of the most successful bombers of the Second World War.

Of mostly orthodox design, it was a mid-wing monoplane of which probably the most recognisable feature was its tail unit featuring twin fins and rudders. The Halifax also featured all-metal construction with a smooth, stressed skin covering the majority of the exterior surfaces; the only exception being the flight control surfaces which were fabric-covered instead. The slab-sided fuselage contained a 22-foot bomb bay which contained the majority of the Halifax's payload, while the cockpit was flush with the upper fuselage.

The Halifax was powered by four engines, two spaced evenly on each wing. The Merlin engines were replaced on later models by the larger Bristol Hercules radial engines that each drove a Rotol-built compressed wood, constant speed propeller, enabling the Halifax B.I to attain a maximum speed of 265 MPH at 17,500 feet. With a typical payload of 5,800lbs of bombs and 2,242 Imp gallons of fuel, it had a range of 1,860 miles. The defensive armaments included power-assisted gun turrets in various positions located across the aircraft with different models of the Halifax using different numbers and combinations of turrets, effectively trading speed for firepower and vice versa. This versatile aircraft was used, not just as a bomber but also to deploy mines and as a glider tug as well as parachuting agents and arms into occupied Europe for the Special Operations Executive (SOE).

Avro Lancaster:

The Avro Lancaster was a British four-engine bomber, designed and manufactured by Avro as a contemporary of the Handley Page Halifax, both bombers having been developed to the same specification, as well as the Short Stirling, all three aircraft being four-engine heavy bombers adopted by the Royal Air Force.

The Lancaster has its origins in the twin-engine Avro Manchester, which had been developed during the late 1930s in response to the Air Ministry Specification P.13/ 36 for a capable medium bomber. The Manchester had proved troublesome in service however and was retired in 1942. The Lancaster was designed by Roy Chadwick and powered by four Rolls Royce Merlin engines in one version and by Bristol Hercules engines in another.

A long, unobstructed bomb bay meant that the Lancaster could take the largest bombs used by the RAF, including the 4,000 lb (1,800 kg), 8,000 lb (3,600 kg) and 12,000 lb (5,400 kg) blockbusters. During its wartime service the Lancaster flew an estimated 156,000 sorties and delivered 608,612 tons of bombs.

The Lancaster was also the aircraft chosen to equip the famous 617 Squadron and was modified to carry the Upkeep "bouncing bomb" designed by Barnes Wallis for operation "Chastise," the attack on the German Ruhr Valley dams.

Although the Lancaster was primarily a night bomber, it excelled in many other roles as well, including daylight precision bombing, for which some Lancasters were adapted to carry the 12,000 lb "Tallboy" bomb and then the 22,000 lb "Grand Slam" earthquake bombs, also designed by Wallis. This was the largest payload of any bomber in the war.

In 1943, a Lancaster was converted to become an engine test bed for many new engines, including turbo-props and turbo-jets. After the war the Lancaster's role was taken over by a larger version of itself, the Avro Lincoln.

In March 1946, a Lancaster of British South American Airways flew the first scheduled flight from the new London Heathrow Airport.

Avro Lancaster
Darren Harbar Photography

Airspeed Horsa Glider:

Airspeed Horsa 1948

I mentioned that the Halifax bomber was sometimes used as a glider tug and the glider it would have pulled was the Airspeed Horsa. The first two Horsa prototypes were built at Salisbury Hall and first flown from Fairey Aviation's aerodrome at Harmondsworth on 12th September 1941, towed behind an Armstrong Whitworth Whitley. Five additional prototypes were assembled and flown later at the Airspeed works in Portsmouth.

Allocated the designation AS.51, around 3,800 Horsa assault gliders were built, 695 of these at Christchurch, with the type also being widely subcontracted.

Production of the AS51 Horsa I comprised 470 at Christchurch, 300 by Austin Motors and 1,461 by a production group coordinated by Harris Lebus Ltd. Seating up to 30 troops, the Horsa was much bigger than its U.S. contemporary (the Waco CG-4A) which had a capacity of only 12. Additionally, the Horsa had the flexibility to carry a Jeep or even a 6-pounder ant-tank gun.

By far the most famous sortie carried out by six Horsa Gliders was the delivery of the Paratroopers responsible for securing the bridge at Bénouville over the Caen Canal in Normandy (now known as Pegasus Bridge) during Operation Deadstick, on the evening of 5th June 1944, the night before the D-Day landings.

The AS.53 Horsa Mk II was designed for vehicle carriage and featured a reinforced floor and a hinged nose section. The Horsa II also featured twin nosewheels and a modified towing strop attachment; and the all up weight for this version was also increased. Production of the Horsa II comprised 65 by Austin Motors and 1,271 by Harris Lebus Ltd.

Barbara Cartland:

An interesting and possibly little-known fact about the history of gliding is the fact that, although the practise of aerotowing gliders in order to launch them first took place in Germany, the idea of towing gliders long distances for the transport of goods was first proposed in 1931 by none other than Dame Mary Barbara Cartland, DBE, CStJ (1901 – 2000) the famous author.

Barbara Cartland in 1925

She had taken a keen interest in the early gliding scene and in 1931 participated in a two-hundred-mile tow in a two-seater glider. It was actually her idea that led to the troop-carrying gliders of World War two. In 1984 she was awarded the Bishop Wright Air Industry Award for this contribution to aviation and in 1991 she was invested by Queen Elizabeth 11 as a Dame Commander of the Order of the British Empire (DEB) in honour of her almost 70 years of literary, political and social contributions. She regularly attended Brooklands aerodrome and motor-racing circuit during the 1920s and 30s, and the Brooklands Museum has preserved a sitting-room from that era and named it after her.

Air Transport Auxiliary

The Air Transport Auxiliary (ATA) was a British civilian organisation set up during the Second World War and based at White Waltham Airfield. Its purpose was to ferry new, repaired and damaged military aircraft between factories, assembly plants, transatlantic delivery points, maintenance units, scrap yards, and active service squadrons and airfields, although not to naval aircraft carriers.

It also flew service personnel on urgent duty from one place to another and performed some air ambulance work. Some of the ATA pilots were women and in 1943 it was possibly the first time in Britain that women received the same pay as their male co-workers.

Initially, in order to comply with the Geneva Convention, because most of the pilots were civilians, aircraft were ferried with guns or other armament unloaded. However, after encounters with German aircraft in which the ferried aircraft were unable to fight back, RAF aircraft began to be ferried with guns fully loaded.

One such pilot was Mary Ellis (1917 – 2018) who was one of the first women to fly Spitfires, heavy bombers and jet aircraft, however, as she once recalled in a television interview, her contribution to the war effort was not always appreciated at the time. At one RAF base, the ground crew refused to believe she was the pilot of the Wellington bomber she had just landed. "They actually went inside the aeroplane and searched it," she recalled, "Everybody was flabbergasted that a little girl like me could fly these big aeroplanes all by oneself."

Mary Ellis (1917-2018)

Events of the Forties

1940   Evacuation of Dunkirk
        Battle of Britain
1942   First jet combat aeroplane
1945   VE day
        Atomic bomb dropped
1946   Pan-Am starts scheduled New York – London service
1947   International Civil Aviation Organisation established
        Sound barrier broken (Chuck Yeager in the Bell X-1)
1948   Berlin airlift
1949   NATO formed

Engine Development

Chapter Seven

Engine Development

Sometimes dubbed the Golden Age of Aviation, the inter war years were characterised by a progressive change from the slow wood-and-fabric biplanes of World War One, to the fast, streamlined metal monoplanes that were bringing about a huge change in both commercial and military aviation.

This revolution was made possible, not just by the advances in aircraft technology and design but also, by the continuing development of ever more powerful, reliable and lightweight aero engines.

The jet engine had begun development during the 1930s but was now beginning to meet its real potential. It was a time of record setting flights for speed and distance and a time when many commercial airlines were being started, issuing in a time of long-distance luxury flights, at least for those well off enough to be able to afford the fare.

Many of the early services had used airships, but after the Hindenburg disaster of 1937 put many off flying, it was the flying boat that came to dominance.

Earlier in the book I explained that in aviation, an inline engine meant any engine that was not radial or rotary but here I want to show some examples of the various different types of inline aero-engine, including the straight inline, the V configuration and the horizontally opposed.

Straight or inline 4   V-6   Horizontally Opposed 4

Aero-engine configurations

One example of a straight inline engine built in the 1930s is the Ranger L-440 air-cooled, six-cylinder, inverted engine shown here.

The greatest advantage of an inline engine is that it allows the aircraft to be designed with a low frontal area to minimize drag and if the engine crankshaft is located above the cylinders, (inverted inline engine,) this allows the propeller to be mounted high up to increase ground clearance, thus enabling shorter landing gear.

Ranger L-440 air cooled, six cylinder inverted engine

An example of a V configuration is the Rolls-Royce Merlin V-12 Engine that powered the Supermarine Spitfire.

Cylinders in a V engine are arranged in two in-line banks, typically tilted 60–90 degrees apart from each other and driving a common crankshaft. The vast majority of V engines are liquid-cooled. The V design provides a higher power-to-weight ratio than a straight inline engine, while still providing a small frontal area.

Roll-Royce Merlin V-12

UL260i horizontally opposed engine

A horizontally opposed engine, also called a flat or boxer engine, has two banks of cylinders on opposite sides of a centrally located crankcase. The engine can be either air-cooled or liquid-cooled, but air-cooled versions predominate. Opposed engines are mounted with the crankshaft horizontal in aeroplanes, but may be mounted with the crankshaft vertical in helicopters. Due to the cylinder layout, reciprocating forces tend to cancel each other out, resulting in a very smooth-running engine.

Opposed-type engines have high power-to-weight ratios because they have a comparatively small, lightweight crankcase. In addition, the compact cylinder arrangement reduces the engine's frontal area and allows a streamlined installation that minimizes aerodynamic drag. These engines always have an even number of cylinders, since a cylinder on one side of the crankcase "opposes" a cylinder on the other side.

Opposed, air-cooled four and six-cylinder piston engines are by far the most common engines used in small general aviation aircraft requiring up to 400 horsepower (300 kW) per engine. Aircraft that require more than 400 horsepower (300 kW) per engine tend to be powered by turbine engines.

An H configuration engine is essentially a pair of horizontally opposed engines placed together, with the two crankshafts geared together.

A word about propellers

It occurs to me that although I have mentioned a little about engine development, I have rather neglected the other rather important component of the none jet power plant, the propeller, so I will attempt to redress the omission now.

The Wright Brothers had realized that a propeller is essentially the same as a wing and were able to use data from their earlier wind tunnel experiments on wings, introducing a twist along the length of the blades in order to maintain a more uniform angle of attack for the blade along its full length.

Mahogany was the preferred wood for propellers through World War One but wartime shortages meant that Walnut, oak, cherry and ash where often used in its place. Alberto Santos Dumont, had been designing propellers for his airships before the Wright Brothers, although they were not as efficient and he applied the knowledge he gained from experiences with airships to make a propeller with a steel shaft and aluminium blades for his 14 biz biplane. Some of his designs used a bent aluminium sheet for blades, thus creating an aerofoil shape. They were heavily under cambered and this, plus the absence of lengthwise twist, made them less efficient than the Wright propellers. Even so, this was perhaps the first use of aluminium in the construction of a propeller.

Originally, a rotating aerofoil behind the aircraft, which pushes it forward, was called a propeller, while the one which pulled from the front was called a tractor. Later the term "pusher" became adopted for the rear mounted device in contrast to the tractor configuration and both were then referred to as propellers or airscrews.

Typically, US propellers rotate clockwise when viewed from the rear of the aircraft but many other aircraft have propellers that rotate in the opposite direction. Sometimes aircraft have opposite hand rotating propellers, that is, they rotate in the opposite direction to their counterpart on the other wing in order to balance the torque. Propellers that rotate in opposite directions on the same propeller shaft are called, counter rotating propellers. Opposite hand propellers generally rotate inwards towards the fuselage, (clockwise on the left engine and counter-clockwise on the right).

The Variable-pitch propeller

Blade pitch refers to the angle between the propeller blade chord line and the plane of rotation of the propeller. Fine pitch, refers to a fine or low pitch angle which is good for low speed acceleration during take-off and climb, whereas coarse pitch, refers to a coarser or higher pitch angle which supplies optimum high-speed performance and fuel economy during cruising.

A propeller is said to be feathered when it is at a right angle to the line of travel and supplies no thrust.

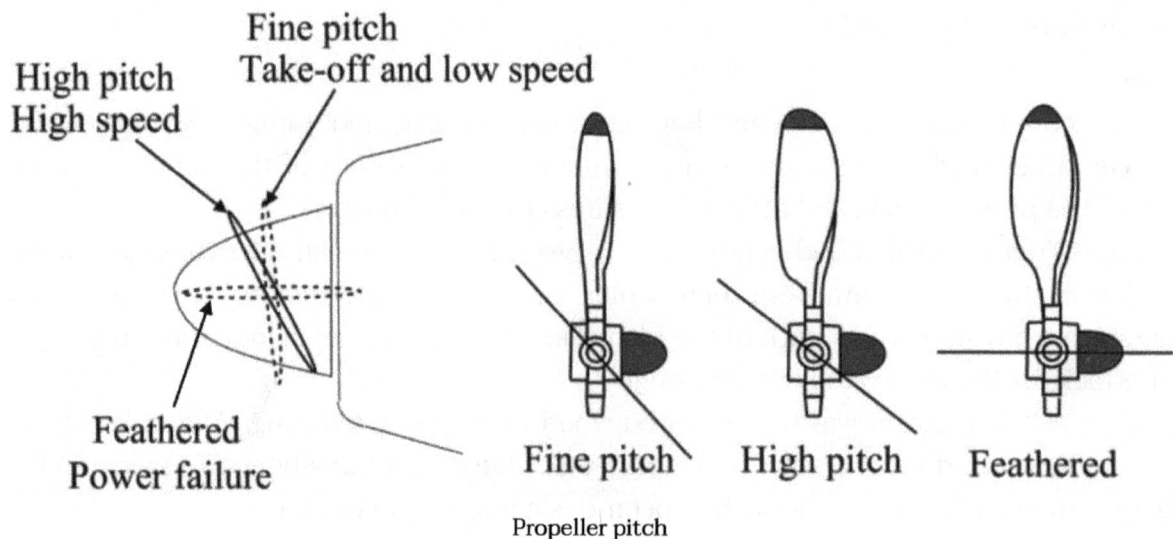

High pitch
High speed

Fine pitch
Take-off and low speed

Feathered
Power failure

Fine pitch   High pitch   Feathered

Propeller pitch

Propellers whose blade pitch could be adjusted while the aircraft was on the ground were used by a number of early aviation pioneers, including Sir Edwin Alliott Verdon Roe OBE, founder of the Avro Aircraft company that produced the Lancaster bomber, and the French aircraft firm Levasseur displayed a variable-pitch propeller at the 1921 Paris Air-show, which it claimed, had been tested by the French government in a ten-hour run and could change pitch at any engine RPM.

Dr Henry Selby Hele-Shaw and T. E. Beacham patented a hydraulically operated variable-pitch propeller in 1924 and presented a paper on the subject before the Royal Aeronautical Society in 1928, though it was received with scepticism as to its worth. The propeller had been developed with Gloster Aircraft Company as the Gloster Hele-Shaw Beacham Variable Pitch Propeller and was demonstrated on a Gloster Grebe, where it was used to maintain a near-constant RPM.

The Gloster Grebe

The French firm Ratier pioneered variable-pitch propellers of various designs from 1928 onwards. Several designs were tried, including a small bladder of pressurized air in the propeller hub, providing the necessary force to resist a spring that would drive the blades from fine pitch for take-off, to coarse pitch for level cruising. At a suitable airspeed, a disk on the front of the spinner would press sufficiently on the bladder's air-release valve to relieve the pressure and allow the spring to drive the propeller to coarse pitch. These "pneumatic" propellers were fitted on the DH88 Comet aircraft, winner of the famed long distance 1934 Mac Robertson race and in the Caudron C.460, winner of the 1936 National Air Races, flown by Michel Detroyat and shown here. Use of these pneumatic propellers required them to be set to fine pitch prior to take-off by pressurizing the bladder with a bicycle pump.

A Cauldron C.460

A common type of controllable-pitch propeller is hydraulically actuated; it was originally developed by Frank W. Caldwell of the United Aircraft Company and de Havilland subsequently bought up the rights to produce Hamilton propellers in the UK, while the British company Rotol was formed to produce its own propellers. In France, Pierre Levasseur also produced controllable pitch propellers, as did the Smith Engineering Co. in the United States.

An electrically operated system was developed by Wallace R Turnbull and refined by the Curtiss-Wright Corporation before being patented in 1929. This system was popular with pilots because even when the engine was no longer running the propeller could be feathered. On hydraulically-operated propellers, the feathering had to happen before the loss of hydraulic pressure in the engine. Feathering simply means that the propeller blade is rotated parallel to the airflow to stop rotation and reduce drag when the engine fails or is deliberately shut down.

An improvement on the automatic type was the constant speed propeller that automatically adjusts the blade pitch according to the engine speed, thereby maintaining a constant engine speed for any given manual control setting. Constant-speed propellers allow the pilot to set a rotational speed according to the need for maximum engine power or maximum efficiency, and a propeller governor acts as a controller to vary the propeller pitch angle as required to maintain the selected engine speed. In most aircraft this system is hydraulic, with engine oil serving as the hydraulic fluid, however, electrically controlled propellers were developed during World War Two and saw extensive use on military aircraft.

The propellers on some aircraft can operate with a negative blade pitch angle, and thus reverse the thrust from the propeller. This is known as Beta Pitch. Reverse thrust is used to help slow the aircraft after landing and is particularly advantageous when landing on a wet runway as wheel braking suffers reduced effectiveness.

The Jet Engine

Frank Whittle

A jet engine works by sucking air into the engine through an intake at the front, normaly with rotating fan blades. This air is then driven through the engine by compressor blades which squeeze it into a smaller space, where fuel is sprayed in, mixed with the air and ignited. The hot gases produced generate energy and turn the turbine blades and in turn the turbine produces the power to drive the compressor. The gases blow out of the exhaust at the back of the engine, thrusting the engine and aeroplane forward.

In England in 1928, Frank Whittle, (1907 – 1996) then a cadet at RAF College Cranwell, formally submitted his ideas for a turbo-jet to his superiors and further developed his ideas over the following months. Then on 16th January 1930, Whittle submitted his first patent but had to wait until 1932 for it to be granted.

The patent showed a two-stage axial compressor, feeding a single-sided centrifugal compressor, but later, Whittle would concentrate on the simpler centrifugal compressor only for a variety of practical reasons. He had his first engine up and running in April 1937. Some accounts state that Whittle's team experienced near panic when the engine failed to stop, accelerating even after the fuel was switched off. As it turned out, fuel had apparently leaked into the engine and accumulated in pools.

In 1935, Hans von Ohain started work on a similar design in Germany and it is often claimed that he was unaware of Whittle's work. Ohain maintained that he had not read Whittle's patent, and Whittle believed him, however, the Whittle patent was available in German libraries at the time and Whittle's son had suspicions that Ohain had either read it or heard of it. Years later, it was admitted by von Ohain in his biography that he had been aware of and read Whittle's patent.

His first device was strictly experimental and could only run under external power but he was able to demonstrate the basic concept. Ohain was then introduced to Ernst Heinkel, who immediately saw the promise of the design. Heinkel had recently purchased the Hirth engine company, and he set Ohain and his master machinist Max Hahn up there, forming a new division of the Hirth company.

Their first centrifugal engine, the HeS1, was up and running by September 1937. Unlike Whittle's engine, Ohain's engine used hydrogen as fuel, supplied under external pressure but their subsequent designs used gasoline and this resulted in the HeS3 which was then fitted to Heinkel's simple and compact He178 aircraft and flown by Erich Warsitz on the morning of 27th August 1939, from Rostock-Marienehe aerodrome. This was an impressively short time for development and the He 178 was the world's first turbojet-powered aircraft to fly.

HeS3 engine : Courtesy of Baier

He 178 First Turbo powered aircraft

The world's first turbo-prop was the Jendraaik Cs-1 designed by the Hungarian mechanical engineer Gyorgy Jendrassik , It was produced and tested in the Ganz factory in Budapest between 1938 and 1942 and was intended to fit into the Varga RMI-1 X/H twin-engined reconnaissance bomber designed by László Varga in 1940 but the program was cancelled.

Perhaps now is a good time to look at the different types of jet engines, there are five basic types but they all employ the same elements of, compression, combustion and exhaust. The simplest form of jet is the Ramjet.

Ramjet.

A ramjet is a form of air-breathing jet engine that uses the engine's forward motion to compress the incoming air without either an axial or centrifugal compressor. Because ramjets cannot produce thrust at zero airspeed, they cannot move an aircraft forward from a standstill. A ramjet-powered vehicle, therefore, requires an assisted take-off like a rocket perhaps, to accelerate it to a speed where it begins to produce thrust. Ramjets work most efficiently at supersonic speeds and can operate at speeds as high as Mach 6, making them particularly useful in applications requiring a small and simple mechanism for high-speed use, such as a missile.

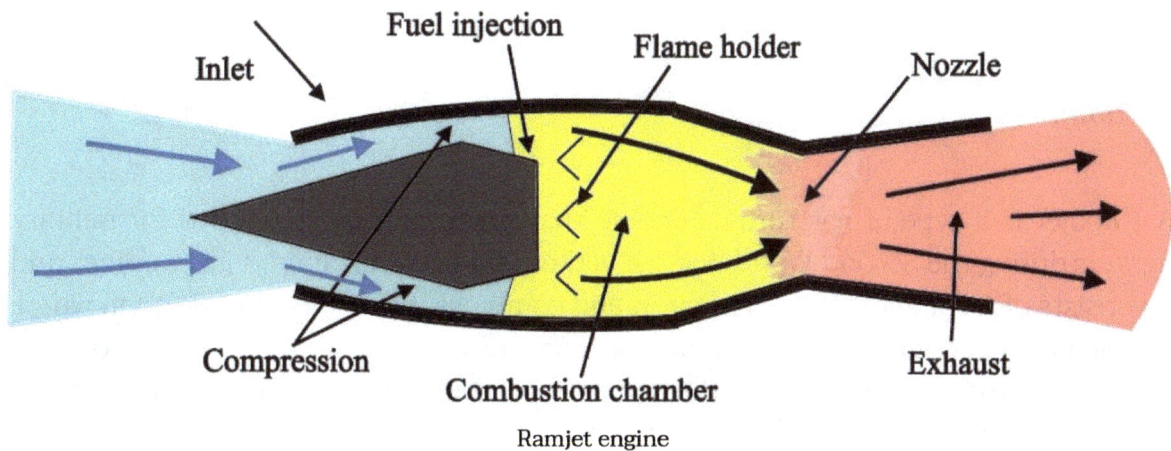

Ramjet engine

The Compressor

Other forms of jet engine have a compressor section in the form of an impeller or rotor, that forces air into the combustion chamber to increase the pressure of the air and to provide conditions favourable for combustion and expansion of the hot gases through the turbine.

At first glance, one may wonder why an engine needs a compressor at all. However, without a compressor, the engine could never develop static thrust, just like a ramjet, and would need to be accelerated up to speed before they can work. For this reason, a compressor-driven engine is useable over a much wider range of conditions.

The compressor stage is made up of the impeller, or rotor, and the diffuser, or stator and in most devices, pressure rises occur across both portions of the stage.

Compressors fall into two broad categories. The first type of compressor is the **centrifugal or annular compressor**. With this type, the impeller accelerates the flow of air by thrusting it outward and so increasing the pressure. The pressure is further increased, and the flow is slowed, when it meets the diffusers that ring the impeller.

The advantages of the centrifugal compressor are that it is easier to design and manufacture, and it can often increase the pressure enough for efficient combustion with only one stage. However, the airflow for a centrifugal compressor is much lower than for an axial, and its pressure ratio is generally lower, meaning it is much less effective for creating thrust and it is less fuel-efficient. Hence, it is more often seen in small engines, where the ease of manufacturing advantages outweighs the performance disadvantages.

The other type of compressor is the **axial flow compressor**. While axial compressors can accommodate more airflow than a centrifugal design of the same size, the rotor/stator stage doesn't generally provide enough compression for most applications. For this reason, modern engines can use as many as 10 or 15 compressor stages.

The advantages of the axial compressor are its higher flow rate and greater pressure ratio, which results in higher thrust and fuel efficiency. This makes it better suited to applications where the thrust of the engine itself is the motive force for the aircraft.

Turbojet

A turbojet is a type of gas turbine engine that was originally developed for military fighters during the Second World War. It is the simplest of all aircraft gas turbines and It consists of a compressor to draw air in and compress it, a combustion section where fuel is added and ignited and then one or more turbines that extract power from the expanding exhaust gases to drive the compressor, and an exhaust nozzle that accelerates the exhaust gases out the back of the engine to create thrust.

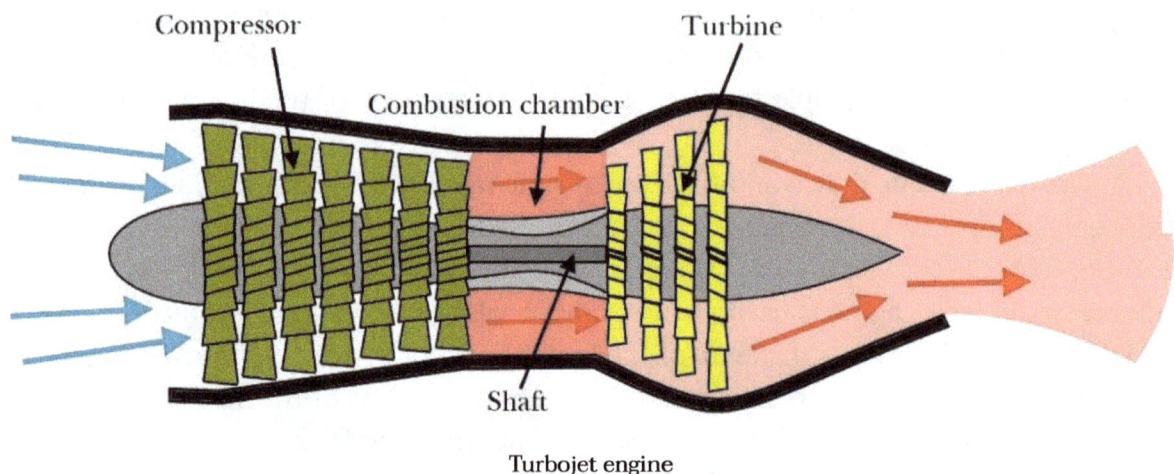

Turbojet engine

When turbojets were first introduced, the top speed of fighter aircraft equipped with them was at least 100 miles per hour faster than competing piston-driven aircraft but in the years following the war, the drawbacks of the turbojet gradually became apparent. At speeds below Mach 2, turbojets use large amounts of fuel and create tremendous amounts of noise. Early designs also responded very slowly to power changes, a fact that caught out many experienced pilots when they attempted the transition from piston powered aircraft to jets. These drawbacks eventually led to the downfall of the pure turbojet, and only a handful of types are still in production. The last airliner that used turbojets was the Concorde, whose Mach 2 airspeed permitted the engine to be highly efficient.

Turbofan

The **turbofan** or **fanjet** is a type of airbreathing jet engine that is now widely used in aircraft propulsion. As the word "turbofan" implies, the engine has both a gas turbine, that derives mechanical energy from combustion and a ducted fan that uses the mechanical energy from the gas turbine to accelerate air rearwards. Thus, whereas all the air taken in by a turbojet passes through the combustion chamber and turbine, in a turbofan, some of that air bypasses these elements. A turbofan, can thus be thought of as a turbojet being used to drive a ducted fan, with both of these contributing to the thrust.

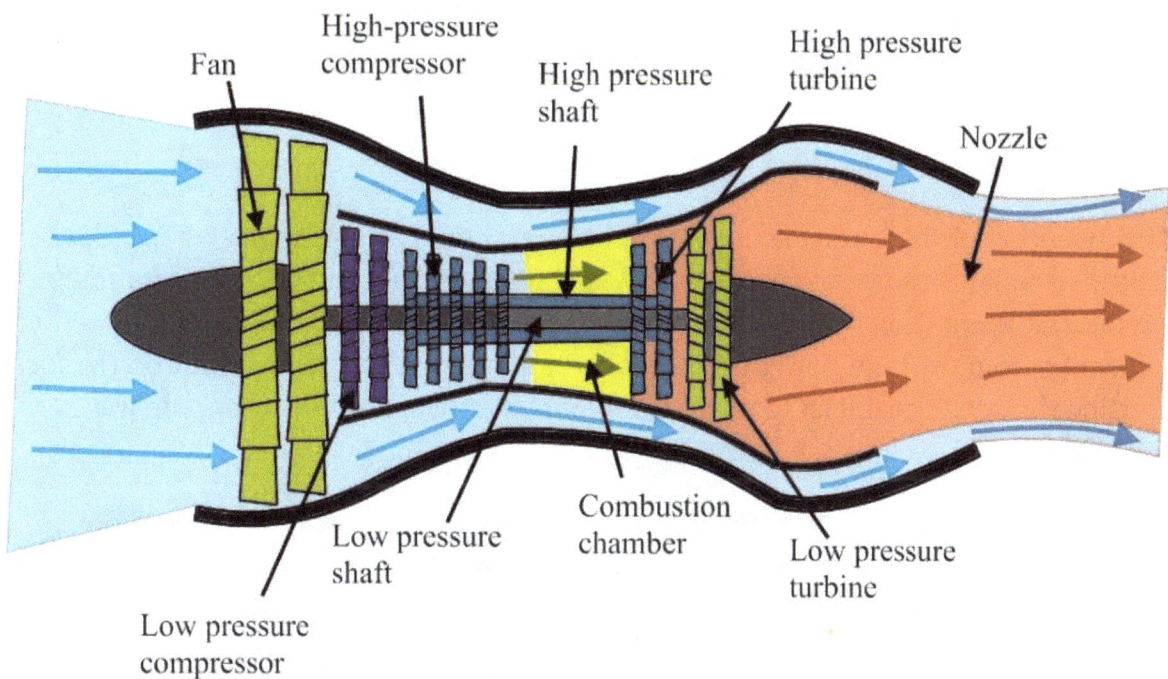

Turbofan or Fanjet engine

The ratio of the mass-flow of air bypassing the engine core divided by the mass-flow of air passing through the core is referred to as the bypass ratio. The engine produces thrust through a combination of these two portions working together and engines that use more jet thrust relative to fan thrust are known as *low-bypass turbofans*, conversely those that have considerably more fan thrust than jet thrust are known as *high-bypass*.

Most commercial aviation jet engines in use today are of the high-bypass type and most modern military fighter engines are low-bypass.

Turbofans were initially invented to overcome the undesirable characteristic of turbojets being inefficient for subsonic flight.

Because the turbine has to also drive the fan, the turbine is larger and has larger pressure and temperature drops, and so the exhaust nozzles are smaller. This means that the exhaust velocity of the core is reduced. The fan also has lower exhaust velocity, giving much more thrust per unit energy (lower specific thrust). The overall effective exhaust velocity of the two exhaust jets can be made closer to a normal subsonic aircraft's flight speed. In effect, a turbofan emits a large amount of air more slowly, whereas a turbojet emits a smaller amount of air quickly, which is a far less efficient way to generate the same thrust.

Afterburners, that are designed to provide an increase in thrust, usually for supersonic flight, take-off or some combat situations and operate by injecting additional fuel into the flow after it has passed the turbine, are not used on high-bypass turbofan engines but may be used on either low-bypass turbofan or turbojet engines. Afterburning significantly increases thrust without the weight of an additional engine, but at the cost of very high fuel consumption and decreased fuel efficiency limiting its practical use to short bursts.

Turboprop

The invention of the jet engine meant that aircraft could attain far greater speeds than they ever could with piston engines and was of course a substantial benefit for military aircraft but less so for civil aviation. However, the designers of civil aircraft still wanted to benefit from the high power that a gas turbine can generate, so they hit on the idea of using the power of the jet to turn a traditional propeller and the turboprop was born.

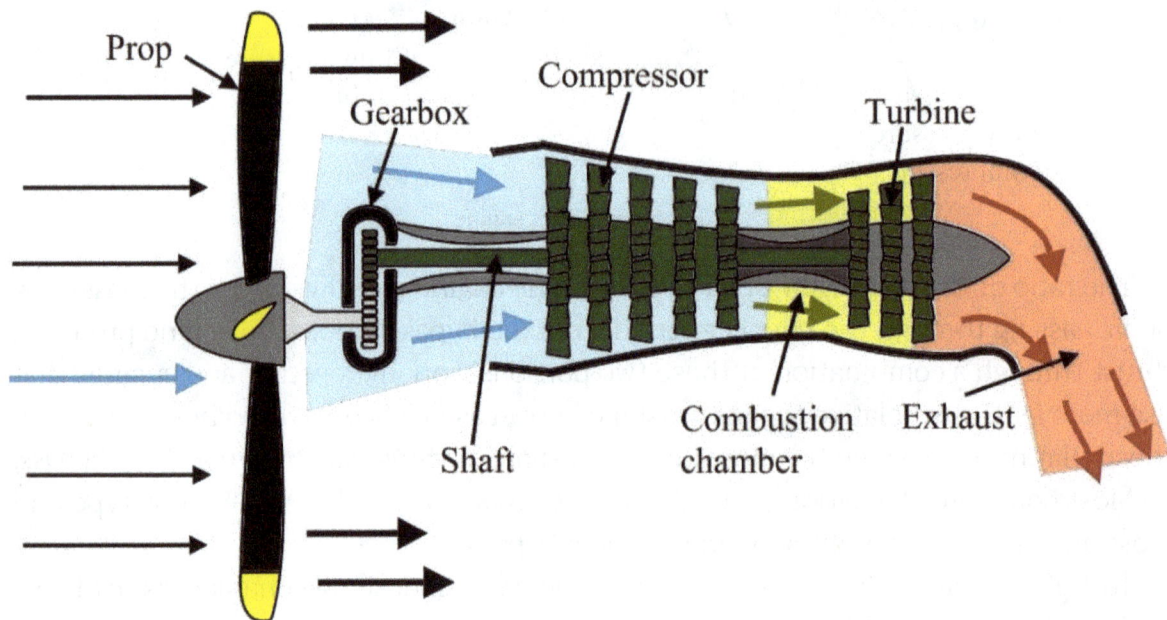

Turboprop engine

Because turbines spin at relatively high speeds compared to propellers, turboprop engines have a gearbox to lower the speed of the shaft and prevent the propeller tips from reaching supersonic speeds. A turboprop is very efficient when operated within the realm of the cruise speeds it was designed for, which is typically 200 to 400 mph (320 to 640 km/h).

Turboshaft

A turboshaft engine is a form of gas turbine that is designed to power a shaft rather than supply jet thrust. In concept, turboshaft engines are very similar to turboprops with only minor differences, and a single engine is often sold in both forms.

Turboshaft engines are commonly used in applications that require a sustained high-power output, high reliability, small size, and light weight. These applications include helicopters, ships, tanks and hovercraft.

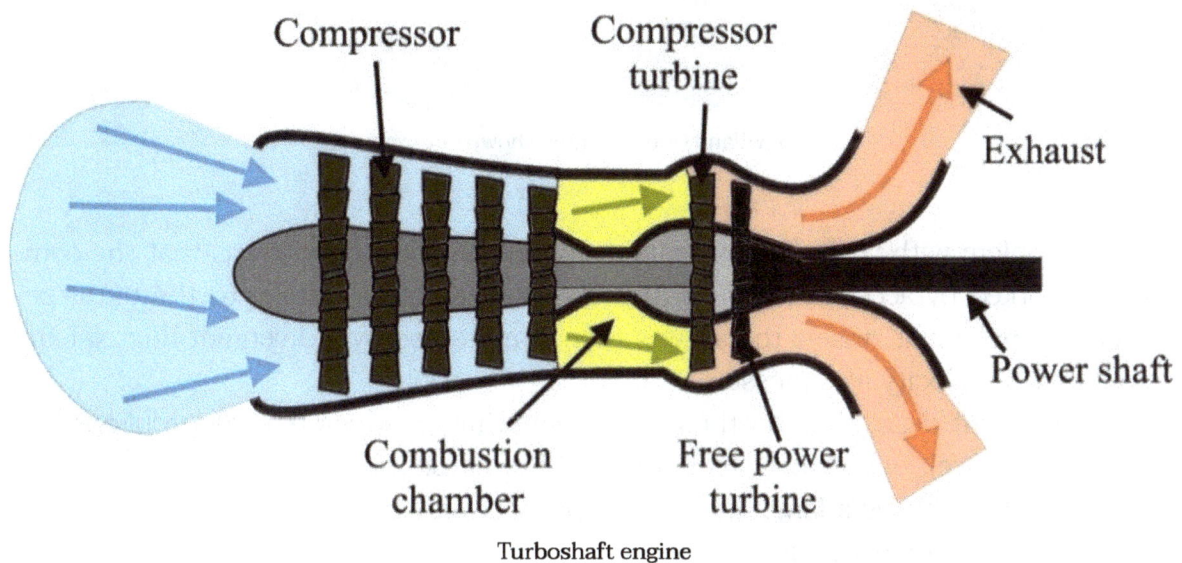

Turboshaft engine

In 1941 British engine designer Frank Halford working from Whittle's ideas, developed a "straight through" version of the centrifugal jet and his design became the de Havilland Goblin shown below.

De Havilland Goblin engine shown cut-away

One problem with both of these early, centrifugal-flow designs, was that the compressor worked by accelerating air outward from the central intake to the outer periphery of the engine, where the air was then compressed by a divergent duct set-up, converting its velocity into pressure.

Although this design had been used for some time in superchargers on piston engines and was well understood, technological limitation of the time meant the compressor needed to have a large diameter to produce the required power and the large engine diameter produced a lot of drag.

A further disadvantage of the earlier Whittle designs was that the air flow was reversed through the combustion section and again to the turbine and tailpipe, all of which added complexity and lowered efficiency. Nevertheless, these engines were light weight and reliable and development rapidly progressed to practical airworthy designs.

The problems of the centrifugal-flow designs were addressed with the introduction of the axial-flow compressor by Austrian Anselm Franz of Junkers engine division.

Franz designed the "Junkers Jumo 004", the world's first mass-produced, operational turbojet engine. Apart from being the world's first jet engine with an axial-flow compressor, it was also the first to have an afterburner and a variable area exhaust nozzle.

The original 004 A model flew for the first time in 1942, but it was not suitable for production because it was too heavy and used alloys that were in short supply in Germany at the time.

The 004 B production model was easier to manufacture, weighed less, and used air cooling for the combustor, turbine blades, and exhaust nozzle. The engine powered the Messerschmitt Me 262, which was the first operational jet fighter.

Messerschmitt Me 262 : Darren Harbar Photography

The first operational jet bomber and reconnaissance aeroplane and the Arado 234. Volume production of the 004 B began in early 1944 and Junkers manufactured nearly 6,000 Jumo 004 engines by the end of World War Two, although the fighter arrived too late to affect the outcome of the war.

In the UK, the first axial-flow engine, was the Metrovick F.2 built by Metropolitan-Vickers and first flown in 1943 powering the Gloster Meteor.

Although more powerful than the centrifugal designs at the time, the Air Ministry considered the Metrovick F.2, too complex and unreliable, however the work at Metropolitan-Vickers led to the development of the Armstrong Siddeley Sapphire engine that was later built in America as the J65.

At the end of the war the allies had a chance to study German aircraft in detail and found that although the Germans had been advanced aerodynamically, they had also been short of materials such as tungsten, chromium and titanium for high-stress components such as turbine blades.

Russia, America and Britain greatly benefited from examining the advances Germany had made during the war, and many German designers and scientist took up positions in these countries after the war.

One, quite extraordinary man who had a chance, not just to examine the German aircraft but to fly them, both in service planes and top-secret experimental craft, was Captain Eric "Winkle" Brown, CBE, DSC, Hon FRAeS, RN, the most decorated pilot in the history of the Royal Navy, (see Appendix).

Arado 234 : Courtesy of GFDL.

Gloster Meteor
Darren Harbar Photography

The Turboprop

The world's first turboprop was designed by Gyorgy Jendrassik, a Hungarian mechanical engineer, who patented his invention in 1928 and built a small-scale, 100Hp. gas turbine in 1938.

A larger version, the Jendrassik Cs-1, with a predicted output of 1,000 bhp, was produced and tested at the Ganz Works in Budapest between 1938 and 1941 but problems with combustion limited its output and during the war the factory was turned over to conventional engine production and the project was abandoned.

Rolls-Royce RB 50 Trent

The first British turboprop engine was the Rolls-Royce Trent, a converted Derwent 11 fitted with reduction gear and a Rotol five-bladed propeller. Two Trents were fitted to a Gloster Meteor EE227 making it the first turboprop powered aircraft, albeit a testbed not intended for production. It was first flown on 20th September 1945 and with the imformation gathered, Rolls-Royce developed the Rolls-Royce Clyde "the first turboprop engine to be fully type certificated for military and civil use" and the Dart, which became one of the most reliable turboprop engines ever built.

Dart production continued for more than fifty years and the Dart-powered Vickers Viscount was the first turboprop aircraft of any kind to go into production. The world's first single engine turboprop aircraft was the Armstrong Siddeley Mamba powered, Boulton Paul Balliol, which first flew on 17th May 1948.

Rolls-Royce RB 53 Dart

The Vickers Viscount

The first turboprop airliner was the Vickers Viscount. It was first flown in 1948 and entered service in 1953 when it was well received by passengers because of the cabin conditions which included pressurisation, low noise and vibration, and panoramic windows. It became one of the most successful and profitable of the first post-war transport aircraft with 445 being built for a range of international customers, including in North America.

Vicker viscount. First Turboprop airliner

The first design in June 1945 was based on the Viking with four turboprop engines and 24 seats and designated the VC 2 or Type 453. Later, a double-bubble fuselage was proposed to give extra underfloor cargo space. It was soon realised that for economical operation an altitude of above 20,000 ft was needed and thus cabin pressurisation was required. The decision for pressurisation resulted in the double-bubble and elliptical fuselage designs being abandoned and a circular cross-section variant was offered at the beginning of 1946. The resulting 28-seat VC-2 was financed by the Ministry of Supply with an order for two prototypes, but before the contract was signed, the government asked for the capacity to be increased to 32. This stretched the fuselage increase from 19.94 m to 22.71 m and meant an increased wingspan of 27 m.

The contract for the aircraft was signed on 9th March 1946 and Vickers allocated the designation Type 609 and the name *Viceroy*. Although George Edwards, the Chief Designer, had always favoured the 800 hp Rolls-Royce Dart, other engines were considered, including the Armstrong Siddeley Mamba which the government had specified for the two prototypes. The choice of the Mamba engine increased the weight but Vickers made sure that the engine nacelle would fit either the Mamba or Dart engines. Because the Dart progressed better in development, the government asked in August 1947 for the second prototype to be Dart-powered. The second prototype was designated the 630 and was named as the *Viscount*. The first prototype already under construction was also converted to the Dart as a 630 as well.

The Tupolev Tu-95

After the Second World War, the Russians, building on work developed by Junkers Motorenwerke, produced the Tupolev Tu-95, known to NATO as the "Bear". This strategic bomber and missile platform was powered by four Kuznetsov NK-12 turboprop engines, each with two contra-rotating propellers.

First flown in 1952 it entered service with the Soviet Union in 1956 and is still in use today, together with a maritime patrol version, the Tu-124 and a passenger airliner derivation, the Tu-114.

The Tu-95 is one of the loudest military aircraft, particularly because the tips of the propeller blades move faster than the speed of sound and, as far as I know, it is the only propeller driven aircraft with swept-back wings, with the exception of the recent Airbus Defence and Space A400M.

Tupolev Tu-95 "The Bear" : Courtesy of RAF/MOD Open Government Licence

In November 2015, fifty-nine years after entering service, the Tu-95 finally saw combat as a bomber. Videos from the Russian Ministry of Defence in the autumn of

2015 show them launching cruise missiles that went on to pound the positions of Syrian rebels. The Russian military today maintains a diverse fleet of bombers capable of carrying heavier payloads and flying at faster speeds than the Tu-95. However, the venerable Bear remains well adapted to the job of hauling heavy cruise missiles and keeping a watchful eye over the Pacific and Atlantic.

The Tu-95 also had tremendous fuel capacity and could fly over nine thousand miles without refuelling. After the initial production variant, later types added the distinctive in-flight refuelling probe, giving it an even further greater range. Typical patrols during the Cold War lasted ten hours, but some Tu-95 flights lasted nearly twice as long.

Tu-95 had crew of six to eight depending on the type, including two pilots and two navigators, while the remaining crew operated guns or sensor systems. The original version of the Bear had two twin-barrelled twenty-three-millimetre cannons in the belly and tail, and a single fixed gun in the nose, all intended to ward off enemy fighters. This kind of armament became increasingly obsolete in the age of long-range air-to-air missiles, so the later models got rid of all but the tail gun.

The Tu-95s was also used in nuclear weapon tests with one dropping the largest nuclear weapon ever detonated over Severny Island in 1961, the fifty-megaton "Tsar Bomba". Deployed by parachute, Tsar detonated four kilometres above the ground, sending a mushroom cloud over forty miles into the sky.

The first American turboprop engine was the General Electric XT31 that was first used in the experimental Consolidated Vultee XP-81 The XP-81 first flew in December 1945, the first aircraft to use a combination of turboprop and turbojet power. Two prototype aircraft were ordered on 11th February 1944 that were designated XP-81. The engine selection was an attempt to couple the high-speed capability of the jet engine with the endurance offered by the propeller engine. The XP-81 was designed to use the General Electric TG-100 turboprop engine (later designated XT31 by the US military) in the nose, driving a four-bladed propeller and a GE J33 turbojet mounted just above the rear fuselage. The turboprop would be used for normal flight and cruising and the turbojet added for high-speed flight.

Although promising, the lack of suitable engines combined with the end of World War Two ended the project. More successful was the Allison T56, a single-shaft, modular design military turboprop with a 14-stage axial flow compressor driven by a four-stage turbine. It was originally developed by the Allison Engine Company to power the Lockheed C-130 Hercules transport entering production in 1954. It has been a Rolls-Royce product since 1995 when Allison was acquired by Rolls-Royce. The commercial version is designated 501-D and over 18,000 engines have been produced since 1954, logging over 200 million flying hours. It has also been used to power the Lockheed Electra Airliner and its military derivative the P-3 Orion.

Allison T56 engine shown cut-away : Courtesy of Steven Fine.

The C-130 Hercules was an American four-engine turboprop military transport aircraft designed and built originally by Lockheed (now Lockheed Martin). Capable of using unprepared runways for takeoffs and landings, the C-130 was originally designed as a troop, medevac, and cargo transport aircraft. It became the main military transport for many forces worldwide with more than 40 variants being bult, including civilian versions marketed as the Lockheed L-100, operate in more than 60 nations.

The C-130 Hercules is the longest continuously produced military aircraft at over 60 years, with the updated Lockheed Martin C-130J Super Hercules.

The Lockheed L-188 Electra was the first large turboprop airliner built in the United States and was first flown in 1957. Initial sales were good, but after two fatal crashes that led to expensive modifications to fix a design defect, no more were ordered. With its unique high power-to-weight ratio, huge propellers and very short wings. Large Fowler flaps significantly increased effective wing area when extended, and the airplane had airfield performance capabilities unmatched by many jet transport aircraft even today, particularly on short runways and high field elevations. Jet airliners soon supplanted turboprops for many purposes, and many Electras were modified as freighters.

C-130 Hercules : Darren Harbar Photography

Impression of a Lockheed Electra Airliner

Some events of the Fifties

1950	Korean War begins
1951	First successful flight of Bloodhound ground to air missile
	First direct unrefuelled crossing of Atlantic by jet
1952	First flight of Britannia airliner
1953	Korean War ends
	First Woman to break the sound barrier (Jackie Cochran in a Canadair Sabre)
1956	Suez crisis
1957	Sputnik 1 put into orbit
	Dog Laika launched in Sputnik 2
1959	Astronaut capsule for NASA's Mercury programme tested
	First run of Pegasus VTOL engine

Turbine blade technology

The blades in a modern gas turbine aero-engine are something of a man-made miracle, the technology involved in their production being like something out of science fiction. The blades operate in an extreme environment, sometimes at temperatures that are above the point of plastic deformation and even above their melting point! Which means that exotic alloys and sophisticated cooling schemes are required.

The high temperatures that fan blades operate in has increased over the years through developments in the casting and manufacturing process. Originally, polycrystalline metals were used to make fan blades but now, developments in material science have seen blades being made from aligned metallic crystals and more recently single crystals to operate at higher temperatures with less distortion and now these alloys, together with Nickel based superalloys are employed in most modern jet engines.

The blades in Sir Frank Whittle's prototypes were made entirely of steel and steel is great for strength and surface hardness, but if you need high-temperature performance it isn't the best, 450–500°C being about its limit. Nickel on the other hand melts at 1,455°C and is resistant to corrosion, both valuable assets to have in terms of aero engines

Even more important is its ability to form alloys, and the particular property of one of those alloys, a compound known as gamma-prime, in which nickel combines with aluminium, is the ability to retain its strength at high temperatures.

With steel or even titanium, the strength rapidly drops off as you reach 40–50 per cent of the melting point but Nickel alloys retain their strength at temperatures even up to 85 per cent of the melting point.

Now the blades need to operate in an environment several hundreds of degrees hotter than the melting point of the nickel alloy itself, so to stop them melting, the metal must be cooled. This is done via two mechanisms, firstly, the blades are coated with a low-conductivity ceramic and secondly, they are riddled with a complex, branching structure of internal channels.

Air is drawn from the high-pressure compressor, routed through the core of the engine and into the root of the blades. It passes through the cooling channels and exits through a myriad of holes in the surface of the blade, this creates an envelope of cooler air around each blade so that the metal is never above its melting point, even though the immediate environment is.

This cooling air isn't actually that cool, being at about 600–650°C, and that's because it has to be taken from the hot core of the engine so it has enough pressure to get through the channels and out of the holes but it's still enough to keep the blade temperature down to about 1,150°C.

Normally, metals are composed of many crystals, ordered structures of atoms arranged in a regular lattice, which form naturally as the metal cools from a molten state. These crystals are typically of the order of tens of microns in size, positioned in many orientations, one micron being one millionth of a metre.

At high temperatures and under strain, the crystals can slide against each other, and impurities can diffuse along the boundaries between the grains. This is known as creep, and it badly affected early turbine blades, which were forged from steel and later nickel bars.

The first stage in development was to get rid of any grain boundaries at right angles to the centrifugal loading and this led to the development of blades that were cast so that the metal crystals all ran from top to bottom. Later, this was optimised further by casting single crystals, with no grain boundaries at all.

When it crystallises, nickel forms a structure known as face-centred cubic; each cube has a face with five atoms, one at each corner and one in the middle.

When alloys are made, generally the atoms just swap in and out of the face-centred cubic lattice. But under the right conditions, aluminium and nickel combine in such a way that nickel goes to the centre of the faces and aluminium to the corners. This is known as a precipitate; it forms islands of greater order within the bulk of the alloy, about half a micron in dimension, packed closely together in a rectilinear formation. Because the size of the lattices of the precipitate and the less ordered bulk alloy are almost identical, they are all part of the same crystal.

But this doesn't just happen naturally. To make the blades, the first stage is a ceramic "core", of the form of the tortuous internal cooling channels. Wax is injected around this to form the shape of the aerodynamic blade, plus several other features that assist in the casting process. Platinum pins are inserted to support the core inside the wax; then the form is 'shelled' by coating it in a slurry of alumina-silicate material to form a ceramic coat. Several more coats of different compositions are applied and then the wax is melted out to leave a void in the shape of the blade. This is investment or 'lost-wax' casting, the same technique Ancient Greek sculptors used to make Bronzes.

Molten metal is then poured into the mould, which is placed inside a furnace to keep the metal molten. At the base of the mould is one of the additional casting features: a helical structure about the same shape as three turns of a standard corkscrew. Known as the pigtail, this is attached to a plate that is cooled by water.

Once filled, the mould is slowly withdrawn from the furnace into a cooler chamber. The metal starts to solidify at the chilled plate, and crystals begin to grow into the pigtail. The crystals grow in a straight line in the direction that the mould is being withdrawn, but because of the pigtail's twisted shape, all but the fastest-growing crystals are eliminated. Only a crystal with the correct orientation emerges into the blade mould proper, and the gradual withdrawal of the mould ensures the crystal continues growing through the melt into the rest of the space.

The formation of the vital precipitates results from careful control of the external temperature and from the design of the mould; those multiple layers of ceramic determine how fast the heat from the molten metal can dissipate, and this provides the extra finesse to achieve the required internal structure. The platinum pins holding the core in place diffuse into the alloy without affecting its properties.

Once solidified, the casting is removed from the mould and the first of some 20 processes begins to prepare it for assembly into an engine. First, the ceramic cores are dissolved away with caustic alkalis. Then the extra features for casting are machined away. The holes for the cooling air to escape are drilled using electrical discharge machining, which forms the required hole geometry to direct the air to the points where it is needed. Finally, the blade receives its insulating ceramic.

Nickel high pressure turbine blades with cooling holes in order to operate in environments above their melting point

By the mid to late 1950s not only were nearly all combat aircraft powered by jet engines it wouldn't be long before all large civilian aircraft were also jet powered, leaving the piston engine to light aircraft and cargo planes.

The ascension of the jet engine from its first flight to almost universal use in larger aircraft took less than twenty years.

Civil Aviation Post War

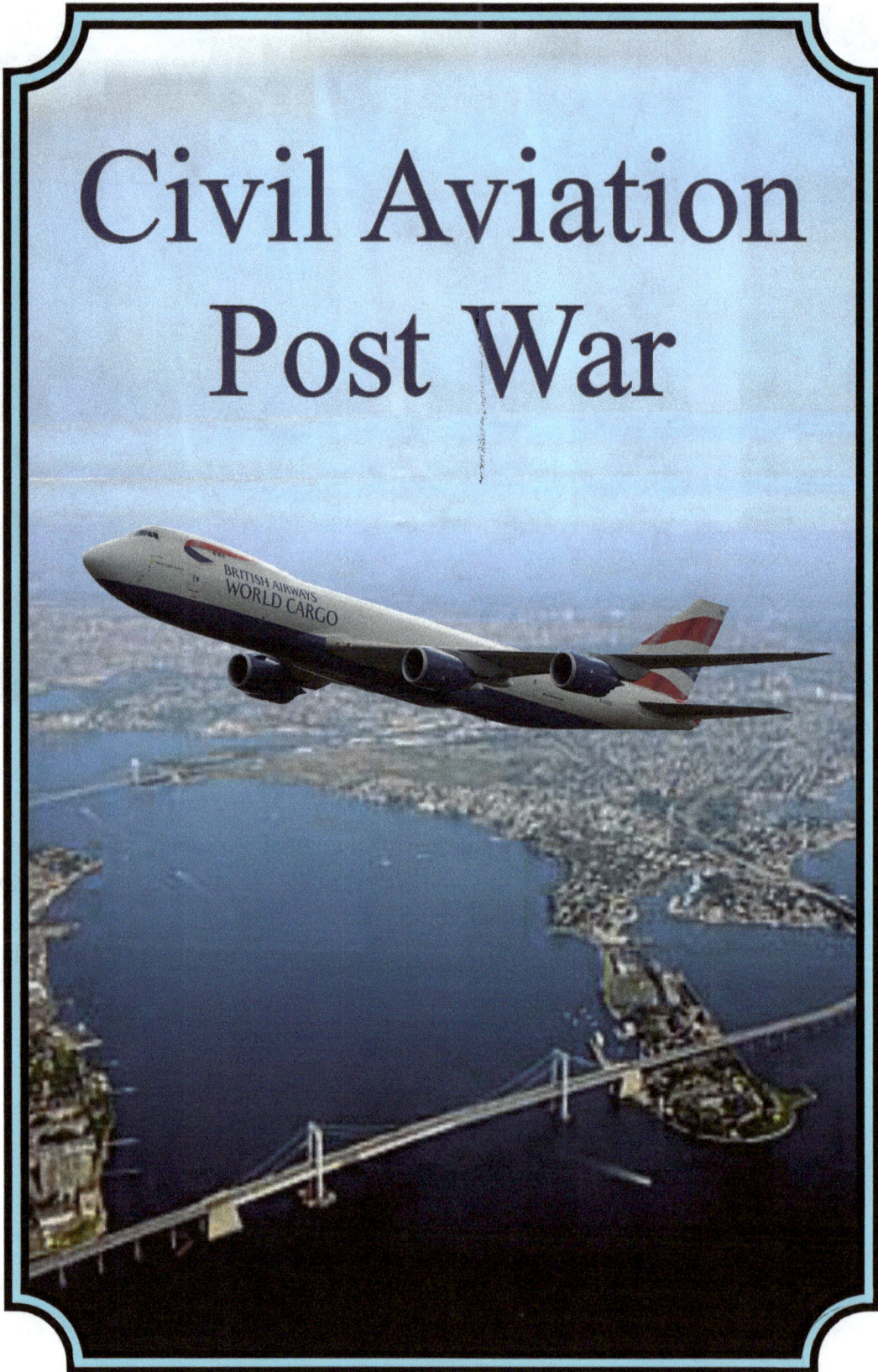

Chapter Eight

Civil Aviation Post War

As early as 1943 a committee was formed to plan for post-war civil aviation. Chaired by J T C Moore-Brabazon, it worked on the assumption that the Allies would be victorious in the war. At first, the Bristol Aeroplane Company (BAC) was not among the group of aircraft manufacturers who were invited to join the consultation but after protests, Leslie Frise, (designer of the Bristol Beaufighter and the Frise Aileron) was invited to attend the first meeting on January 14th 1943 in London.

Bristol Brabazon

Bristol Brabazon outside its specially built hanger at Filton

One of the committee's recommendations was for a large transatlantic airliner and BAC was asked to look into it, provided that it didn't interfere with the company's important war work.

Construction of the Brabazon prototype began in October 1945 and was planned along the lines of the pre-war Imperial Airways flying boats with an onboard cinema, lounge bar and sleeping quarters for around 100 1st class passengers.

Being 54 metres long with a wingspan of 70 metres, the Brabazon required a stronger and longer runway than other aircraft of the time, not just for normal take-offs but also in case of emergency landings and brake failures. This meant that the existing runway at the BAC Filton works had to be lengthened.

It was agreed that the village of Charlton, that comprised of some 88 homes, a public house and a post office that was adjacent to the airfield, would have to be demolished and the existing residents re-housed in council accommodation in Patchway, paying a subsidised rent. It is said that construction of the extended runway used so much cement that it caused a shortage in the South West of England. Eventually the runway, although it only saw limited use with the Brabazon, proved an enormous asset for BAC with their future projects. As a Bristolian and aviation enthusiast, I find it sad to see the Filton runway unused, large areas of the airfield sold off for housing and now proposals for the Brabazon hanger to become a music venue, but I digress.

The Brabazon was powered by a total of eight Bristol Centaurus 18-cylinder radial engines, the most powerful British-built piston engines available at the time, each being capable of generating 2,650 hp. These engines were installed in a unique arrangement where each was paired with another, but instead of sharing a common crankshaft, the paired engines each had their driveshafts angled towards an enormous central gearbox. Between them they drove a series of eight paired contra-rotating propellers which were set on four forward-facing nacelles.

The maiden flight, piloted by Chief Test Pilot Bill Pegg, took place on the 4th September 1949 and on 15th June 1950, the aircraft gave demonstration flights at London Airport.

Brabazon was destined to be the wrong aircraft at the wrong time however, airline companies were looking to move into the jet age and in America, manufacturers were busy converting their large bombers into civil airliners with great success and were meeting the current demand. Unable to find buyers, BAC sold the only existing Brabazon for scrap after it had completed only 400 hours flying time.

The Brabazon had not been a commercial success but neither was it a complete loss, the research and manufacturing experience gained in building and flying such a large technically advanced aircraft were invaluable to BAC. The lessons about pressurised cabins, hydraulic power controls, electrical generation and engine controls were later used on the development of several other aircraft.

Lockheed Constellation

The Lockheed Constellation was a propeller-driven, four-engine airliner built by Lockheed between 1943 and 1958 at Burbank, California. Lockheed built 856 in numerous models, all with the same triple-tail design and dolphin-shaped fuselage and most were powered by four 18-cylinder Wright R-3350 Duplex-Cyclone engines. The Constellation was used as a civil airliner as well as a military and civilian air transport. The Constellation series was the first pressurized-cabin civil airliner series to go into widespread use. Its pressurized cabin enabled large numbers of commercial passengers to fly well above most bad weather for the first time, thus significantly improving the general safety and ease of air travel and it was used as the presidential aircraft for Dwight D. Eisenhower during his time in office.

Lockheed Constellation : Darren Harbar Photography

The aircraft that were entering construction for TWA when World War Two broke out were quickly converted to fulfil an order of 202 C-69 Constellation military aircraft for the United States Army Air Force and the first prototype flew on 9th January 1943.

The de Havilland 106 Comet:

The de Havilland 106 Comet was the world's first commercial jet airliner. Developed by de Havilland at its Hatfield Aerodrome in Hertfordshire, it was powered by four de Havilland Ghost turbojet engines, semi-concealed in the wings, giving it an extremely sleek and streamlined appearance.

The Comet featured square windows and a pressurised cabin, offering a great deal of passenger comfort. Several of the Comet's avionic systems were also new to civil aviation. One such feature was the "irreversible powered flight control", which increased the pilot's ease of control and the safety of the aircraft by preventing outside forces from changing the directed positions and placement of the aircraft's control surfaces. Additionally, a large number of the control surfaces, such as the elevators, were equipped with a complex gearing system as a safeguard against accidentally over-stressing the surfaces or airframe at higher speeds.

At its debut in 1952 the Comet seemed to be heading for unrivalled commercial success. but tragedy was to strike within twelve months of its entering service.

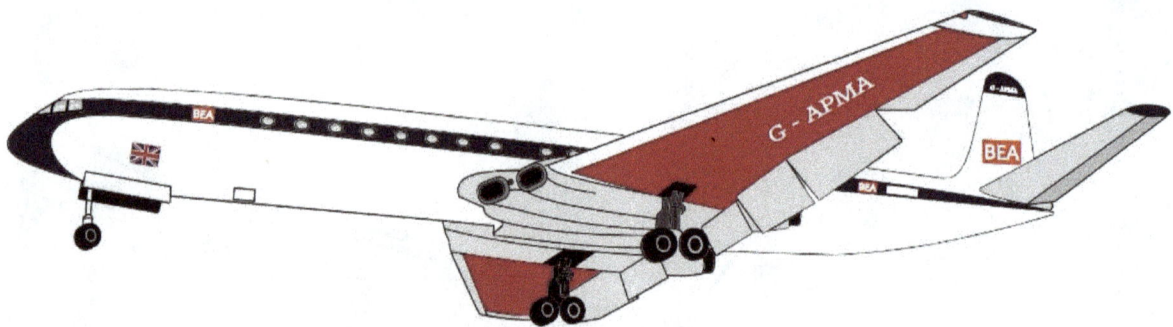

de havilland Comet

On May 7th 1953 a Comet, BOAC flight 783, broke up in mid-air and crashed near Calcutta, India, after flying into a thunderstorm; all 43 on board were killed. As if that tragedy wasn't enough, on January 10th 1954, BOAC flight 781 flying from Rome to London on the last leg of a flight from Singapore, disintegrated in mid-air.

BOAC voluntarily grounded its Comet fleet and engineers suggested 60 immediate modifications to the design to rectify some of the design flaws that were believed to have caused the accident and Comet flights resumed again on March 23rd 1954, however, only two weeks later on April 8th, another Comet, South African Airways flight 201, flying from Rome to Cairo bound for Johannesburg, disintegrated in mid-air, killing all 14 passengers and seven crew.

The entire Comet fleet was then grounded, its Certificate of Airworthiness revoked and the line production at de Havilland in Hatfield suspended.

A number of investigations led by Sir Arnold Hall at the Royal Aeronautical Establishment in Farnborough, UK followed. Most critically, this included a full-scale cyclic internal pressurisation test of the fuselage in a water tank and the aircraft G-ALYU was selected for this purpose. G-ALYU had accumulated 1,221 internal pressurisation cycles in service and after a further 1,836 cycles in the water tank, the cabin ripped open after a proof-test loading 33% higher than the nominal pressurisation cycle loading. Evidence of fatigue cracking was found that originated from the aft lower corner of the forward escape hatch and also from the right-hand aft corner of the windows.

Metal fatigue was a phenomenon that was not very well understood at the time but as a result of the tests the Comet was extensively redesigned, with oval windows, structural reinforcements and other changes. Rival manufacturers meanwhile heeded the lessons learned from the Comet while developing their own aircraft.

Although sales never fully recovered, the improved Comet 2 and the prototype Comet 3 culminated in the redesigned Comet 4 series, which flew in 1958 and remained in commercial service until 1981. The Comet was also adapted for a variety of military roles as well as for VIP flights, medical and passenger transport, as well as surveillance and the last Comet 4, which was used as a research platform, made its final flight in 1997.

The most extensive Comet modifications resulted in a specialised maritime patrol derivative, the Hawker Siddeley Nimrod. This was in response to a requirement issued by the Royal Air Force to replace its fleet of ageing Avro Shackletons.

Avro Shackleton

The Nimrod MR1/MR2s were primarily to be used for anti-submarine warfare operations, with secondary roles including maritime surveillance and anti-surface warfare. It served from the early 1970s until March 2010. The intended replacement was to be an extensively rebuilt Nimrod MR2s, designated Nimrod MRA4, however, due to considerable delays, repeated cost overruns, and financial cutbacks, the development of the MRA4 was abandoned in 2010.

Nimrods remained in service with the Royal Air Force however until 2011, over 60 years after the Comet's first flight.

Hawker Siddeley Nimrod : Darren Harbar Photography

Britain's aviation industry, although in the ownership of private companies, was more or less managed by the government and during the Second World War the design and manufacture of civil and transport aircraft had largely been abandoned to ensure the production of sufficient combat aircraft.

During the 1950s, the government required the aviation industry to consolidate and in consequence only two engine makers were left by 1959, Rolls-Royce and Bristol Siddeley. From 1959 to 1961 the British government forced the consolidation of a further twenty or so British aviation firms, including Vickers and English Electric's aviation interests, into three larger groups with the threat of withheld contracts and the lure of project funding. While the majority of fixed-wing aircraft design and construction lay in the British Aircraft Corporation and the Hawker Siddeley Group, the helicopter divisions of Bristol, Fairey and Saunders-Roe, with their hovercraft, were merged with Westland to form Westland Helicopters in 1961. Hawker Siddeley later merged with BAC in 1977

The British government was in control of route-licensing for private airlines and also oversaw the newly established and publicly owned British Overseas Airways Corporation (BOAC) for long-range flights and the British European Airways (BEA) for short and medium-range flights.

Bristol Britannia

In the early fifties, BOAC required an airliner that could take off from short runways in order to service its long-haul Empire routes and Bristol built the Britannia airliner to fulfil these requirements.

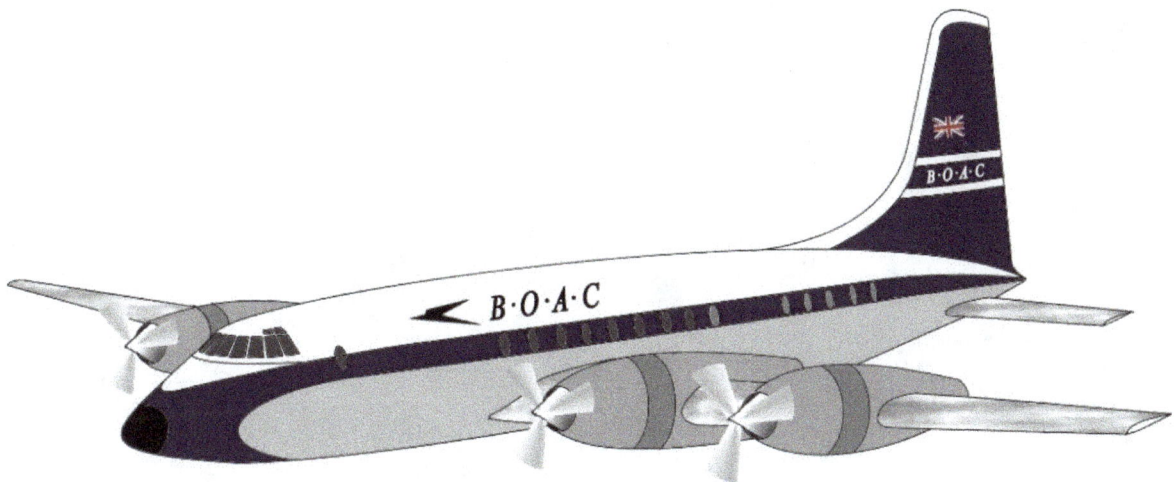

Impression of a Bristol Brtannia

The first pair of prototypes, were powered by the early series Proteus 625 engine. This was the direct follow-up to the 600 series engine that had already successfully completed its type trials, having been originally designed to replace the piston engines on the Brabazon. The maiden flight, that took place on August 16th 1952 with Chief Test Pilot Bill Pegg at the controls, turned out to be a rather eventful one, as the over-sensitive flying controls led to a wild pitching before Pegg managed to regain control. During the landing approach, smoke filled the cockpit and the main undercarriage bogie was stuck in its cycle, only fully deploying seconds before landing. These "snags" however, proved to be minor and by September, the prototype was cleared to perform at the 1952 SBAC (Society of British Aerospace Companies) display at Farnborough, where spectators commented on the "quietness" of the giant airliner, leading to it becoming known as "The Whispering Giant.

However, in 1953 and 1954, after the crash of the three de Havilland Comets, the Air Ministry demanded that the Britannia undergo lengthy tests. Further delays still were attributed to teething problems with the engine and in February 1954, Bill Pegg was flying the second prototype, G-ALRX, with potential buyers from KLM on board, when an engine fire, caused by a failed reduction gear threatened to engulf the entire wing. Bill Pegg was concerned that the intense heat could melt the main spar so he took the decision to land on the mud flats on the Severn Estuary. In his autobiography he says, "*Whilst we succeeded in putting out the first fire by turning off the fuel, the fire-extinguisher system failed to cope with the oil tank blaze.*" Needless to say, KLM did not purchase any Britannia aircraft.

Britannia after landing on the mud flats

Issues of icing were highlighted by BOAC after they had taken delivery of the Britannia and although this problem was easily overcome by simply selecting a different cruising height to the one specified, they were exaggerated publicly by the company, who had now changed their mind and wanted the Boing 707 instead of Britannia, virtually killing off its sales prospects. The Britannia was retired in 1975 and only 85 were ever built. It's probable that sales to other companies would have been few anyway, simply because the Britannia was designed specifically for the needs of one company, BOAC and didn't necessarily meet the needs of others, the result possibly of too much government control. Other companies were more generally competitive and designing aircraft to meet the needs of many airlines, not just one, with a view to overall sales.

Boeing 707

The biggest opposition faced by the likes of Comet and Britannia was the American Boeing 707, a mid to long-range narrow body four engine jet airliner.

Boeing 707 : Courtesy of Jett Clipper Johnny

Although it was not the first jetliner in service, the 707 was the first to be commercially successful and dominated passenger air transport in the 1960s and remained successful throughout the 1970s. It established Boeing as one of the largest manufacturers of passenger aircraft, and led to the later series of airliners with 7-7 designations. The later 720, 727, 737 and 757 all share elements of the 707's fuselage design.

Developed from the Boeing 367-80 a prototype 707 jet first flew in 1954. A larger fuselage cross-section, along with other modifications, resulted in the initial-production 707-120, powered by Pratt & Whitney J57 (Pratt & Whitney designation JT3C) turbojet engines, taking to the skies on December 20th 1957. Regular service began with Pan American World Airways in October 1958.

Several derivatives followed, including a stretched version, powered by Rolls-Royce Conway Turbofans that entered service in 1960. Military derivatives include the E-3 Sentry airborne reconnaissance aircraft and the C-137 Stratoliner VIP transports. A total of 865 Boeing 707s were produced and delivered along with over 800 military versions.

E-3 Sentry airborne recnnaissance aircraft.

Vickers VC-10

In 1951, the British Government asked Vickers-Armstrong to consider a military transport development of the Valiant V Bomber with transatlantic range, as a successor to the de Havilland Comet. The concept interested BOAC, who then entered into discussion with Vickers and the RAF and in October 1952, Vickers were contracted to build a prototype, which they designated the Vickers V-1000, followed in June 1954 by a production order for six aircraft for the RAF.

The planned civil airliner was known as the VC7, (the seventh Vickers civil design). Development was delayed by the need to meet the RAF's requirements for short take-off and a self-loading capability.

VC 10 : Courtesy of Steve Fitzgerald.

Work started on the prototype but by 1955 the aircraft's increased weight required a more powerful engine, causing BOAC to question the engine development cycle. In 1955, the government cancelled the RAF order in a round of defence cuts.

Vickers and the Ministry of Supply hoped that BOAC would still be interested in the VC7 but they were reluctant to support the production of another British aircraft following delays in the Britannia programme and the crashes involving the de Havilland Comet.

Although BOAC had ordered modified Comet 4s, it viewed the type as an intermediate rather than a long term type and in 1956, ordered 15 Boeing 707s. These were oversized and underpowered for BOAC's medium-range Empire, African and Asian routes, which involved destinations with what were known as "Hot and High" airports that reduced aircraft performance, notably between Karachi and Singapore, and they could not lift a full load from high-altitude airports like Kano or Nairobi.

Several companies proposed a suitable replacement but after carefully considering the routes, Vickers offered the VC10. Crucially, Vickers was the only firm willing to launch its design as a private venture, instead of relying on government financing.

The VC10 was a new design but used some production ideas and techniques, as well as the Conway engines, developed for the V.1000 and VC7. It had a generous wing equipped with wide chord Fowler flaps and full span leading edge slats for good take-off and climb performance; its rear engines gave an efficient clean wing and reduced cabin noise. The engines were also further from the runway surface than an underwing design, an important factor in operations from rough runways such as those common in Africa; wide, low-pressure tyres were also adopted with this same concern in mind.

The VC10 was capable of landing and taking off at slower speeds than the rival Boeing 707 and its engines could produce considerably more thrust, providing good hot and high performance; it was also considered to be a safer aircraft.

The onboard avionics and flight-deck technology were extremely advanced, with a quadruplicated automatic flight control system (a "super autopilot") that was intended to enable fully automatic zero-visibility landings (though the auto-land system did not work smoothly and was finally removed from the Super VC10s.). Capacity was up to 135 passengers in a two-class configuration.

Despite some misgivings about operating costs, BOAC ordered 25 aircraft. Vickers calculated that it would need to sell 80 VC10s at about £1.75 million each to break even so, apart from BOAC's 25, another 55 remained to be sold.

Vickers offered a smaller version, the VC11, to BEA for routes like those to Athens and Beirut but this was rejected in favour of the Hawker Siddeley Trident, shown here.

Hawker Siddeley Trident : Courtesy of Christian Volpal.

On 14th January 1958, BOAC increased its order to 35, with options for a further 20 aircraft, the largest civil order ever placed in Britain at that time, these were to have smaller 109-seat interiors and more first-class seating. To offer greater economy, Vickers began work on the *Super* 200 development of the VC10 with more powerful engines and an 8.1 m longer fuselage offering up to 212 seats, 23 more than the Boeing 707–320 series.

By January 1960, Vickers was experiencing financial difficulties and was concerned that it would not be able to deliver the 35 VC10s without making a loss. It offered to sell ten Super 200s to BOAC at £2.7 million each only to find that BOAC was now unconvinced it had a role for the already ordered 35 VC10s and doubted the airline's ability to fill all 200 seats.

The whole project looked to be facing cancellation but the government stepped in, supporting Vickers with an order for Super 200s being placed on 23rd June 1960. The Super 200 extension was cut down to 3.9 m for the finalised Super VC10, the original design retrospectively becoming the Standard VC10.

In accordance with its contract with Vickers, in May 1961, BOAC amended its order to 15 Standard and 35 Super VC10s, eight of the Supers having a new combi configuration with a large cargo door and stronger floor. In December the order was reduced again to 12 Standards.

By the time deliveries were ready to begin in 1964, airline growth had slowed and BOAC wanted to cut its order to seven Supers. In May, the government intervened, placing an order for VC10s as military transports to absorb over-production.

This lengthy, well-publicised trouble eroded market confidence in the VC10 and BOAC chairman Gerard d'Erlanger and managing director Sir Basil Smallpeice resigned, defending the opinion that the airline was a profit-making company, not a sponsor of indigenous aircraft. BOAC's incoming chairman Sir Giles Guthrie was also anti-VC10; he proposed that the Vickers programme be shelved in favour of more Boeing 707s and this led to BOAC being referred to in some quarters as the "Boeing Only Airways Corporation".

The prototype Standard, G-ARTA, rolled out of the Weybridge factory on 15th April 1962 and on 29th June, after two months of ground, engine and taxi tests, it was first flown by Vickers' chief test pilot G R 'Jock' Bryce, and co-pilot Brian Trubshaw, later to be Chief Test Pilot on the Concorde, and flight engineer Bill Cairns. It was flown from Brooklands to Wisley for further testing.

By the end of the year, two more aircraft had been flown and flight tests revealed a serious drag problem, which was addressed via the adoption of Küchemann wingtips, which feature a large radius curve from the leading edge to a sharp corner at the trailing edge when viewed from above and "beaver tail" engine nacelle fairings, as well as a redesigned basal rudder segment for greater control effectiveness; these aerodynamic refinements considerably elongated the testing process.

The certification programme included visits to Nairobi, Khartoum, Rome, Kano, Aden, Salisbury and Beirut. A VC10 flew across the Atlantic to Montreal on 8th February 1964. By this point, seven of the original 12 Standards were complete and the production line was preparing for the Supers.

A Certificate of Airworthiness was awarded on 23rd April 1964 and the plane was introduced to regular passenger service between London and Lagos on 29th April.

The VC-10 achieved the fastest crossing of the Atlantic by a jet airliner, a record still held to-date for a sub-sonic airliner, of 5 hours and 1 minute, only the supersonic Concorde has been faster. The VC-10 is often compared to the larger Soviet Ilyushin Il-62, among others, because of the use of a rear engine quad layout. Some smaller business jets like the Lockheed JetStar, also have this engine arrangement.

Soviet Ilyushin Il-62

Although only a relatively small number of VC10s were built, they provided long service with BOAC and other airlines from the 1960s to 1981. They were also used from 1965 as strategic air transports for the Royal Air Force and ex-passenger models and others were used as aerial refuelling aircraft, a role that was only taken over in 2013 by the Airbus Voyager.

By the end of 1964, all production requirements had been fulfilled; Vickers (now part of BAC) retained the prototype and the first Super VC10 was first flown from Brooklands on 7th May 1964. Although the Super was really only a minor development of the Standard model with an extra fuel-tank in the fin, testing was prolonged by the need to move each engine pair 27 cm outboard as well as up and giving them a 3-degree twist. This redesign resolved the tailplane buffeting and fatigue issues incurred by operating the thrust reversers.

When BOAC and BEA combined in 1972 to form British Airways, the new company began retiring the Super VC10s from trans-Atlantic flights in 1974, mainly due to the 1973 oil crisis and retirement of their Super VC10 fleet began in April 1980, being completed the following year.

After failing to sell them to other airlines, British Airways sold 14 of the 15 survivors to the RAF in May 1981 (one went for preservation at Duxford). The VC10 served its intended market for only fifteen years although it could have continued in airline service much longer despite its high fuel consumption, but high noise levels also sounded its death-knell.

The first RAF aircraft were delivered for testing on 26th November 1965. These VC10s were all named after Victoria Cross medal holders, the names being displayed above the forward passenger door. The decision to name the fourteen RAF VC10s started with the first CO of the VC10 era, Wing Commander Mike Beavis. He proposed around 1967 that the aircraft, with its VC10 designation, would be most suited for commemorating Victoria Cross recipients. This idea was approved but it also created a bit of a headache, as there were then 51 VCs which had been won by airmen, and only fourteen VC10s so difficult decisions had to be made about who to exclude. No doubt there were long debates and disagreements before the final fourteen were chosen.

One of the VC10s, named after VC medal holders

In addition to the strategic transport role, the VC10 routinely served as the aeromedical aircraft during evacuations and in its VIP role, the aircraft was commonly used by members of the British Royal family, and by several British Prime Ministers, Margaret Thatcher reportedly insisted on flying by VC10.

The aircraft proved capable of being flown non-stop by two flight crews, enabling several round-the-world flights, and one such VC10 circumnavigated the globe in less than 48 hours. In 1982, VC10 C1s formed a part of the airbridge between RAF Brize Norton and Wideawake Airfield on Ascension Island during operation Corporate, the campaign to retake the Falkland Islands. Used, or at least deployed in most theatres involving British forces several times since then, the remaining VC10s were withdrawn from Iraq in June 2009 along with most other British military assets.

Boeing 747

1969 saw the first flight of the Boeing 747, a wide-body, long–range, commercial jet airliner and cargo aircraft. The first wide-body airplane produced; it was the first plane to be referred to as a "Jumbo Jet". The distinctive hump over the upper deck along the forward part of the aircraft, has made it one of the world's most recognizable aircraft alongside Concorde.

The reason the 747 came into being was because in 1963, the United States Air Force started a series of study projects on a very large long range strategic transport aircraft

Boeing, Douglas, and Lockheed were given study contracts for the airframe and General Electric and Pratt & Whitney for the engines. As the proposed aircraft needed to be able to be loaded from the front, a door had to be included where the cockpit was usually sited and all of the companies solved this problem by moving the cockpit above the cargo area. Douglas had a small "pod" just forward and above the wing, Lockheed used a long "spine" running the length of the aircraft with the wing spar passing through it, while Boeing blended the two, with a longer pod that ran from just behind the nose to just behind the wing.

These studies led to initial requirements for the CX-Heavy Logistics System (CX-HLS) in March 1964, and In 1965, Lockheed's aircraft design and General Electric's engine design were selected for the new C-5 Galaxy transport, which became the largest military aircraft in the world at the time.

Sometime before Boeing lost the contract for the CX-HLS it had been asked by Juan Trippe, the president of Pan American Airways (Pan Am), one of their most important airline customers, to build a passenger aircraft that would be more than twice the size of the 707. During this time, there was a great deal of airport congestion, worsened by an increasing number of passengers being carried on relatively small aircraft, a problem that Trippe thought could be addressed by a new larger aircraft.

In response, Boeing would carry the nose door and raised cockpit concepts of the CX-HLS over to the design of a new large airliner and in 1965 Joe Sutter was transferred from Boeing's 737 development team to manage the design studies for the new airliner, already assigned the model number 747.

Cargo version of a Boeing 747 Lumbo Jet : Darren Harbar Photography

Sutter began a design study with Pan Am and other airlines, to better understand their requirements. In the freighter role, the clear need was to support the container-ised shipping methods that were being widely introduced at about the same time. Standard shipping containers are 8 ft (2.4 m) square at the front (slightly higher due to attachment points) and available in 20 and 40 ft (6.1 and 12 m) lengths. This meant that it would be possible to support a 2-wide stack of containers two or three ranks deep with a fuselage size similar to the earlier CX-HLS project.

In the end, Boeing, and many others were proved wrong about subsonic airliners becoming obsolete and the 747 ended up being widely used by most of the world's major airlines.

The 747 has an upper and lower deck configuration for part of its length and is available in passenger, freighter, and other versions. Boeing designed the 747's hump-like upper deck to serve as either a first-class lounge or to accommodate extra seating, and to allow the aircraft to be easily converted to a cargo carrier by removing seats and installing a front cargo door.

It would seem that Boeing expected supersonic airliners, the development of which was announced in the early 1960s, to render the 747 and other subsonic airliners obsolete, while the demand for subsonic cargo aircraft would remain robust well into the future.

Although the 747 was expected to become obsolete after 400 were sold, production passed 1,000 in 1993 and by June 2019, 1,554 aircraft had been built, with 20 of the 747-8 variants remaining on order at the time writing this book.

The most common variant of the 747 in service is the 747-400, this has a high subsonic cruise speed of Mach 0.85 to 0.855 (up to 570 mph or 920 km/h) with an intercontinental range of 7,260 nautical miles. The newest version of the aircraft, the 747-8, received certification in 2011 and deliveries of the 747-8F freighter version began in October 2011 and deliveries of the 747-8I passenger version began in May 2012.

Boeing 737 Max

Introduced in May 2017 the aircraft was offered in four variants, offering 138 to 204 seats in typical two-class configurationand a 3,215 to 3,825 nautical mile (5,954 to 7,084 km) range. The 737 MAX 7, MAX 8 and MAX 9 are intended to replace the 737-700, -800, and -900, respectively and an additional length is offered with the further stretched 737 MAX 10.

After two Boeing 737 MAX 8 aircraft crashed in October 2018 and March 2019, causing 346 deaths, aviation authorities around the world have grounded the aircraft series until further notice. Boeing announced in December 2019 that it would suspend production of the Boeing 737 MAX beginning in January 2020 but have been hugely criticised for not grounding the fleet for investigation after the first crash.

At time of writing production of the 737 MAX is suspended, but who knows what the future holds.

Boeing 737 Max : Courtesy of Acefitt

Boeing 777X

Boeing 777X : Courtesy of Dan Nevill

The Boeing 777X is the latest series of the long range wide-body, twin engine 777 family from Boeing and is in response to the latest revamp of the Airbus A350. The 777X features new GE9X engines, new composite wings with folding wingtips, greater cabin width and seating capacity, and technologies from the Boing 787 Dreamliner that was introduced in October 2011. The 777X was launched in November 2013 with two variants: the 777-8 and the 777-9. The 777-8 provides seating for 384 passengers and has a range of 8,730 nmi (16,170 km) while the 777-9 has seating for 426 passengers and a range of over 7,285 nmi (13,500 km).

The 777-9 first flew on January 25th 2020, with deliveries expected to commence in 2021.

****

In 1997, Europe was supporting three times the number of contractors on less than half the budget of the United States and governments wanted to see their defence manufacturers merge into one single entity, a European Aerospace and Defence Company.

As early as 1995 the German aerospace and defence company Daimler Chrysler Aerospace (DASA) and its British counterpart British Aerospace were keen to create a transnational aerospace and defence company. They envisaged including the French company Aerospatiale, the other major European aerospace company, but only after its privatisation. The first stage of this integration was seen as the transformation of Airbus from a consortium of British Aerospace, DASA, Aerospatiale and the Spanish manufacturer Construcciones Aeronautics SA (CASA) into an integrated company, in this aim BAe and DASA were united against the various objections of Aérospatiale.

As well as Airbus, British Aerospace and DASA were also partners in the Panavia Tornado and Eurofighter Typhoon projects. Merger discussions began between British Aerospace and DASA in July 1998, just as French participation became more likely with the announcement that Aérospatiale was to merge with Matra and emerge with a reduced French government shareholding. A merger was agreed between British Aerospace Chairman Richard Evans and DASA CEO Jürgen Schrempp in December 1998, however, when the British General Electric Company put its defence electronics business Marconi Electronics Systems (MES) up for sale on 22nd December 1998, British Aerospace abandoned the DASA merger in favour of purchasing its British rival.

The merger of British Aerospace and MES to form BAE Systems was announced on 19th January 1999 and completed on 30th November. DASA and the Spanish aircraft company Construcciones Aeronautics SA agreed to merge on 11th June 1999. On 14th

October 1999 DASA agreed to merge with Aérospatiale-Matra to create the European Aeronautic Defence and Space Company, (EADS)

In July 2001 the partners in Airbus Industries formed Airbus SAS and BAE Systems held a 20% stake but in September 2006 they sold their stake in Airbus, leaving it wholly owned by EADS and in 2008 GKN bought Airbus' Filton wing making faciality.

****

Airbus

While many European aircraft were innovative and at the forefront of technology, even the most successful had small production runs compared to American companies such as Boeing. Factors favouring American aircraft manufacturers included, the fact that the size of the United States made air transport popular, and a 1942 Anglo-American agreement, entrusting transport aircraft production to the US and the World War Two legacy of a profitable, vigorous, powerful and structured aeronautical industry in America.

Even though, by the mid-1960s, several European aircraft manufacturers had drawn up competitive aircraft designs, they were all aware of the risks of a new project. For example, in 1959, Hawker Siddeley had advertised an "Airbus" version of the Armstrong Whitworth AW.660 Argosy, which would be able to lift as many as 126 passengers on ultra-short routes at a direct operating cost of just a few pence per seat mile but the company was beginning to accept, along with others and governments, that collaboration was required to develop such an aircraft if it was to compete with the more powerful US manufacturers.

Negotiations began over a European collaborative approach and at the 1965 Paris Air show, the major European airlines informally discussed their requirements for a new "Airbus" capable of transporting 100 or more passengers over short to medium distances at a low cost.

The same year, Hawker Siddeley (at the urging of the UK government) teamed up with Brequet and Nord to study Airbus designs. The Hawker Siddeley/Breguet/Nord group's HBN 100 became the basis for the continuation of the project.

By 1966 the partners were Sud Aviation, later Aerospatiale (France) Arbeitsgemeinschaft Airbus, later Deutsche Airbus (West Germany) and Hawker Siddeley (UK). A request for funding was made to the three governments in October 1966 and on 25th July 1967, the three governments agreed to proceed with the proposal.

In the two years following this agreement, both the British and French governments developed doubts about the project. The French government threatened to withdraw from the project due to its concern over funding all of the Airbus A300, Concorde and the Dassault Mercure concurrently, but in the end, they were persuaded to maintain their support.

With its own concerns at the A300B proposal in December 1968, and fearing it would not recoup its investment due to lack of sales, the British government withdrew on 10th April 1969 but West Germany stepped in and took this opportunity to increase its share of the project to 50%. Given the participation by Hawker Siddeley up to that point, France and West Germany were reluctant to take over its wing design, so the British company was allowed to continue in the role of a privileged subcontractor. Hawker Siddeley invested £35 million in tooling and, requiring more capital, received a £35 million loan from the West German government.

The first project was to be a proposed 320 seat, twin engine airliner designated Airbus A300 and in 1967 Roger Béteille was appointed as the technical director. Béteille developed a division of labour that would be the basis of Airbus' production for years to come.

France would manufacture the cockpit, flight control and the lower centre section of the fuselage; Hawker Siddeley, whose Trident technology had impressed him, was to manufacture the wings, West Germany should make the forward and rear fuselage sections, as well as the upper centre section, the Dutch would make the flaps and spoilers and finally Spain, who had yet to become a full partner, would make the horizontal tailplane.

On 26th September 1967 the West German, French and British governments signed a "Memorandum of Understanding" in London which allowed continued development studies. This also confirmed Sud Aviation as the "lead company", that France and the UK would each have a 37.5% work share with West Germany taking 25%, and that Rolls-Royce would manufacture the engines.

Airbus A 300 : Courtesy of Bill Abbott

As it turned out, there was little support from the airlines for a 300 plus seat liner so Airbus submitted proposals for a 250-seat airliner, powered by pre-existing engines. Designated A250 at first but later becoming the A300B

This dramatically reduced development costs, as the Rolls-Royce RB207, that was to be used in the A300 represented a large proportion of the costs.

The RB207 had also suffered difficulties and delays, since Rolls-Royce was concentrating its efforts on the development of another jet engine, the RB211, for the Lockheed L-1011 and was going into administration due to bankruptcy in 1971. The A300B was smaller but lighter and more economical than its three-engined American rivals, the Lockheed L-1011 and the McDonnell Douglas DC-10.

Lockheed L-1011 : Courtesy of Steve Fitzgerald

McDonnell Douglas DC10

The launch of the A300 saw only a small number of sales but these picked up largely due to a good marketing strategy and by 1979, there were 256 orders on the books. Compare this to the launch of the A320 in 1984, when Airbus boasted 272 confirmed orders on the books with over 100 more uncommitted options before it had even flown.

A320

Airbus A320 : Courtesy of Jetstar Airways

The Airbus A320 pioneered the use of digital fly-by-wire and side-stick flight controls in airliners and in October 2019, it surpassed the Boeing 737 to become the highest-selling airliner and as of December 2019, a total of 9,247 aircraft have been delivered to more than 330 operators including low-cost carriers, with 8,796 aircraft remaining in service. American Airlines is the largest operator with 412 aircraft.

In June 1977 a new *Joint European Transport* (JET) programme was set up, established by two teams from the UK (BAC) British Aircraft Corporation, (HAS) Hawker Siddeley Aviation, one team from France, Aerospatiale, and two teams from Deutsche Airbus representing it's constituent companies(VFW Fokker) Vereiniate Flugtecnische Werke & Fokker and (MBB) Messerschmitt-Bölkow-Blohm. The team was led byDerek Brown, previously head of projects at HAS Hatfield.

It was based at the then British Aircraft Corporation site in Weybridge, Surrey UK. A plan for a 162-seater aircraft was established by the end of 1977 and initially known as JET 2 in order to allow for a smaller version of around 130 seats to be designated JET 1.

Airbus was looking at two categories for future programmes, a single aisle fuselage with 6 abreast seating and a twin aisle with 8/9 abreast seating. JET 2 was a conventual concept and the prospect for sales looked good but Airbus was wasn't very well known at the time and their rivals, Boeing and Douglas already had strong sales figures around the world.

Eventually JET 2 became the basis for the A320 with a slightly enlarged fuselage and after a great many meetings JET 2 (now renamed SA2 for single aisle) as well as the proposed TA9 and the TA11, which eventually became the A330 and A340 respectively the SA2 was again renamed, this time the A320.

The project was launched in March 1984 and immediately received orders from Air France, Air Inter, British Caledonian Airways, Cyprus Airways and Inex Adria of the former Yugoslavia.

A word about Fly-by-wire.

The A320's fly-by-wire technology not only improved flight controls and reduced weight it also enabled Airbus to take safety to a new level by introducing, "flight envelope protection." Pilots flying the A320 were free to operate it as normal but the flight envelope protection system prevented the aircraft from performing manoeuvres outside its performance limits. Fly-by-wire also established "commonality". No matter how aircraft differ in size and weight from each other the pilot can fly them in the same way because the computer drives the aircraft's flight controls and this leads to a reduction in the time, and therefore the cost of training pilots.

A330

1994 saw the introduction of the Airbus A330, essentially a lengthened A300 but with an all new wing designed to be capable of having either two or four engine arrangement, (as in the A340 that was introduced in March 1993) and coupled with the powerful, Rolls-Royce Trent 700 engine. It was targeted at the growing demand for high-capacity, medium-range, transcontinental trunk routes, offering the same range and payload as the McDonnell Douglas DC-10 but with 25 per cent more fuel efficiency, it was seen as a viable replacement for the DC-10 and the Lockheed L-1011 TriStar.

Airbus A330 : Courtesy of Masakatsu.

A350

Entering service in January 2015 with Qatar Airways the A350 XWB is the first Airbus mostly made of carbon fibre reinforced polymer. Its new fuselage is designed around a nine-abreast economy cross-section, up from the eight-abreast A330/A340.

The A350 XWB has two variants: the A350-900, typically flying 300 to 350 passengers over a 15,000 kilometres (8,100 nautical miles) range and a 280 ton MTOW (maximum take-off weight), and the longer A350-1000, accommodating 350 to 410 seats over 16,100 km (8,700 nautical miles) with a higher 319 t (703,200 lb Maximum Take-off Weight), supported by a six-wheel main landing gear.

Airbus A350 : Courtesy of Gerard van der Schaaf.

A380

Airbus A380 : Courtesy of Damien Aiello.

The world's largest passenger airliner is the Airbus A380, first delivered to Singapore Airlines on 15th October 2007 and entering service on 25th October.

Production peaked at 30 per year in 2012 and 2014, however, Airbus concedes that its $25 billion investment for the aircraft cannot be recouped. In February 2019, after Emirates reduced its last orders in favour of the A350 and A330, Airbus announced that A380 production would end by 2021.

The full-length double deck aircraft has a typical seating capacity of 525, though it is certified for up to 853 passengers. It is powered by either four Engine Alliance GP7200 or Rolls-Royce Trent 900 turbofan engines. As of December 2019, Airbus had received 251 firm orders and delivered 242 aircraft.

A220

Airbus A220 : Courtesy of Markus Eigenheer.

Introduced into service with Swiss International Air lines in 2016 the A220 was originally designed by Bombardier Aerospace and marketed as the Bombardier C Series.

It was purchased by Airbus and is now marketed by Airbus Canada Limited Partnership, a joint venture between Airbus and the Quebec Government's investment arm, Investissement Québec.

Early operators recorded better-than-expected fuel consumption and dispatch reliability, as well as positive feedback from passengers and crew.

The Sound Barrier

Chapter Nine

The Sound Barrier

As aircraft designers and manufacturers continued to strive for faster and faster speeds, it became obvious that propeller driven thrust was not going to achieve the ultimate goal, that of faster than sound flight. The speed at which the tips of propellers rotated was already reaching transonic speeds and as a result the propellers were experiencing decreased performance due to the shockwaves. Although it is true that some propeller driven aircraft were able to get close to the speed of sound in dives, they suffered serious problems when doing so, such as control reversal, and flutter on curved surfaces. It was also very hard for the pilots to pull out of the resulting dive and there were many recorded fatalities.

During World War Two and immediately after, there were a number of claims that the sound barrier had been broken in a dive. The majority of these (purported) events however, can be dismissed as instrumentation errors. The typical airspeed indicator uses air pressure differences between two or more points on the aircraft, typically near the nose and at the side of the fuselage, to produce a speed figure. At high speed, the various compression effects that lead to the sound barrier also cause the ASI to go non-linear and produce inaccurately high or low readings, depending on the specifics of the installation. This effect became known as "Mach jump." Before the introduction of Mach meters, accurate measurements of supersonic speeds could only be made externally, using ground-based instruments and many claims of supersonic speeds were found to be far below this speed when so measured.

In 1942, a press release was issued, stating that Lieutenants Harold E. Comstock and Roger Dyar had exceeded the speed of sound during test dives in their P-47 Thunderbolt, but it is widely agreed that this was due to inaccurate ASI readings. In similar tests, the North American P-51 Mustang, a higher performance aircraft, demonstrated limits at Mach 0.85, with every flight over Mach 0.84 causing the aircraft to be damaged by vibration.

One of the highest recorded instrumented Mach numbers attained for a propeller aircraft is that of Mach 0.891 for a Spitfire PR X1, flown during dive tests at the Royal

Aircraft Establishment, Farnborough in April 1944. The Spitfire was flown by Squadron Leader J. R. Tobin to this speed, corresponding to a corrected true airspeed of 606 mph. In a subsequent flight, Squadron Leader Anthony Martindale achieved Mach 0.92, but it ended in a forced landing after over-revving damaged the engine.

In the 1990s, Hans Guido Mutke claimed to have broken the sound barrier on 9th April 1945 in a Messerschmitt Me 262 jet aircraft. He states that his ASI pegged itself at 1,100 kilometres per hour (680 mph). Mutke reported, not just transonic buffeting but the resumption of normal control once a certain speed was exceeded and then a resumption of severe buffeting once the Me 262 slowed again. He also reported engine flame out. His claims are widely disputed however, even by other pilots in his unit.

In England in October 1943 the Miles Aircraft Company was issued with a contract to produce an aircraft in accordance with Air Ministry Specifications E.24/43. The programme was highly ambitious for its time, aiming to produce an aircraft and engine capable of the unheard-of speeds of at least 1,000 miles per hour (1,600 km/h) during level flight, and involved a very high proportion of cutting-edge aerodynamic research and innovative design work that resulted in the turbojet powered Miles M.52. The pilot selected for the M.52 project was Captain Eric "Winkle" Brown. (See Appendix)

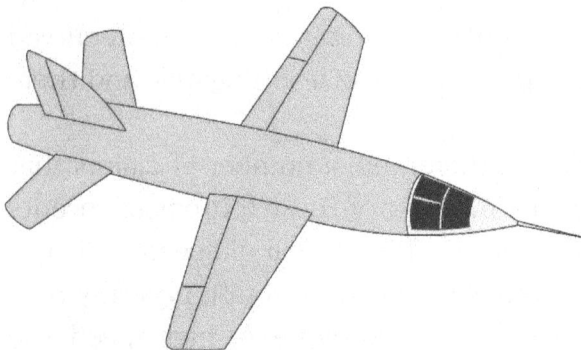

Impression of the M 52

Between 1942 and 1945, all work on the project was shrouded in secrecy and in February 1946, the programme was terminated by the new Labour government of Clement Attlee, seemingly due to budgetary reasons, but it probably had just as much to do with a disbelief, held by some ministry officials, on the viability of supersonic aircraft in general. In September 1946, the existence of the M.52 was revealed to the general public and this led to calls for an official explanation as to why the project had been terminated. The Air Ministry, partially in response to the demands, controversially decided to revive the design, but this time as a series of unmanned rocket-powered 30 per cent scale models, instead of the original manned full-scale aircraft that had been previously under development. These unmanned scale models were air-launched from under a modified de Havilland Mosquito aircraft.

During one successful test flight, Mach 1.38 was achieved by a scale model in normally controllable transonic and supersonic level flight, a unique achievement at that time, which validated the aerodynamics of the M.52, at which point, the ministry again cancelled that project and issued a new requirement, which would ultimately result in the English Electric Lightning interceptor aircraft that was to replace the Gloster Javelin all weather interceptor.

The British Air Ministry then signed an agreement with the United States to exchange all high-speed research data and designs and as a direct result of that agreement, the American Bell Aircraft company was given access to all the drawings and research on the M.52. The United States, however, reneged on the agreement and no data was forthcoming the other way.

Bell's supersonic design at the time was still using a conventional tail and they were battling the problem of control. However, they utilized the information on the Miles 52 to initiate work on the Bell X-1, an aircraft that although rocket powered rather than jet, turned out to be very similar in design to the original Miles M.52 and featuring the variable-incidence tail of the M.52. The XS-1 was later known as the X-1 and was the aircraft in which Chuck Yeager is credited with being the first person to break the sound barrier in level flight on October 14th 1947, flying at an altitude of 45,000 ft (13.7 km).

The rocket-powered aircraft, that Yeager had christened "Glamorous Glennis" after his wife, was launched from the bomb bay of a specially modified B-29 and glided to a landing on a runway. Bell X-1 flight number 50 is the first one where the X-1 recorded supersonic flight, reaching Mach 1.06 (1,299 km/h, 807.2 mph) peak speed. However, Yeager and many other

The Bell X1

personnel believe that Flight 49, also with Yeager piloting, which reached a top recorded speed of Mach 0.997 (1,221 km/h), may have in fact, exceeded Mach 1, although the measurements were not accurate to three significant figures and no sonic boom was recorded for that flight.

Chuck Yeager
photographed in 1951

As a result of the X-1's initial supersonic flight, the National Aeronautics Association voted its 1948 Collier Trophy to be shared by the three main participants in the program. Honoured at the White House by President Harry S. Truman for their contributions were Larry Bell for Bell Aircraft, Captain Yeager for piloting the flights, and John Stack for the National Advisory Committee for Aeronautics (NACA)

In his book "Aces Wild: The Race for Mach 1 (1998), fellow North American test pilot, Al Blackburn speculates that George Welch may have broken the sound barrier two weeks before Chuck Yeager in an early flight of the XP-86 prototype. However, this claim is disputed by others, including, Bob Hoover who was a chase pilot for both Welch and Yeager and Welch himself never made that claim. The XP-86 did however, officially achieved supersonic speed on April 26th 1948.

The first woman to break the sound barrier was Jackie Cochran (see Appendix) on May 18th, 1953, in a Canadair Sabre with Yeager as her wingman.

Some Events of the Sixties

1960 Bristol Aircraft Ltd. joins Vickers-Armstrong and English Electric to form British Aircraft Corporation.
Sputnik 5 makes 18 Earth orbits.
1961 First Pegasus transition from vertical take-off to level flight to vertical landing.
First non-stop flight between Britain and Australia.
First man in space.
1962 Concorde development agreement signed between BAC and Sud Aviation.
First US astronaut orbits the Earth.
Cuban Missile Crisis.
Telstar launched.
1964 First female solo flight around the world.
Bluebird breaks land speed record.
1966 Bristol Siddeley merges with Rolls-Royce.
First man-made object lands on the Moon.
1967 Apollo 1 capsule destroyed on launch pad by fatal fire.
1969 First man lands on the Moon.
Concorde's first flight at Filton, Bristol.
First Harrier jump-jet delivered to the RAF.

As the science of high-speed flight became more widely understood, a number of changes in design were seen, such as swept wings and the application of the area rule. These changes led to the eventual understanding that the "sound barrier" is easily penetrated with the right aircraft design and by the 1950s, many combat aircraft could routinely break the sound barrier in level flight, although they still often suffered from control problems when doing so, such as "Mach tuck", (the tendency for the nose to drop as the shock wave moves back over the wing creating high lift further back and causing the aircraft to tuck or pitch nose-down).

By the late 1950s, the issue was so well understood that many companies started investing in the development of supersonic airliners, believing that to be the next "natural" step in airliner evolution.

Concorde
Courtesy of Edward Marmet

Concorde

The 1950s was the decade of supersonic flight. The sound barrier had been broken and the race was on to build a supersonic airliner. At BAC in Bristol, Archibald E Russell led a team that designed the Bristol Type 198 aircraft. Powered by six Rolls-Royce Olympus engines the team was confident the aircraft would reach at least Mach 2.2 but it was never built. The government thought it too expensive and suggested BAC should turn their efforts towards something smaller. The next project Russell's team took on was the four engine Type 223 which turned out to be similar in design to an aircraft being developed by Sud Aviation in France, the Super Caravelle, and so on the 29th November 1962 the British and French governments agreed to finance a joint project to develop a supersonic civil airliner.

At the very start of the project there was some disagreement. Russell wanted to build a large intercontinental airliner, but Pierre Satre of Sud Aviation wanted a small transcontinental design. In the end the resulting, small, 100 seat, intercontinental Concorde was a compromise.

The division of responsibility between the British and French teams was set at 40/60 for the airframe and 60/40 for the engines and the two production lines were established at Filton in Britain and Toulouse in France. The fully equipped forward and rear fuselages were built at Weybridge, the centre fuselage and wings at various sites across France, with Filton building the nacelles (engine casings), air intake and engine bay. The Olympus 593 engine was jointly developed by SNECMA and Bristol Siddeley that was soon to become part of Rolls-Royce.

As a rule, delta wing aircraft have to keep their nose up when landing but landing tests in BAC's highly advanced flight simulator showed that Concorde's long nosecone would obscure the pilot's view when the plane was in that attitude. At first it was suggested that a television camera could be used to give the pilot a view of the runway but this idea was unpopular so in the end it was decided that the nose and visor would be lowered for landing using hydraulic controls.

Another considerable problem faced was the fact that no jet engine can accept air in its compressors at supersonic speeds, which is of course required for a supersonic Mach 2 airliner.

So the engineers had to come up with an answer to how they could slow the air down and the answer was the eleven foot long Air Intake Control System that slows the air down from Mach 2 to Mach 0.5 (which is about 1,350 mph to about 500 mph) at which point it is at a suitable speed at which to enter the engines.

The air-intake assemblies are the most critical part of the whole powerplant. Assuming that they are operating correctly, they produce 63% of the net positive thrust of the engines.

Concorde incorporated many new and interesting technical features but the variable geometry air intake system, that allows Concorde to cruise at Mach 2 without the continued use of the engine reheats, has to be one of the most innovative of them all.

The systems ensure that the Olympus engines get just the right amount of air moving at the correct speed through a wide variety of airspeeds. The air in-take is rectangular in cross section and is of variable geometry, in that it embodies two moving ramps in the top surface, the ramps forward and aft, do not meet but move up and down to control airflow. The in-takes also have two smaller doors which either let in more air or spill it out when not required by the engines. The moving parts of the air in-takes are operated hydraulically under computer control; this was found to be necessary during the prototype development stages. See diagram showing Concorde's engine air intake management system.

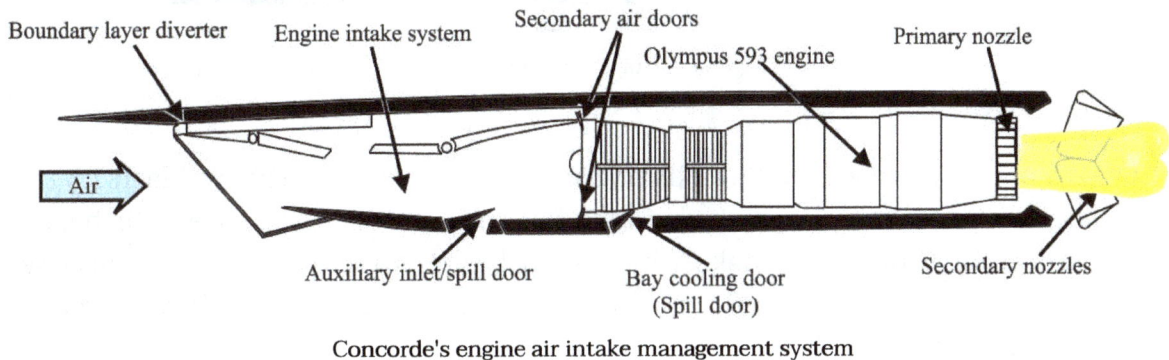

Concorde's engine air intake management system

During take-off the engines require the maximum airflow so the secondary air doors are closed (diagram A), which means that the engine bay is isolated from the intake airflow; this causes all the intake air to flow into the engine. The ramps are now fully up, the auxiliary inlet vane (which is part of the spill door assembly) is wide open and held open aerodynamically allowing extra airflow into the engine. While Concorde is travelling at slow speeds all the air which is required goes into her engines and is known as primary airflow, this means the secondary doors are closed during this time. This also stops the engine from ingesting any of its own exhaust gases.

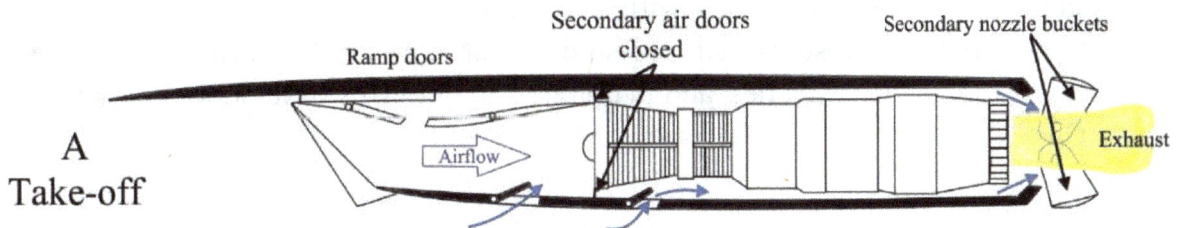

Diagram A: Take-off

Once Concorde has taken off, it enters a period of flight known as the noise abatement procedure, this sees the afterburners turned off and power reduced. The secondary nozzles remain in their take-off position when the engines are throttled for noise reduction.

As the aircraft accelerates the secondary exhaust buckets begin to open such that by M=1.1 the secondary nozzles are fully open forming the divergent part of the back of the engine. The secondary air doors are also open at this stage of flight, allowing the air to bypass the engine (see the diagram B).

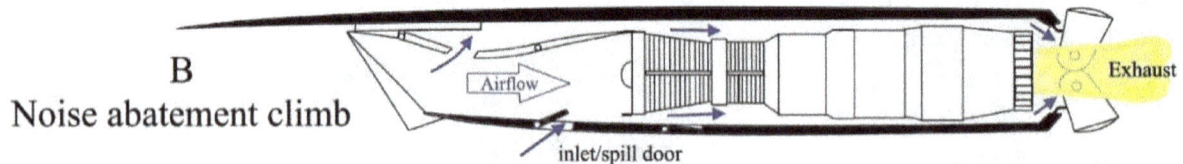

B
Noise abatement climb

Diagram B: Noise abatement climb

Once Mach 0.93 is reached the auxiliary inlet is closed, and then above Mach 1.3 the in-take ramps come into play, by lowering to form a series of shock waves which start from the bottom lip of the air intake, which is machined to a fine sharp point. This now has the effect of slowing the air down. Once Concorde has reached Mach 2, the ramps would have moved over half their possible travel distance.

Once the aircraft is at cruising speed, the airflow is not only slowed down by the in-takes, it is also compressed and considerably raised in temperature. The compression at this stage of flight is helpful because it means that the engine's own compressors have less work to do, but the rise in temperature of about 200C leads to the necessity for special metals in the engine, such as titanium and Nimonic 90 nickel alloy.

While Concorde is in flight, it meets all the changes with air temperature and pressure which causes disturbances to the wave pattern in the in-takes. The computers can sense these changes during the flight and make any final necessary adjustments to the ramp positions in the in-takes, which maintain the airflow required by Concorde's four engines. Equally, any changes in engine power settings require some changes in the airflow and Concorde's computers deal with this in the same way.

Each in-take, then, presents high-pressure hot air at Mach 0.5 to the first stage of the Olympus 593 mk610 engines, and in doing so the in-takes have done their job (Diagram C).

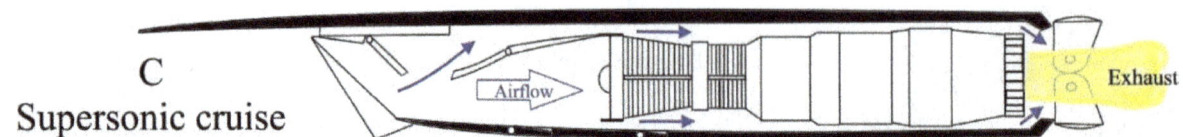

C
Supersonic cruise

Diagram C: Supersonic cruise

After touch down the engines move to reverse thrust mode. The auxiliary inlet vane along with the ground running flap will all be in their open position and the secondary nozzle buckets move to the closed position directing airflow forwards to slow the aircraft down (Diagram D).

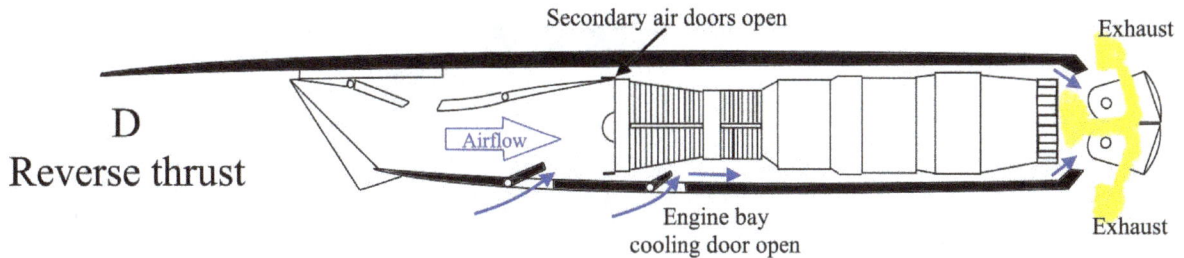

Diagram D: Reverse thrust

If Concorde were to suffer an engine failure during supersonic flight, which could theoretically cause a catastrophic failure of the airframe, the engines would suddenly require little or no air so the ramps would go down fully, diverting some air over the top of the engine, while the spill door would open downwards to pour air out of the underside. The speed of this operation would obviously be critical and Concorde's ability to deal with this sort of problem is impressive by any standard. Slam-closure of a throttle at Mach 2 makes Concorde react, but the engine doesn't even hiccup.

The sudden need to dump air produces the one odd flying characteristic of the aircraft. If an engine fails at supersonic speed, Concorde banks the wrong way. Any aircraft, Concorde included, will yaw towards the dead engine because the thrust on that side has suddenly been lost, and the engine has become a producer of drag. As a result, the wing on the side opposite to the failed engine will temporarily move faster, gain lift and rise.

The combined effect is both roll and yaw towards the dead engine. But at Mach 2 there is all the excess air to get rid of so the spill door opens and the in-take air is deflected downward (Diagram E). This causes the wing to rise and Concorde to bank away from the dead engine. The technique for dealing with this situation is first to level the wings, then to counter the yaw with the rudder. The auto-stabilizers will already have applied some rudder so it is not a difficult process for the pilot.

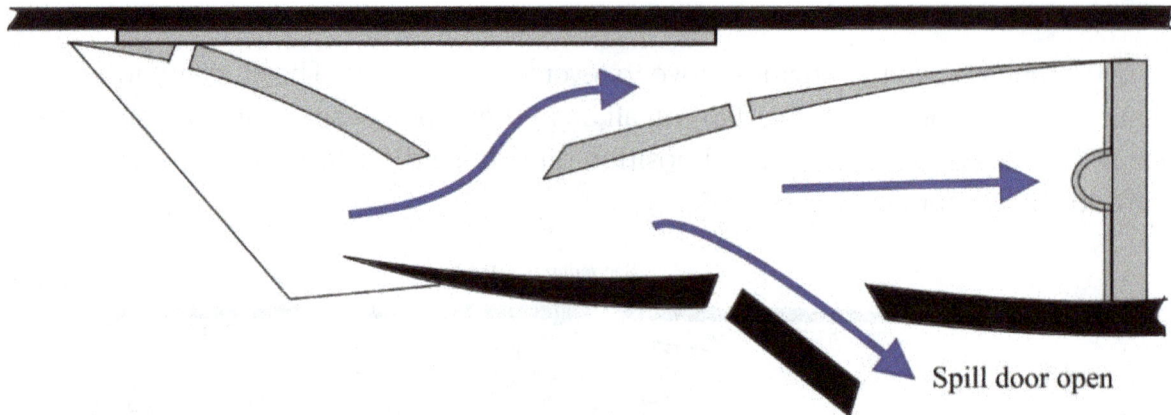

Diagram E: Engine failure

An interesting Concorde anecdote:

When we moved to Winterbourne, many years ago, I discovered that our next-door neighbour, Graham Clark, was heavily involved with Concorde and he would sometimes have interesting stories to tell. One in particular sticks in my mind, but why don't I let Graham tell it in his own words.

"In 1985, an Olympus 593 Rolls-Royce colleague was coming back through Orly Airport. He saw Air France Concorde 02 on display in concrete blocks and was amazed to see that the Bulkhead between engines 1 and 2 was showing signs of wood grain.

*When this colleague and I met, I explained the unexpected situation. In June 1981 a Bristol Siddeley pre-production Concorde coming from New York towards Heathrow had a **severe** fire alarm in engine 1 with very excessive vibration.*

The fire extinguishers shut down the engine and because engine 2 had become very hot, shut that down also. The aircraft now diverted to Shannon, (an emergency aerodrome set up for any problems) at subsonic speed on two engines.

Subsequent investigation showed that number 1 engine had lost the front bearing out through the dump doors into the Atlantic. The engine tried to carry on running, on the LP compressor blade tips, causing excessive heat to go back into the HP casing, outside of which were the fuel manifolds.

This heat was sufficient to burn a small hole in the Bulkhead between number 1 and number 2 engines, accounting for the overheating and shutting down of engine number 2.

Both engines came back to number 4 shop at Patchway where number 1 was found to be a right-off but number 2 was inspected and put back into service, leaving just the problem of the hole in the Bulkhead.

At this time Air France was retiring one of its test aircraft to use as a static exhibit outside of Orly Airport. The aircraft usage was finished but the Bulkheads were still serviceable.

In order to use a good Bulkhead from this aircraft for our Concorde 002, we made an agreement with Snecma that we could have it if we made a replacement. So we made one in plywood in number 4 shop, Patchway, and painted it with aircraft grey, so that it could not be easily detected. Not until after five or six years of weathering anyway, when the wood grain started to be visible!"

Graham Clark

American SST design

In 2016, NASA announced it had signed a contract for the design of a modern low noise supersonic transport or SST, with Lockheed Martin Aeronautics.

In the early 1960s, various executives of US aerospace companies were telling the US public and Congress that there were no technical reasons why a Supersonic liner could not be produced. In April 1960, Burt C Monesmith, a vice president with Lockheed, stated to various magazines that such an SST aircraft, constructed of steel weighing 250,000 pounds (110,000 kg) could be developed for $160 million. But it was the Anglo-French development of the Concorde that set off panic in the US industry, where it was thought that Concorde would soon replace all other long-range designs, especially after Pan Am took out purchase options on the Concorde. Congress was soon funding a supersonic design effort, selecting the existing Lockheed L-2000 and the Boeing 2707 designs, to produce an even more advanced, larger, faster and longer range design.

The Boeing 2707 design was eventually selected for continued work, with design goals of ferrying around 300 passengers and having a cruising speed near to Mach 3.

The US government decided in the end not to continue with the project due to the expense of development as well as the fact that they were some years behind the French and British project, and also the inescapable fact that supersonic flight produces sonic bangs, something the American people would almost certainly object to.

Tupolev Tu-144

The Soviet Union, on the other hand, did produce its own design, the TU-144. This was an aircraft remarkably similar to Concorde in design, so much so in fact that the western press nicknamed it the "Concordski", the most noticeable difference being the large "canards" (see Appendix) on the Russian design.

A total of sixteen airworthy Tupolev TU-144s were built; a seventeenth Tu-144 (reg. 77116) was never completed. There was also at least one ground test airframe for static testing in parallel with the prototype 68001 development.

The TU-144 or "Concordski" : Courtesy of NASA.

While superficially the Tu-144 looked very similar to Concorde, there were many differences, most of which were due to less sophisticated solutions to the problems Concorde's designers had also solved.

There is no doubt that Soviet thinking on the Tu-144 was heavily influenced by Concorde, the absence of a horizontal stabiliser (tail planes), for example, which was a radical departure from previous Soviet designs. The engine configuration was also noticeably different and overall, the Tu-144 needed to be more rugged to cope with tougher operating conditions.

Although industrial espionage may well have played a role in the Tu-144's development, the Soviets were still capable of exploring their own avenues to solve the multitude of technical problems thrown up by the project. The result was an aircraft which broadly resembled Concorde but which differed substantially in refinement and detail.

A Tu-144 crashed dramatically at the Paris Air Show in 1973, delaying its further development but the aircraft was introduced into commercial service on 26th December

1975. In May 1978, (another Tu-144,) an improved version, the Tu-144D, crashed on a flight while being delivered. However it remained in use as a cargo plane until 1983, when the Tu-144 commercial fleet was grounded. The Tu-144 was later used by the Soviet space program to train pilots of the Buran spacecraft. The Tu-144 made its last flight on 26th June 1999.

There are several theories as to why the Tu-144 crashed, one being that it manoeuvered to avoid a French Mirage that was attempting to photograph its unique canards. Initial French reports denied the existence of the Mirage but more recent reports have admitted it. What we know for sure is that the aircraft made what seemed to be a landing approach with the landing gear down and the canards extended but then climbed rapidly on full power. The aircraft pitched over and went into a steep dive. It was when pulling out of the dive that the aircraft broke up and crashed, killing six people on board and a further eight on the ground. Sixty people received severe injuries.

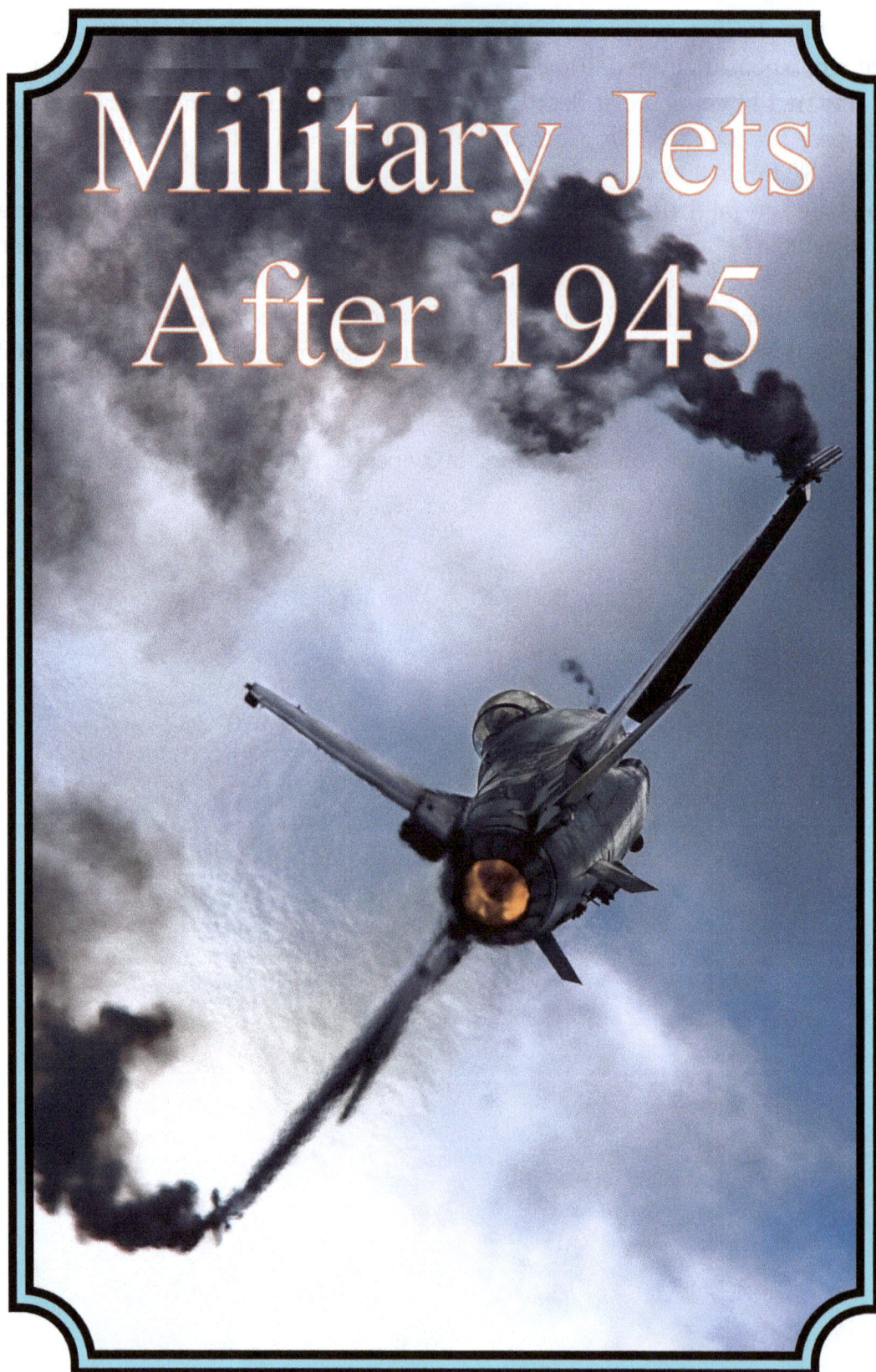

Military Jets After 1945

Chapter Ten

Military Jets After 1945

MiG-15

By the 1950s almost all combat aircraft were powered by jet engines, including the MiG-15, one of the first successful jet fighters to incorporate swept wings to achieve high transonic speed and in combat over Korea, it outclassed straight-winged jet fighters, which were largely relegated to ground-attack roles. The Mig-15 was quickly countered however by the similar swept-wing, North American F-86 Sabre.

MiG-15 Two seater trainer : Darren Harbar Photography

When refined into the more advanced Mig-17, the aircraft design would again surprise the West when it proved effective against supersonic fighters such as the Republic F-105 Thunderchief and the McDonnell Douglas F-4 Phantom 11 in the Vietnam War of the 1960s.

The F-86 Sabre

F-86 Sabre : Darren Harbar Photography

The North American F-86 Sabre, sometimes called the Sabrejet, was a transonic jet fighter produced by North American Aviation and is best known as the United States' first swept wing fighter, participating in some of the earliest Jet-to-jet battles in the history of aviation. Considered one of the best and most important fighter aircraft in the Korean war, the F-86 is also rated highly in comparison with fighters of other eras. Although it was developed in the late 1940s and was outdated by the end of the 1950s, the Sabre proved versatile and adaptable and continued as a front-line fighter in numerous air forces until the last active operational examples were retired by the Bolivian Air Force as late as the 1990s.

Its success led to an extended production run of more than 7,800 aircraft between 1949 and 1956, in the United States, Japan, and Italy. In addition, 738 carrier-modified versions were purchased by the US Navy and variants were also built in Canada and Australia making it one of the worlds most produced jets.

Gloster Javelin

Gloster Javelin : Courtesy of Richard Vandervord.

The Gloster Javelin puts in an appearance in February 1956 having first flown in 1951, this was a twin-engined, T-tailed, Delta wing subsonic night and all-weather interceptor that served with the Royal Air Force from the mid-1950s until the late 1960s and was the last aircraft design to bear the Gloster name. It was introduced in 1956 after a lengthy development period and received several upgrades during its lifetime to its engines, radar and weapons, which included the De Havilland "Fire-streak" air-to-air missile.

The first prototype was completed in 1951. An unusual feature of the prototypes was the opaque canopy over the rear cockpit. It had been believed that visibility out-side the cockpit was unnecessary and even a hindrance to the observer; the only external view available was through two small portholes. The opaque canopy was changed however on the production modal.

Following a month of ground testing in November 1951, the first prototype con-ducted its first flight at Moreton Valence Airfield. Bill Waterton, Gloster's Chief Test Pilot, would later describe the Javelin as being "as easy to fly as an Anson", although also expressing concern over its inadequate power controls. Disaster nearly struck during one test flight when aerodynamic flutter caused the elevators to detach in mid-flight but despite the lack of control surfaces, Bill Waterton was able to land the aircraft using tailplane trimming and engine thrust for pitch control. He was awarded the George Medal for his actions to retrieve flight data from the burning aircraft.

The second prototype (WD808) received a modified wing in 1953. After initial testing by Waterton, it was passed to another Gloster test pilot, Peter Lawrence for his opinion, but tragically, on 11th June 1953, the aircraft crashed during testing.

Lawrence had ejected from the aircraft, but too late (at about 400 ft (120 m)), and was killed. The Javelin had experienced a deep stall, and the wing, acting like an air-brake, had drastically reduced forward motion and at the same time degraded the airflow over the elevators, leaving them useless. Without elevator control, Lawrence was unable to regain control and the aircraft dropped from the sky. A stall warning device was later developed and implemented for future Javelins

The Javelin was succeeded in the interceptor role by the English Electric Lightning, a supersonic aircraft capable of flying at more than double the Javelin's top speed, which was introduced into the RAF only a few years later. The Javelin served for much of its life alongside the Lightning; the last Javelins were withdrawn from operational service in 1968 following the introduction of successively more capable versions of the Lightning.

The V Bombers

The first response to Russia developing an atomic capability was the development of the Canberra medium range jet bomber by English Electric but what was really needed was a long-range jet bomber capable of carrying an atomic bomb.

English Electrc Canberra Bomber : Courtesy of SAC A K Benson

The first contract for such an aircraft was given to Vickers-Armstrong at Weybridge and resulted in the first of the V-bombers which was named the Valiant. Contracts were also placed with Avro and Handley-Page.

Vickers Valiant

104 Valiants were built with the first being delivered to the RAF in January 1955 on schedule, indeed all the ordered Valiants were delivered on or before their scheduled delivery date, a somewhat rare occurrence both then and now.

Vickers Valiant V bomber

Initially operating at high altitude to avoid missiles the Valiant was at first painted in a white anti-flash coating, but with the development of missiles that were capable of reaching those high altitudes it was decided to operate them at low level with a full camouflage paint finish. This change in operational height led to cracks appearing in the wings and its withdrawal from service in 1965, but it remains the only British built bomber to carry and drop atom bombs in trials.

Avro Vulcan

Avro Vulcan : Darren Harbar Photography

Despite its radical and unusual shape, the Vulcan airframe was built along traditional lines. Except for the most highly stressed parts, the whole structure was manufactured from standard grades of light alloy.

Each Vulcan had four Rolls-Royce Olympus engines buried in the wings, positioned in pairs close to the fuselage. It carried a five-man crew, the first pilot, co-pilot, navigator radar, navigator plotter and air electronics officer (AEO) all of whom were accommodated within the pressure cabin on two levels

The two pilots sat on Martin-Baker ejector seats, whilst on the lower level, the other crew members sat facing rearwards and would abandon the aircraft via the entrance door. A rudimentary sixth seat forward of the navigator radar was provided for an additional crew member and the B.2 had an additional seventh seat opposite the sixth seat and forward of the AEO. These seats were no more than cushions, a full harness and an oxygen and intercom facility.

Fuel was carried in 14 bag tanks, four in the centre fuselage above and to the rear of the nosewheel bay and five in each outer wing. The tanks were split into four groups of almost equal capacity, each normally feeding its respective engine although cross-feeding was possible.

Despite being designed before a low radar cross-section and other stealth factors were ever a consideration, a Royal Aircraft Establishment technical note of 1957 stated that of all the aircraft so far studied, the Vulcan appeared by far the simplest radar echoing object, due to its shape, only one or two components contributed significantly to the echo at any aspect, compared with three or more on most other types.

One memorable incident that I remember being talked about in Bristol, during my last year of school, happened on 2nd December 1962. A Vulcan was being used at Filton, Bristol, as a test-bed for the Olympus 320 engine when the shaft failed and the whole turbine was flung off, cutting the airframe in half and setting the aircraft alight. As the airframe and the Olympus engine both contained magnesium alloy, observers recalled that, "*the whole thing went up like a firework display.*" When a wing then collapsed due to the heat, it allowed burning oil to run down the runway and engulf the BAC fire engine that was in attendance and it too, was engulfed by fire and utterly destroyed.

1962 Test-bed fire at Filton.

Handley Page Victor

Handley Page Victor : Darren Harbar Photography

Introduced in April 1958, the Handley Page Victor was a British strategic bomber which saw service during the Cold War era. It was the third and final V-bomber to be operated by the Royal Air Force, the other two being the Avro Vulcan and the Vickers Valiant. The Victor had been developed as part of the United Kingdom's airborne nuclear deterrent but in 1968, it was retired from the nuclear mission and the nuclear deterrent role was given to the Royal Navy's submarine launched Polaris missiles in 1968 and many of the Vickers were converted into re-fuelling tankers. The Victor was the last of the V-bombers to be retired, the final aircraft being removed from service on 15 October 1993.

The Victor had a five-man crew, comprising the two pilots seated side-by-side and three rearward-facing crew, these being the navigator/plotter, the navigator/radar operator, and the air electronics officer (AEO). Unlike the Vulcan and Valiant, the Victor's pilots sat at the same level as the rest of the crew, due to a larger pressurised compartment that extended all the way to the nose. As with the other V-bombers, only the pilots were provided with ejection seats; the three systems operators relying on "explosive cushions" inflated by a CO_2 bottle that would help them from their seats and towards a traditional bail out in the event of high g-loading, but despite this, escape for the three crew in the back seats was extremely difficult.

While assigned to the nuclear delivery role, the Victor was finished in an all-over anti-flash white colour scheme, designed to protect the aircraft against the damaging effects of a nuclear detonation. The white colour scheme was intended to reflect heat away from the aircraft; paler variations of RAF's roundels were also applied for this same reason. When the V-bombers were assigned to the low-level approach profile in the 1960s, the Victors were soon repainted in green/grey tactical camouflage to reduce visibility to ground observation; the same scheme was applied to subsequently converted tanker aircraft.

The Victor had fully powered flying controls, i.e. ailerons, elevators and rudder, with no manual reversion which, therefore, required a back-up system, i.e. duplication. Since they were fully powered an "artificial feel" unit was needed, fed by ram air from the pitot (air-flow detector) in the nose.

The Victor B.1 was powered by four Armstrong Siddeley Sapphire turbojet engines that were embedded in pairs in the wing roots. Difficulties were encountered with the Sapphires when stationed in tropical environments as several engines were destroyed by the turbine blades striking the outer engine casing, which could occur when flying through dense cloud or heavy rain. The Victor B.2 was powered by the newer Rolls-Royce Conway turbofan, which at one point held the distinction of being the most powerful non-afterburning engine outside of the Soviet Union. The Conway had significantly higher thrust than the Sapphire engine in the B.1.

English Electric Lightning

The English Electric Lightning was a fighter aircraft that served as an interceptor during the 1960s, the 1970s and into the late 1980s. It remains the only fully UK-designed-and-built fighter capable of Mach 2. The Lightning was designed, developed, and manufactured by English Electric, which was later absorbed by the newly-formed British Aircraft Corporation and later the type was marketed as the BAC Lightning. It was operated by the Royal Air Force, the Kuwait Air Force and the Royal Saudi Air Force.

A unique feature of the Lightning's design is the vertical, staggered configuration of its two Rolls Royce Avon turbojet engines within the fuselage. The Lightning was initially designed and developed as an interceptor to defend the V bomber airfields from attack by anticipated future nuclear-armed supersonic Soviet bombers such as that which emerged as the Tupolev Tu-22, but it was subsequently also required to intercept other bomber aircraft such as the Tupolev Tu-16 and Tu-9. The Lightning had an exceptional rate of climb, ceiling and speed and many pilots described flying it as like "being saddled to a skyrocket".

English Electric Lightning : Darren Harbar Photography

The Lightning had several distinctive design features, the primary being the twin-engine arrangement, notched wing and low-mounted tailplane. The vertically stacked and longitudinally staggered engines were the solution devised to meet the conflicting requirements of minimising frontal area, providing undisturbed engine airflow across a wide speed range, and packaging two engines to provide sufficient thrust to meet performance goals.

The unusual over/under configuration allowed for the thrust of two engines, with the drag equivalent to only 1.5 engines mounted side-by-side, a reduction in drag of 25% over more conventional twin-engine installations. The engines were fed by a single nose inlet with the flow split vertically aft of the cockpit, and the nozzles tightly stacked, effectively tucking one engine behind the cockpit. The result was a low frontal area, an efficient inlet, and excellent single-engine handling with no problems of asymmetrical thrust. The only real drawback to this arrangement was that because the engines were close together, an uncontained failure of one engine was likely to damage the other. If desired, an engine could be shut down in flight and the remaining engine run at a more efficient power setting which increased range or endurance, however this was rarely done operationally because there would be no hydraulic power if the remaining engine failed.

Production aircraft were powered by various models of the Rolls-Royce Avon engine. Later models of the Avon featured, in addition to increased thrust, a full variable reheat arrangement. A special heat-reflecting paint containing gold was used to protect the aircraft's structure from the hot engine casing which could reach temperatures of 600 °C. Under optimum conditions, a well-equipped maintenance facility took four hours to perform an engine change so specialised ground test rigs were developed to speed up maintenance and remove the need to perform a full ground run of the engine after some maintenance tasks.

The stacked engine configuration complicated maintenance work, and the leakage of fluid from the upper engine was a recurring fire hazard. The fire risk was reduced, but not eliminated, following remedial work during development. For removal, the lower No.1 engine was removed from below the aircraft, after removal of the ventral tank and lower fuselage access panels, by lowering the engine down, while the upper No.2 engine was lifted out from above via removable sections in the fuselage top.

The fuselage was tightly packed, leaving no room for fuel tanks or main landing gear. The notched wing contained a fairly conventional three-section main fuel tank and leading-edge tank. The operational range was severely compromised by its limited fuel capacity so an additional fuel tank was added under the fuselage, but range still remained short.

The main landing gear was sandwiched outboard of the main tanks and aft of the leading-edge tanks, with the flap fuel tanks behind. The long main gear legs retracted towards the wingtip, necessitating an exceptionally thin main tyre inflated to the high pressure of 330–350 psi (23–24 bar; 2,300–2,400 kPa). On landing the No. 1 engine was usually shut down when taxiing to save brake wear, as keeping both engines running at idle power was still sufficient to propel the Lightning to 80 mph if brakes were not applied.

The Tornado

The Panavia Tornado is a family of twin-engine, variable-sweep-wing, multi-role combat aircraft jointly developed and manufactured by Italy, the United Kingdom, and West Germany. There are three primary variants, the Tornado ECR for electronic combat and reconnaissance, the Tornado ADV, (air defence variant) interceptor and the IDS (interdictor/strike) aircraft. An interdictor aircraft, also known as deep air support (DAS), is one that uses preventative tactical bombing attacks against enemy targets, often well inside enemy lines, that are not an immediate threat, in order to delay, disrupt or hinder later enemy engagement of friendly forces.

Panavia Tornado
Darren Harbar Photography

The angle of the wings in relation to the fuselage can be altered in flight by the pilot and the variable wing can adopt any sweep angle between 25 degrees and 67 degrees, with a corresponding speed range for each angle. Some Tornado ADVs were fitted with an automatic wing sweep system to reduce pilot workload. When the wings are swept back, the exposed wing area is lowered and drag is significantly decreased, which is conducive to performing high speed low-level flight. The weapons pylons pivot with the angle of the variable-sweep wings so that the armaments point in the direction of flight and do not hinder any wing positions.

During development, Germany in particular encouraged that significant attention be given to the Tornado's short-field take-off and landing performance and so for shorter take-off and landing distances, the Tornado can sweep its wings forward to the 25 degree position and deploy its full-span flaps and leading edge slats to allow the aircraft to fly at lower speeds. These features, in combination with the thrust reverser equipped engines, give the Tornado excellent low-speed handling and landing characteristics. Including all variants, 992 aircraft were built.

Due to its multirole design, the Tornado was able to replace several different types of aircraft in the adopting air forces but the only operator outside the three original partner nations was the Royal Saudi Air Force.

The Tornado was also operated by the Royal Air Force, the Italian Airforce and the Royal Saudi Airforce during the Gulf War of 1991 as well as in the Bosnian and Kosovo Wars, the Iraq War and the Libyan Civil War, it also saw action in Afghanistan, Yemen and Syria.

The Typhoon

The Typhoon's development effectively began in 1983 with the Future European Fighter Aircraft programme, a multinational collaboration among the UK, Germany, France, Italy and Spain. Disagreements over design authority and operational requirements led France to leave the consortium and go on to develop the Dassault Rafale independently.

The first prototype of the finalised Eurofighter made its first flight on 27th March 1994 and the aircraft's name, Typhoon, was adopted in September 1998; the first production contracts were also signed that same year.

Political issues within the partner group significantly delayed the Typhoon's development and the sudden end of the Cold War, reduced European demand for fighter aircraft, and initiated further debate over the aircraft's cost and work share. The Typhoon eventually entered operational service in 2003, with the air forces of Austria, Italy, Germany, Britain, Spain and Saudi Arabia, with the air forces of Oman, Kuwait and Qatar expected to follow, bringing the procurement total to 623 aircraft as of 2019.

Typhoon : Darren harbar Photography

Dassault Rafale

Originally scheduled to enter service in 1996, the French Rafale also suffered significant delays due to post-Cold War budget cuts and changes in priorities. The aircraft is available in three main variants: the Rafale C, a single-seat land-based version, Rafale B, a twin-seat land-based version, and the Rafale M, a single-seat carrier-based version. It was developed by the French as an alternative to being involved in the development of the Typhoon and is very similar to it in outward appearance, however there is great debate about which is actually the better aircraft.

The Typhoon is the faster aircraft of the two and has a significantly superior thrust-to-weight ratio, which gives it better acceleration at all altitudes. This also allows the Typhoon to retain and regain energy faster than the Rafale in a horizontal dogfight situation. It also has a significantly higher service ceiling of over 60,000ft which allows it to operate uniquely well alongside the US F-22 Raptors 'high and fast' in the air superiority role which is exactly where it was designed to excel.

Dassault Rafale : Darren Harbar Photography

The Rafale has a significantly superior load-carrying capability and its manoeuvrability at low speeds and altitudes is better than Typhoon's, although the margin is slim except where both aircraft are very heavily loaded. In terms of horizontal manoeuvrability, the Rafale has the better instantaneous turn rate, allowing it to reverse its turns more quickly but the Typhoon can sustain higher g's for longer without losing speed. High alpha performance is similar, with both aircraft limited by their air intake placement and lack of thrust vectoring, although Typhoon's intakes can at least 'gape' slightly to increase airflow at high alpha and low speeds. Range is almost identical at around 2000 nautical miles with three drop-tanks in 'ferry' configuration but in terms of strike missions, Rafale's greater payload capacity allows it to carry greater under-wing fuel loads for a given strike payload. The high availability of aerial refuelling in both air force's standard operating scenarios means the small differences are almost unimportant for overall combat effectiveness.

Airbus A400M

The Airbus A400M Atlas is a European four-engine turboprop transport aircraft developed by Airbus Military (now Airbus Defence and Space) with member countries, UK, France, Germany, Spain, Belgium (including Luxemberg) and Turkey all placing orders simultaneously in the multi nation contract. It was designed to replace older transports such as Transall C-160 and the Lockheed C-130 Hercules. The A400M is a multirole transport aircraft and was designed to carry over 90% of all the inventories of the participating nations, unlike the Hercules that managed less than 60%, the main exceptions being battle tanks and bridge building equipment, for which a much larger aircraft would be needed.

Unlike other military transport aircraft, it can land and take-off from temporary landing strips and can also perform aerial refuelling (including that of helicopters) and medical evacuation when fitted with the appropriate equipment.

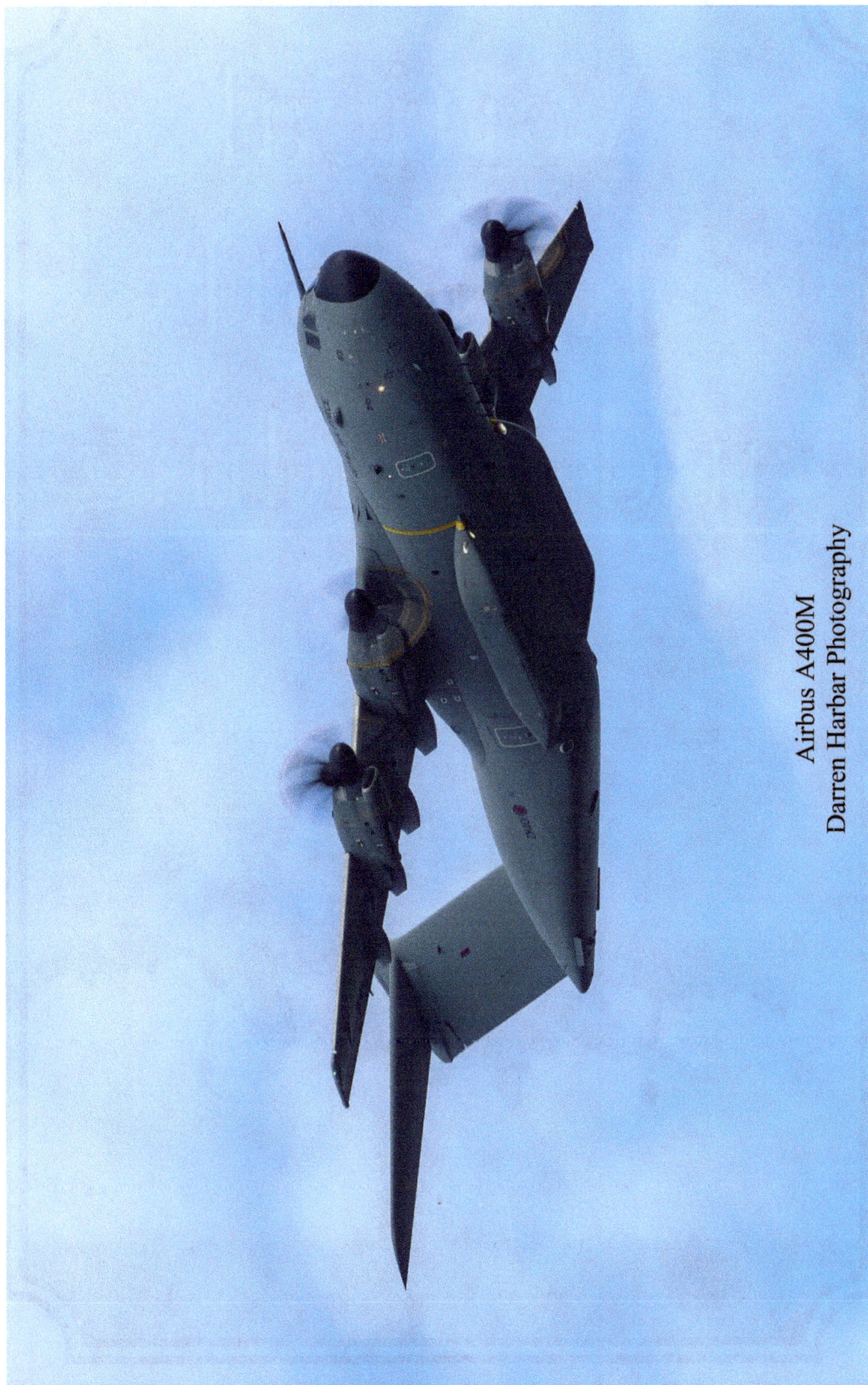

Airbus A400M
Darren Harbar Photography

Vertical Take-off and Landing

Chapter Eleven

Vertical Take-off and Landing

The conventional aeroplane has the drawback of needing a runway, sometimes quite a long one, in order to get sufficient airflow over the wings to take off. This seriously restricts where it can operate from. A helicopter on the other hand can take off vertically from almost anywhere but has the disadvantage of not being able to travel very fast. A modern helicopter can maybe reach speeds of around 200 mph, although in August 2010, a technology demonstrator, known as the Sikorsky X2, reached 435 km/h or 270 miles per hour, unofficially breaking the helicopter speed record. But this is still very slow compared to the speed of a modern jet aeroplane.

Sikorsky X2

A vertical take-off and landing (VTOL) aircraft that can also fly at supersonic speeds is therefore at a great advantage and designers and engineers have been trying to perfect such an aircraft from the earliest days.

Some VTOL aircraft can operate in other modes as well, such as CTOL (conventional take-off and landing), STOL (short take-off and landing), and/or STOVL (short take-off and vertical landing), while others, such as most helicopters, can only operate by VTOL, due to the aircraft lacking landing gear that can handle horizontal motion. VTOL is a subset of V/STOL (vertical and/or short take-off and landing). Electric and hybrid-electric vertical take-off and landing aircraft, or eVTOLs, are currently being developed by companies such as Rolls-Royce in the quest for fully autonomous passenger air vehicles (PAV).

247

Bell Boeing V-22 Osprey : Courtesy of FOX 52.

Besides helicopters, there are currently two different kinds of VTOL aircraft in military service and these are craft using a tiltrotor, such as the Bell Boeing V-22 Osprey and another using directed jet thrust, such as the Harrier and Sea Harrier and new F-35B Lightning ll Joint Strike Fighter (JSF). In the civilian sector, only helicopters are in general use.

Although it wasn't until 1967 that we saw the arrival of the Hawker-Siddeley Harrier Jump Jet, man has been trying to take-off vertically since the earliest times.

Paul Cornu

A manned VTOL aircraft, in the form of primitive helicopter, was first flown in 1907. It was designed and built by bicycle manufacturer Paul Cornu and was an open-framework structure built around a curved steel tube that carried a rotor at either end with the engine and pilot in the middle. Power was transmitted to the rotors by a drive belt that linked both rotors and spun them in opposite directions. Control was to be provided by cables that could alter the pitch of the rotor blades, and by steerable vanes at either end of the machine intended to direct the downwash of the rotors.

Paul Cornu

The Cornu helicopter is reported to have made a number of short hops, rising perhaps 1.5 or 2 metres (5–7 feet) into the air and staying aloft for something less than one minute. This was long enough for Cornu to learn that the control systems he had designed were ineffective, and he abandoned the machine soon after.

Cornu in his helicopter in 1907.

In 1922-1925,Henry Berliner produced an experimental fixed wing VTOL aircraft with a horizontal rotor but the aircraft had only limited controlability.

On September 14th 1939, the VS-300, the world's first practical helicopter, took flight at Stratford, Connecticut. Designed by Igor Sikorsky and built by the Vought-Sikorsky Aircraft Division of the United Aircraft Corporation, the helicopter was the first to incorporate a single main rotor and tail rotor design. Piloted by Sikorsky himself, the September 14th tethered flight lasted only a few seconds.

The Sikorsky helicopter

The first free flight took place on May 13th 1940. The innovative 28-foot diameter, three-blade rotor allowed for variable pitch of the blades with a blade speed of 250 to 300 mph. The concepts demonstrated in the VS-300 provided the basis for the first production helicopters and became the standard for helicopter manufacturing across the world.

The Tiltrotor

A tiltrotor aircraft combines the vertical lift capability of a helicopter with the speed and range of a conventional fixed wing aircraft. For vertical flight, the rotors are angled so the plane of rotation is horizontal, lifting the aircraft the same way a helicopter does. As the aircraft gains speed however, the rotors are progressively tilted forward, with the plane of rotation eventually becoming vertical. In this mode the wing provides the lift, and the rotor provides forward thrust as a propeller, enabling a tiltrotor to achieve higher speeds than a conventional helicopter.

Impression of the Baynes Heliplane.

In the late 1930s British aircraft designer Leslie Everett Baynes was issued a patent for the Baynes Heliplane, a tilt rotor aircraft, and in 1941 German designer Heinrich Focke began work on the Focke-Achgelis Fa 269, which had two rotors that tilted downward for vertical take-off, but wartime bombing halted development.

The Bell XV-3 was first flown on 11 August 1955. Although it was limited in performance, the aircraft successfully demonstrated the tiltrotor concept, accomplishing 110 transitions from helicopter to airplane mode between December 1958 and July 1962. The XV-3 program ended when the remaining aircraft was severely damaged in a wind tunnel accident on 20 May 1966 but the data and experience from the XV-3 program were used to successfully develop the Bell XV-15 which later paved the way for the V-22 Osprey. The Dornier DO 29, also shown here, was an experimental aircraft developed in the 1950s to test tilt-rotor systems, but although the concept proved successful during tests the project was abandoned at the end of the test program.

Bell XV-3 1955

Dornier DO 29 1958

Bell XV -15 1977

Bell-Boeing V-22 Osprey
1989

Four different tiltrotor aircraft

Tailsitters

Both Lockheed and Convair were awarded contracts in May 1951 in an attempt to de-sign, construct, and test two experimental VTOL fighters. Lockheed produced the XFV, and Convair produced the Convair XFY Pogo.

Both experimental programs proceeded to flight status and completed test flights 1954–1955, when the contracts were cancelled. Similarly, the Ryan X-13 flew a series of test flights between 1955 and 1957, but also suffered the same fate. All three aircraft where what was known as tailsitters. Some tailsitters landed conventionally in a hori-zontally-oriented configuration, while others had a much more ambitious goal of land-ing vertically with the aircraft's back to the ground, a highly hazardous procedure, mainly, but not exclusively, because of limited pilot visibility. This led to the concept being abandoned once a more practical form of VTOL appeared, in the form of thrust vectoring.

Lockheed XFV   Convair XFY Pogo   Ryan X-13

Tailsitters

The use of vertical fans driven by engines for vertical take-off was investigated in the 1950s. The US built an aircraft where the jet exhaust drove the fans, while British projects included fans driven by mechanical drives from the jet engines.

Another, far more influential and practical contribution to VTOL research was supplied by Rolls-Royce's Thrust Measuring Rig or "flying bedstead" as it was affectionately known in 1953. This was a pioneering vertical take-off and landing rig developed by Rolls-Royce purely for research purposes. It has the distinction of being the first jet-lift aircraft to fly anywhere in the world.

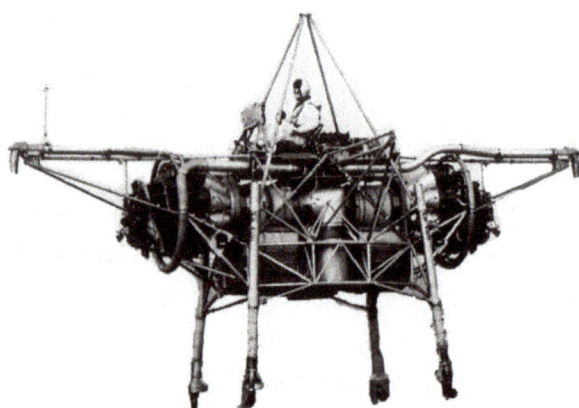

Rolls-Royce Trust Measuring Rig (Flying Bedstead)

The design of the thrust measuring rig was unique. It was powered by a pair of Nene turbojet engines, which were mounted back-to-back horizontally within a steel framework that was raised upon four legs fitted with large castors for wheels. The TMR lacked any lifting surfaces, such as wings. Instead, lift was generated purely by the thrust generated by the Nene engines being directed downwards against the ground. The first flights saw the rig loosely tethered to the ground with chains. The aircraft survived a failure of its thrust vectored control system on the 16th September 1957 whilst being piloted by Wing Commander Stan Hubbard of the RAF but on 29th November 1957, the second TMR, was destroyed during a test flight, resulting in the death of Wing Commander H. G. F. Larsen, who had been piloting the aircraft for the first time.

The TMR had been envisioned specifically for conducting research, specifically to explore the potential applications of the newly developed jet propulsion towards carrying out vertical accents. First flying in August 1954, extensive studies were conducted during a series of test flights into how stabilisation could be performed during the aircraft's hover. It contributed to a greater understanding of the level of power and appropriate manners of stabilisation involved in a VTOL aircraft, as well as proving the feasibility of the concept in general and led to the first VTOL engines as used in the first British VTOL aircraft, the Short SC.1 (1957), which used four vertical lift engines with a horizontal one for forward thrust.

Short SC.1 (1957)

The Short SC.1 was the first British fixed-wing VTOL aircraft. The SC.1 was designed to study the problems with VTOL flight and the transition to and from forward flight in response to a Ministry of Supply request for tender (ER.143T), for a vertical take-off research aircraft issued in September 1953. Short's design was accepted by the ministry and a contract was placed for two aircraft (XG900 and XG905) to meet Specification ER.143D dated 15th October 1954. The SC.1 was also equipped with the first "fly-by-wire" control system for a VTOL aircraft.

This electrically-signalled control system, which also comprised the auto-stabiliser, not only transferred signals from cockpit controls such as the position of the stick, but also monitored feedback signals from the servos to provide stability of the systems itself. A total of three modes of control for the aerodynamic surfaces and/or the nozzle controls were permitted by the system:

The Short SC.1 at Farnborough 1958.

1. Aerodynamic surfaces and air-jet nozzles controlled electrically via three independent servo-motors (with "three-way parallel" or "triplex" fail-safe operation) in conjunction with three auto-stabilizer control systems ("full fly-by-wire").
2. Hybrid-mode, in which the nozzles were controlled by servo/auto-stabilizer and the aerodynamic surfaces were linked directly to the manual controls.
3. Direct mode, in which all controls were linked to the control stick.

Modes 1 and 2 were selected on the ground; whenever the auto-stabilizer was in use, the pilot had an emergency override lever available with which to revert to direct control mode in flight. The outputs from the three control systems were compared and a "majority rule" enforced, ensuring that a failure in a single system was overridden by the other two, presumably correct, systems. Any failure in a "fly-by-wire" pathway was indicated to the pilot as a warning, which he could either choose to ignore or respond to by switching to direct (manual) control.

The Short SC.1 was a single-seat low wing tailless delta wing aircraft of approximately 8,000 lb all-up weight (max. 7,700 lb for vertical flight). It was powered by four vertically-mounted, lightweight Rolls-Royce RB108 lift engines that provided a total vertical thrust of 8,600 lb, along with a single RB.108 cruise engine in the rear of the aircraft to provide thrust for forward flight. The lift engines were mounted vertically in side-by-side pairs in a central bay so that their resultant thrust line passed close to the centre of gravity of the aircraft. These pairs of engines could be swivelled fore-and-aft to produce vectored thrust for acceleration and deceleration along the aircraft's longitudinal axis.

During conventional flight, the lift engines would be shut down and before beginning the transition back from horizontal to vertical flight, they would be started using compressed air from the single cruise engine. The compressed air provided the initial rotation of the engine but a pressure drop from intake to exhaust also had to be present as the compressed air alone was not adequate for reaching idle speed. Considerable wind-tunnel and flight development of the air intake was required because at the start of transition from horizontal flight the vertically-mounted engines have to tolerate a crosswind equal to the forward flight speed without surging or excessive vibrations, problems which were overcome by effective changes to intake and engine design.

The cockpit layout was mainly conventional, but complicated by the large number of systems the pilot had to monitor. For its role as a research aircraft it had comprehensive recording equipment. The common throttle lever for the four vertical lift engines was the only additional primary control in the cockpit; it was operated in a similar manner to that of the collective pitch lever of a helicopter. Two ways to control the attitude of the aircraft were required depending on its forward speed; aerodynamic surfaces were used during conventional flight, and air-jet nozzles for transitioning from horizontal flight, to hovering and vertical flight. Bleed air from the four lift engines (approximately 10 per cent of the intake airflow) was supplied to the variable nose, tail and wing tip nozzles, for pitch, roll and yaw control at low speeds owing to the lack of sufficient airflow over the aerodynamic surfaces for conventional controls to be effective.

The SC.1 flew for over ten years, during which it provided a great deal of data that served to influence later design concepts such as the "puffer jet" controls on the Hawker Siddeley P.1127, the precursor of the Hawker Siddeley Harrier. The flight-testing work relating to vertical take-off and landing techniques and technologies also proved to be invaluable, and helped further Britain's lead in the field. The Short SC.1 was ultimately rendered obsolete by the emerging Harrier which, amongst other things, proved that it was unnecessary to carry an additional four engines solely for the purposes of lift-off and landing.

EWR VJ 101

EWR VJ 101 in 1964 : Courtesy of Ralf Maneufel.

This was an experimental German tilt-jet VTOL fighter aircraft. VJ stood for Versuchsjäger, (German for "Experimental Fighter"). The VJ 101 was one of the first V/STOL designs to have the potential for eventual Mach 2 flight.

The German Federal Government issued a request to the nation's recently revived aviation industries, to look at the possibility of designing a vertical take-off fighter. In 1960 German engine manufacturer MAN Turbo commenced work on a suitable engine in close cooperation with British engine manufacturer Rolls-Royce Limited. Likewise, aircraft firms Heinkel, Bölkow and Messerschmitt performed their own studies before coming together to form a joint venture company, EWR, for the purpose of developing and manufacturing their design for a supersonic VTOL fighter aircraft, which was soon designated as the *VJ 101 D*. The Federal Ministry of Defence were impressed enough to place an order for a pair of experimental prototypes to be produced to demonstrate the design's capabilities.

The two prototypes, X-1 and X-2 were constructed, hopefully as a replacement for the Lockheed F-104G Starfighter interceptors and the plan was to run a five-year test program. However, things were complicated by the changing requirements of the Ministry of Defence and in 1968 development of the VJ 101 was cancelled.

The Harriers

Michel Wibault, a French aircraft designer, had the idea to use vectored thrust for vertical take-off aircraft. This thrust would come from four centrifugal blowers driven by a Bristol Orion turboprop, the exhaust from each blower being vectored by rotating the blower scrolls (outlets). Although the idea of vectoring the thrust was quite novel, the engine propod was considered to be far too heavy so engineers began to explore other engine concepts using components from the existing Orpheus and Olympus engines.

One promising concept was the BE52 which used the Orpheus 3 engine and on a separate coaxial shaft, the first two stages of an Olympus 21 LP compressor, which acted as a fan, delivering compressed air to two thrust vectoring nozzles at the front of engine.

At this point in the design process, the exhaust from the LP turbine discharged through a conventional rear nozzle and there were separate intakes for the fan and core compressor because the fan did not supercharge the core compressor.

Although the BE.52 was a self-contained power plant and lighter than Wibault's concept, the (BE.52) it was still complicated and heavy. As a result, work on the BE.53 started in February 1957. In the BE.53 design, the Olympus stages were fitted close to the Orpheus stages, thus simplifying the inlet ducting. The Olympus stages now supercharged the Orpheus core, improving the overall pressure ratio and creating what is now considered a conventional turbofan configuration.

At first, Bristol designed the engine in isolation, with little feedback from the various airframe manufacturers furnished with data. However, in May 1957 the team received a supportive letter from Sydney Camm of Hawker Aviation who were looking for a replacement for the Hawker Hunter, a transonic British fighter that had been introduced in 1954.

The Hawker Hunter : Darren Harbar Photography.

The 1957 Defence White Paper, which focused on missiles, and not manned aircraft, which were apparently considered "obsolete" in some quarters, was bad news because it signalled the end of government financial support for the development of any new combat aircraft. This prevented any official financial support for the engine or aircraft from the Ministry of Defence.

Fortunately, engine development was financially supported to the tune of 75% from the Mutual Weapons Development Program and Verdon Smith of Bristol Siddeley Engines Limited, (which Bristol Engines had by then become on its merger with Armstrong Siddeley) quickly agreed to pay the remainder.

The first prototype engine ran on 2nd September 1959 and after that date future engine development ran in tandem with the aircraft, the Hawker P.1127. The aircraft first flew in a tethered hover on 21st October 1960, powered by the BE53/3 (Pegasus 2). Free hover was achieved on 19th November of the same year and transition to wing-borne flight occurred in 1961. Later versions of the P.1127 were fitted with the Pegasus 3 and eventually the Pegasus 5 engines.

The Pegasus 5 was also used in the Kestrel, a refinement of the P.1127. Nine Kestrels were built for a Tripartite evaluation exercise, comprising pilots from the United Kingdom, the United States, and West Germany. The Kestrel was subsequently developed into the Harrier combat aircraft by Hawker alone with no government funding.

Harrier Jump Jet : Darren Harbar Photography.

There had been some concerns that it would be difficult for the Harrier to transition from vertical to horizontal flight but testing showed that because of the extreme power to weight ratio it only took a few degrees of nozzle movement to get the aircraft moving forward quickly enough to produce lift from the wing, and that even at a 15 degree angle the aircraft accelerated very well.

The pilot simply had to move the nozzle control forward slowly. During transition from horizontal back to vertical flight the pilot would simply slow to roughly 200 knots and turn the nozzles downward, allowing the engine thrust to take over as the aircraft slowed and the wings stopped producing lift.

Further design and development improvements to the Pegasus to produce ever higher thrusts were continued by Bristol engines beyond 1966, when Rolls-Royce Ltd bought the Company.

A related engine design, the 39,500 lbf (with reheat) the Bristol Siddeley BS100 for a supersonic VTOL fighter, the Hawker Siddeley P.1154, was not developed to production as the aircraft project was cancelled in 1965.

The Sea Harrier

Hawker Sea Harrier : Darren Harbar Photography.

The Royal Navy had already pre-ordered 24 aircraft because of the results being achieved by the RAF and the fact that it would provide a unique short take-off and landing capability at sea. By the time of the first flight this order had increased to 34. The primary role of the Sea Harrier was to provide air defence for aircraft carriers and other surface ships in conflict zones and it gave a good account of itself during the 1992 Falklands conflict as well as in the Gulf and Balkans.

The Space Shuttle

A non-vectored 26,000 lb thrust derivative of the Pegasus engine running on liquid hydrogen, the RB.420, was designed and offered to NASA in 1970 in response to their requirement for an engine to power the projected Space Shuttle on its return from space but in the end, NASA chose a shuttle design using a non-powered gliding return.

F-35 Lightning II

The Lockheed Martin F-35 Lightning II is a family of single-seat, single-engine, all-weather, multirole combat aircraft built by Lockheed Martin along with many subcontractors, including Northrop Grumman, Prat & Whitney and BAE Systems.

The F-35 has three main models: the conventional take-off and landing F-35A, the Short take-off and vertical landing F35B and the catapult-assisted take-off and arrested recovery carrier-based F-35C. The F-35 descends from the Lockheed Martin X-35 Joint Strike Fighter.

Funding for the Lightning come mostly from the US but also from other NATO members such as The United Kingdom, Italy, Australia, Canada, Norway and the Netherlands, all of whom receive contracts to manufacture components for the aircraft.

As the largest and most expensive military program ever, the F-35 became the subject of a lot of scrutiny and criticism in the U.S. and other countries. In 2013 and 2014, critics argued that the plane was "plagued with design flaws", with many blaming the procurement process in which Lockheed was allowed to design, test, and produce the F-35 all at the same time, instead of identifying and fixing defects before firing up its production line. By 2014, the program was $163 billion over budget and seven years behind schedule.

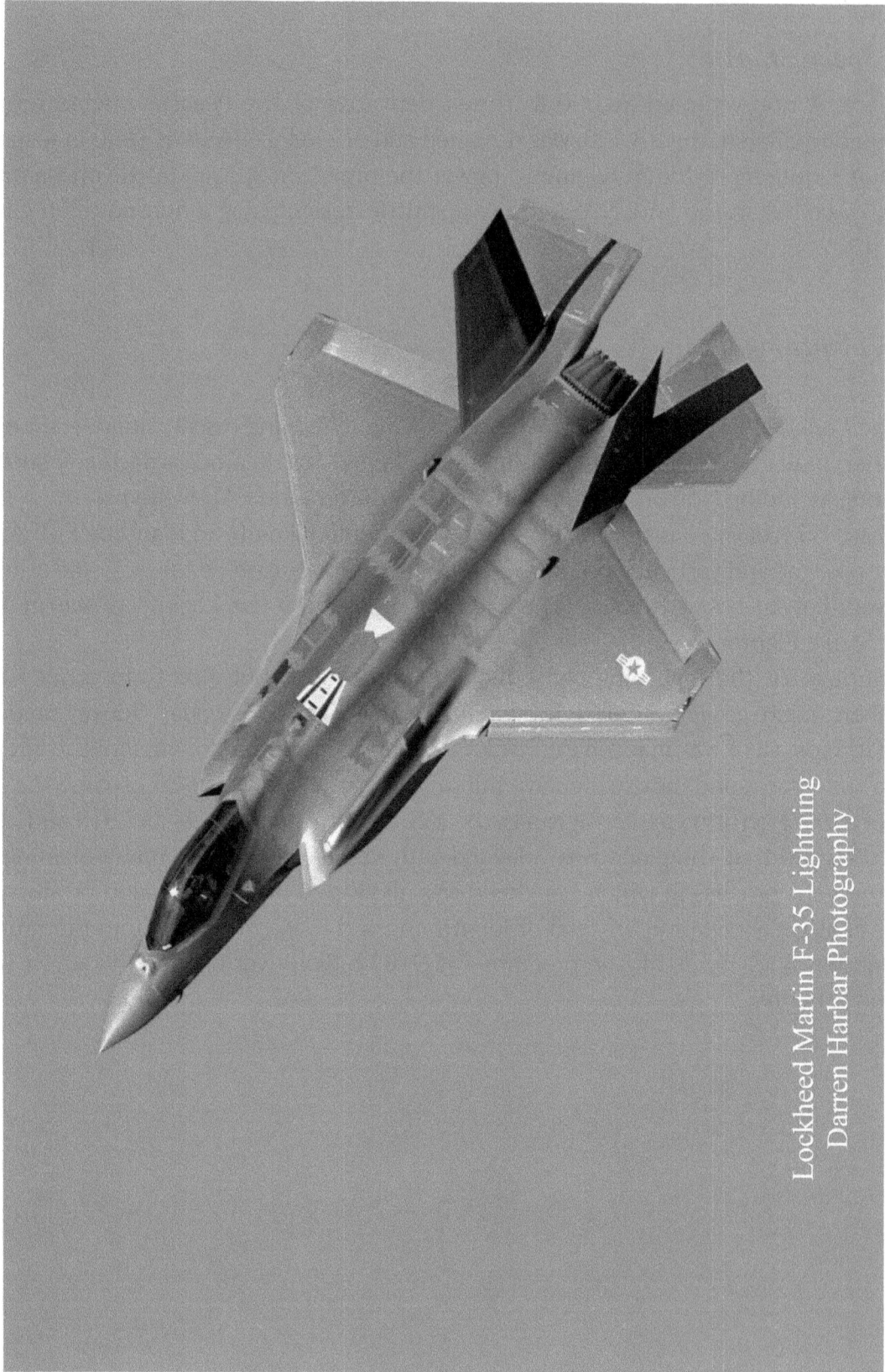

Lockheed Martin F-35 Lightning
Darren Harbar Photography

The F-35 first flew on 15th December 2006 and in July 2015, the US Marines declared its first squadron of F-35B fighters ready for deployment. However, the Department of Defence based durability testing, indicated the service life of early-production F-35B aircraft as being well under the expected 8,000 flight hours, and possibly as low as 2,100 flight hours, so design changes had to be made. The U.S. Air force declared its first squadron of F-35As ready for deployment in August 2016 and the U.S. Navy in February 2019. In 2018, the F-35 made its combat debut with the Israeli Air Force. The U.S. stated plan is to buy 2,663 F-35s, which will provide the bulk of the tactical airpower of the U.S. Air Force, Navy and Marine Corps in coming decades. Deliveries of the F-35 for the U.S. military are scheduled until 2037, with a projected service life up to 2070.

Aircraft Safety

Chapter Twelve

Aircraft Safety

Let's face it, in the early days, flying was a hazardous business and many of the early pioneers of flight gave their lives in the pursuit of the necessary knowledge. Gradually, as more was learnt, it became a little safer, as long as one wasn't fighting in a war that is, but crashes happened and often the reason for it was unknown. If flying was to become more generally accepted and opened up to the wider population, then ways had to be found to make it safer. The most obvious way forward was to make the aircraft themselves stronger, more stable and easier to fly and in fact, progress was constantly being made in that department, however aircraft were also becoming more sophisticated and more complicated and that brought with it its own problems. It inevitably meant there were more ways that things could go wrong and so people started looking at ways, not just of avoiding a crash, but of surviving one if it happened.

The Parachute

Most people know that Leonardo de Vinci sketched a parachute in his Codex Atlanticus towards the end of the fifteenth century but it wasn't until the late eighteenth century that Louise-Sébastien Lenormand made the first recorded public jump in 1783 in France. After making a jump from a tree with the help of a pair of modified umbrellas, Lenormand refined his contraption and on December 26th 1783, he jumped from the tower of the Montpellier observatory, in front of a large crowd that included Joseph Montgolfier, using a 14-foot parachute with a rigid wooden frame. His intended use for the parachute was to help entrapped occupants of a burning building to escape unharmed.

Lenormand jumping from the Montpellier Observatory in 1783.

In 1875 Jean-Pierre Blanchard, using a dog as a passenger, demonstrated how a parachute could be used as a means of safely disembarking from a hot air balloon. These early parachutes were made from linen stretched over a wooden frame but in the late 1790s Blanchard began making parachutes from folded silk and in 1797, André Garnerin made the first descent using a frameless silk parachute. In 1804 Jérôme Lalande introduced a vent in the canopy to eliminate violent oscillations.

We now jump forward in time to 1907 when two key advances in parachute design were demonstrated by Charles Broadwick, who entertained crowds at public events by jumping from hot air balloons. The parachute he used was folded into a pack on his back and was pulled free from it as he jumped by a static line attached to the balloon that then snapped under the strain, allowing him to descend freely. Broadwick was later joined by Georgia Ann Thompson, who at the age of fifteen, was later adopted by Charles to ease travel arrangements and became known as "Tiny Broadwick" due to her small size of just 5 feet tall.

On December 28th 1908, Tiny made her very first jump out of a hot air balloon. Billed as "the doll girl," Tiny began performing aerial skydives and stunts while wearing a "life preserver" designed by her adopted father. The skydiving family travelled around and performed at fairs, carnivals, and parks.

Among her many other achievements, Tiny Broadwick was the first woman to parachute from an airplane, which she is credited with accomplishing on 2nd June 1913 over Los Angeles, with aviator Glen

Tiny Broadwick

L. Martin as the pilot. However, she had previously made at least two jumps from Martin's plane during an exhibition in Chicago's Grant Park the week of September 16th 1912. These early jumps included a well-publicised jump on January 9th 1914, from a plane built and piloted by Martin, 1,000 feet over Griffith Park in Los Angeles, California, that captured the public's imagination. Tiny was also the first woman to parachute into water.

In 1914, she demonstrated parachutes to the U.S. Army and on one of her demonstration jumps, the static line became entangled in the tail assembly of the aircraft, so for her next jump she cut off the static line and deployed her chute manually, thus becoming the first person to jump free-fall. This also demonstrated that pilots could escape from an aircraft and deploy their chute by using what was later called a ripcord.

The first parachute jump from an aeroplane was made in 1911 by Grant Morton, when he jumped from a Wright Model B, piloted by Phil Parmalee at Venice Beach, California. The parachute Morton used was a "throw out" type where he held the parachute in his arms as he left the aircraft.

Not all tests of parachutes were successful of course and on 4th February 1912 Franz Reichelt jumped to his death from the Eiffel Tower during a test of his "wearable" parachute.

Also in 1912, Gleb Kotenikovlev, successfully demonstrated the breaking effects of a parachute, by attaching one to the back seat of a Russo-Balt automobile while driving at speed, thus inventing the drogue-parachute. Kotenikovlev was also the man who invented the first knapsack parachute, although Hermann Lattemann and his wife Käthe Paulus had been jumping from balloons with bagged parachutes in the last decade of the 19th century. Sadly, Lattemann died at the age of 42, when he and his wife jumped out of a balloon named "Fin de Siècle", his parachute failed to open, although his wife's did and she watched in horror as her husband fell to his death.

Štefan Banic patented an umbrella like design that was attached to the body in 1914 but there is no evidence that it was ever used.

The first military use of the parachute was by artillery observers on tethered balloons in World War One. Tethered balloons were tempting targets for enemy fighter aircraft, although difficult to destroy due to their heavy anti-aircraft defences. Because it was difficult to escape from them, and because they were dangerous when on fire, due to the hydrogen gas used to fill them, observers would abandon them and descend by parachute as soon as enemy aircraft were sighted. The ground crew would then attempt to retrieve and deflate the balloon as quickly as possible. The main part of the parachute was in a bag suspended from the balloon with the pilot wearing only a simple waist harness attached to the main parachute. When the balloon crew jumped the main part of the parachute was pulled from the bag by the crew's waist harness, first the shroud lines, followed by the main canopy. This type of parachute was first adopted on a large scale for their observation balloon crews by the Germans, and then later by the British and French.

Observers preparing to descend by parachute.

While this type of unit worked well from balloons, it had mixed results when used on fixed-wing aircraft by the Germans, where the bag was stored in a compartment directly behind the pilot. In many instances where it didn't work the shroud lines had become entangled with the spinning aircraft. although a number of famous German fighter pilots were saved by this type of parachute, including Hermann Göring. No parachutes were issued to Allied aeroplane pilots because it was thought at the time, that if a pilot had a parachute he would jump from the plane as soon as it was hit rather than trying to save the aircraft. It was also true that there was very little room in the cockpit for the addition of a parachute

In 1911, the American, Solomon Lee Van Meter Jr. patented a backpack style parachute that he called the "Aviatory Life Buoy". His self-contained device featured a revolutionary quick-release mechanism, the ripcord, that allowed a falling aviator to expand the canopy when safely away from the disabled aircraft.

Otto Heinecke, a German airship ground crewman, designed a parachute which the German air service introduced in 1918, becoming the world's first air service to introduce a standard parachute. Although many pilots were saved by these, their efficacy was relatively poor. Out of the first 70 German airmen to bail out, around a third died, including aces such as Oberleutnant Erich Löwenhardt, who fell from 3,600 metres (11,800 ft) after being accidentally rammed by another German aircraft and Fritz Rumey who tested it in 1918, only to have it fail at a little over 900 m (3,000 ft). These fatalities were mostly due to the parachute or static line becoming entangled in the airframe of their spinning aircraft or because of harness failure, a problem that was fixed in later versions.

The French, British, American and Italian air services later based their first parachute designs on the Heinecke parachute to varying extents, however, also in the United Kingdom, Sir Frank Mears, who was serving as a Major in the Kite Balloon section of the Royal Flying Corps in France, registered a patent in July 1918 for a parachute with a quick release buckle, known as the "Mears parachute". It was in common use from then onwards.

World War One highlighted the need to develop a parachute design that could be reliably used to exit a disabled aeroplane, even if it was spinning, something a tethered parachute certainly couldn't do. After the war, a team led by Major Edward L. Hoffman of the United States Army and including Leslie Irvin, a stunt man and parachutist, was put together to develop an improved parachute. This new improved design would incorporate three key elements. Firstly, it needed to be worn in a pack on the aviator's back, secondly it needed a ripcord so that it could be opened at a safe distance from the stricken aircraft and lastly it would need to be pulled clear of its pack by means of a pilot chute. The new Type-A parachute was tested successfully in 1919 and Major Hoffman was awarded the Robert J. Collier Trophy in 1926

An early brochure of the "Irvin Air Chute Company" credits William O'Connor as having become, on August 24th 1920, at McCook Field near Dayton, Ohio, the first person to be saved by an Irvin parachute. Another life-saving jump was made, also at McCook Field, by test pilot Lt. Harold H. Harris on October 20th 1922. Shortly after Harris' jump, two Dayton newspaper reporters suggested the creation of the "Caterpillar Club" for successful parachute jumps from disabled aircraft and on July 4th 1924 Gleb Kotelnikov of Russia, became the first parachutist to apply the soft packing of a parachute instead of a hard casing.

Beginning with Italy in 1927, several countries began experimenting with using parachutes to drop soldiers behind enemy lines and after a number of experimental mass jumps, the regular Soviet Airborne Troop were established in1931. By the time World War Two started large airborne forces were trained and used in surprise attacks, such as in the battles for Fort Eben-Emael and The Hague, the first large-scale, opposed landings of paratroopers in military history, by the Germans. This was followed later in the war by airborne assaults on an even larger scale, such as the battle of Crete and Operation Market Garden, the latter being the largest airborne military operation ever. Aircraft crew were by this time routinely equipped with parachutes for emergencies.

The Ejector Seat

It was Romanian inventor Anastase Dragomir who proposed the modern layout for an ejection seat in the late 1920s. The design featured a pilot seat that could be discharged from an aircraft or other vehicle. It was successfully tested on 25th August 1929 at the Paris-Orly Airport and in October that same year at Băneasa near Bucharest. The design was perfected during World War Two. Prior to this, the only means of escape from an incapacitated aircraft was to "bail out" and in many cases this was difficult to achieve due to either injury, the difficulty of egress from a confined cockpit, G-forces or other factors.

The first ejection seats were developed independently during World War Two by Heinkel and Saab. Early models were powered by compressed air and the first aircraft to be fitted with such a system was the Heikel He 280 prototype jet engine fighter in 1940. One of the He 280 test pilots, Helmut Schenk, became the first person to escape from a stricken aircraft with an ejection seat on 13th January 1942 after his control surfaces iced up and became inoperative.

The He 280 was never put into production so the first operational aircraft built anywhere to provide ejection seats for the crew was the Heikel He 219 Uhu night fighter in 1942

Heikel He 219 Uhu night fighter.

In Sweden, an ejector seat using compressed air was tested in 1941 and a gunpowder ejection seat was developed by Bofors and tested in 1943 for the Saab 21. The first test in the air was on a Saab 17 on 27th February 1944, and the first real use was by Lt. Bengt Johansson on 29th July 1946 after a mid-air collision between a Saab J 21 and a Saab J 22.

The first operational military jet to feature an ejector seat was the Heinkel He 162 Spatz in 1942. The Spatz featured a new type of ejection seat, this time fired by an explosive cartridge. In this system, the seat rode on wheels set between two pipes running up the back of the cockpit.

When lowered into position, caps at the top of the seat fitted over the pipes to close them. Cartridges, basically identical to shotgun shells, were placed in the bottom of the pipes, facing upward. When fired, the gases would fill the pipes, popping the caps off the end, and thereby forcing the seat to ride up the pipes on its wheels and out of the aircraft.

Heinkel He 162 Spatz.

After World War II, the need for such systems became pressing, as aircraft speeds were getting ever higher, approaching that of the speed of sound and manual escape at such speeds would be impossible.

The United States Army Air Forces briefly experimented with downward-ejecting systems operated by a spring, but it was the work of James Martin and Captain Valentine Baker who formed the Martin-Baker company that proved crucial.

Martin-Baker investigated ejection seats from 1934 onwards, several years before Germany and Sweden proposed similar systems in 1938. The company concluded that an explosive-powered ejection seat was the best solution. In particular, Baker's death in 1942 during a test flight of the MB3 affected Martin so much that pilot safety became his primary focus and led to the later reorganisation of the company to focus primarily on ejection seats, having previously also designed aircraft.

In 1944, James Martin was asked by the Ministry of Aircraft production to develop methods of escape for pilots from critically damaged aircraft. Martin decided that the best method involved the ejection of the pilot and seat together aided by an explosive charge. After ejection, the pilot would separate from the seat and open his parachute by pulling a ripcord in the usual way.

Studies were conducted to find the limits of upward acceleration that the human body could stand. A test rig was built and the first dummy shot with the seat loaded to 200lb was made on 20th January 1945. Four days later, one of the company's fitters, Bernard Lynch, undertook the first "live" ride, being shot up the rig to a height of 4 feet 8inches. In three further tests, the power of the cartridge was progressively increased until a height of 10 feet was reached, at which stage Lynch reported the onset of considerable physical discomfort.

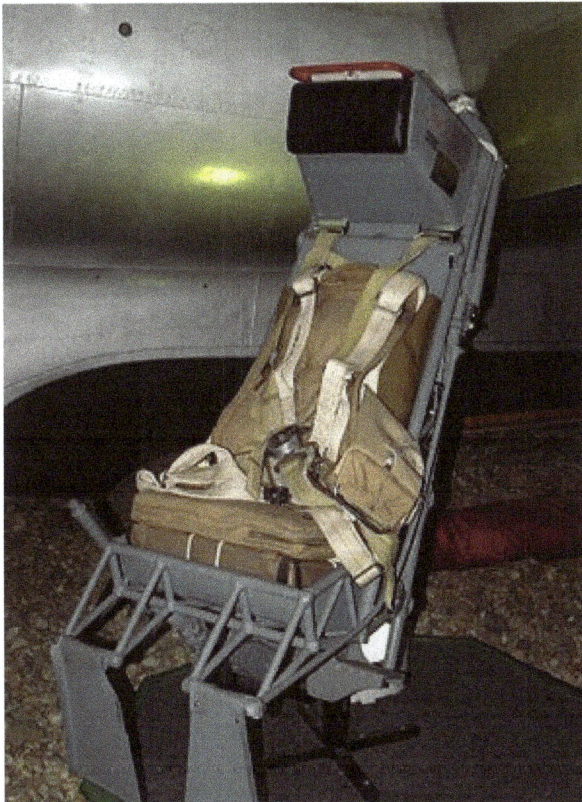

Martin-Baker ejector seat Mk1.

The first seat was successfully live-tested by Lynch on 24th July 1946, when he ejected from a Gloster Meteor travelling at 320 miles per hour (510 km/h) at 8,000 feet (2,400 m) over Chalgrove Airfield in Oxfordshire. The first production Martin-Baker ejection seat, a Rri-Mk 1 was installed in the Saunders-Roe SR.A/1 prototype and the first use of an ejection seat in an actual emergency was by a British test pilot J. O. Lancaster, who was forced to eject from the Armstrong Whitworth A.W.52 flying wing experimental aircraft he was flying in May 1949.

Martin-Baker was a pioneer in expanding the operational envelope of the ejection seat to enable it to be used at low altitudes and airspeeds, leading eventually to a zero-zero capability.

Early examples used a solid propellant charge to eject the pilot and seat by igniting the charge inside a telescoping tube attached to the seat itself. As aircraft speeds increased still further, this method proved inadequate to get the pilot sufficiently clear of the airframe but increasing the amount of propellant risked damaging the occupant's spine.

Experiments with rocket propulsion began in 1958 and the Convair F-102 Delta Dagger was the first aircraft to be fitted with a rocket-propelled seat. Martin-Baker developed a similar design, using multiple rocket units feeding a single nozzle. The greater thrust from this configuration had the advantage of being able to eject the pilot to a safe height, even if the aircraft was on or very near the ground.

J. O. Lancaster ejected from a Armstrong Whitworth A. W. 52 flying wing like the one shown here.

In the early 1960s, deployment of rocket-powered ejection seats designed for use at supersonic speeds began in such planes as the Convair F-106 Delta Dart. Some pilots have ejected at speeds exceeding 700 knots, 810 mph. but the vast majority of ejections occur at fairly low speeds and altitudes, when the pilot can see that there is no hope of regaining aircraft control before impact with the ground.

The "standard" ejection system operates in two stages. First, the entire canopy or hatch above the aviator is opened, shattered, or jettisoned, after which the seat and occupant are launched through the opening. In most earlier aircraft this required two separate actions by the pilot but later egress system designs perform both functions as a single action.

Aircraft designed for low-level use sometimes have ejection seats which fire through the canopy, as waiting for the canopy to be ejected first could prove too slow. Many aircraft types such as the vertical take-off Harrier, use Canopy Destruct systems, which have an explosive miniature Detonation Cord or FLSC (Flexible Linear Shaped Charge), embedded within the acrylic plastic of the canopy. The charge is initiated when the eject handle is pulled, and shatters the canopy over the seat a few milliseconds before the seat is launched. This system was developed for the Hawker Siddeley Harrier family of VTOL aircraft in case ejection was necessary while the aircraft was in the hover, and jettisoning the canopy might result in the pilot and seat striking it. This system is also used in the T-6 Texan 11 and the F-35 Lightning 11.

The system known as Through-Canopy Penetration is similar to Canopy Destruct, but a sharp spike on the top of the seat, known as the shell tooth, strikes the underside of the canopy and shatters it

Encapsulated Seat egress systems were developed for use in the B-58 Hustler and B-70 Valkyrie supersonic bombers. These seats were enclosed in an air-operated clamshell, which permitted the aircrew to escape at airspeeds and altitudes high enough to otherwise cause bodily harm.

Some aircraft designs, such as the General Dynamics F-111, do not have individual ejection seats, but instead, the entire section of the airframe containing the crew can be ejected as a single capsule. In this system, very powerful rockets are used, and multiple large parachutes are used to bring the capsule down and on landing, an airbag is used to cushion the impact and this also acts as a flotation device if the Crew Capsule lands in water.

Airliner Safety

As aircraft have become larger, faster and more complicated, the number of things that can go wrong during a flight have also increased and although devices such as parachutes and ejector seats have helped aircrew to escape doomed aircraft, the majority of people who fly, the passengers, have to rely on the skill of the pilot and his being able to land the stricken plane and then to be able to escape uninjured before any fire can spread through the cabin.

Air-crash investigation has played a major role in improving the reliability of aircraft to both avoid and survive crashes and to enable passengers to survive should the worst happen.

1908

The first air accident report was written by Frank Lahm in 1908 when he investigated and reported on the crash that killed U.S. Army First Lieutenant Thomas Selfridge, the first person to die during powered flight. The Wright Model A, piloted by Orville Wright, was the most technologically advanced aeroplane in the world and Wright had just replaced its two eight-foot, eight-inch diameter propellers with nine-foot ones in order to make the aircraft faster. It was cruising at 40 miles per hour at a height of approximately 125 feet when Wright heard a light tapping noise behind him, he whirled around and saw nothing wrong, but, as he later wrote to his brother, "*soon felt two big thumps, which gave the machine a terrible shaking.*" An observer at the time said that the aeroplane corkscrewed right and pitched up, rocking like a ship in rough water, then nosed dived almost straight down. About 25 feet from the ground, the airplane began easing out of the dive. "*A few feet more,*" Wright wrote, "*and we would have landed safely.*"

Wright was quickly pulled from the wreckage, dazed and in pain from some broken bones but it took several minutes to free the unconscious and more seriously injured Selfridge, who died in surgery some three hours later, the victim of a skull fracture.

Lahm was the obvious choice to conduct the War Department-ordered investigation. He'd flown with Wright a few days before the accident, had seen the crash, and had helped drag Wright from his mangled airplane.

Lahm interviewed about a dozen spectators, including an artilleryman who, Lahm later wrote, "*gave the impression of being a reliable witness*" and Octave Chanute, one of the foremost aviation theorists of the day. Several of them verified what Lahm himself had seen; a chunk from one of the propeller blades break off during flight and fall to the ground. Lahm found and examined the broken propeller, and took precise measurements at the scene, a procedure closely followed today.

Wright was so distraught by the incident that Lahm wasn't able to question him for several weeks, but based on Wright's recollections and the physical evidence, Lahm's conclusion was that the broken propeller had caused damage that rendered the airplane uncontrollable.

"I am of the opinion that due to excessive vibration, this guy wire, (securing the front rudder) and the right hand propeller came into contact," Lahm wrote in his report, issued on February 19th 1909. *"The clicking which Mr. Wright referred to being due to the propeller blade striking the wire lightly several times, when, the vibrations increasing, it struck it hard enough to pull it out of its socket and at the same time to break the propeller."*

The next summer, Wright returned to Fort Myer with an upgraded Model A and with Wright serving as his instructor, Lahm learned to fly in this airplane, and became America's second certified military pilot.

1950s

We have already looked at the tragic mid-air breakups of the three Comets in the 1950s and the investigations led by Sir Arnold Hall at the Royal Aeronautical Establishment in Farnborough. Metal fatigue was a phenomenon that was not very well understood at the time but as a result of the tests the Comet was extensively redesigned, with oval windows, structural reinforcements and other changes. Rival manufacturers also heeded the lessons learned from the Comet tragedy while developing their own aircraft.

1985

After a Lockheed TriStar encountered a thunderstorm while approaching Dallas-Fort Worth and struck the ground far short of the runway, killing 137 people and injuring a further 28 in 1985, investigators found that there was a lack of procedures and training to deal with "microbursts" and or wind shear. A microburst is a small but intense downdraught that occurs in storms and wind shear is a sharp change in wind speed or direction. As a result of the investigation NASA developed a detection and alert system to be installed on commercial aircraft.

On 22nd August 1985 a Boeing 737 caught fire before take-off at Manchester airport, with the loss of 55 lives. It was about to begin its flight to Corfu, in Greece but before take-off, one of the engines failed, causing the fire, and the captain instructed the crew to evacuate the plane. There were 82 survivors with most of the deaths being caused by smoke inhalation. The accident brought about industry-wide action on aeroplane design, including changes to the seating layout near exits; fire-resistant seat covers; floor-level emergency lighting; fire-resistant wall and ceiling panels; increased numbers of extinguishers; and clearer rules on evacuation procedures.

Evacuation slides

The first aircraft evacuation slide was developed and produced by Air Cruisers, founded by James F. Boyle, inventor of the World War Two life vest, the "Mae West". The patent for the inflatable escape chute assembly was submitted by Boyle in 1954 and the designs was patented in 1956. Today Air Cruisers is part of Zodiac Aerospace and ultimately owned by Safran who are the world's largest provider of evacuation slides. Prior to inflatables, some passenger aircraft utilized canvas type slides which required the crew to undertake an extensive rigging procedure.

Fires

Fires have caused the deaths of many aircraft passengers, even though the accidents were otherwise survivable. Post-accident investigation indicates that often these deaths do not result from the fire itself but rather, death results from the inhalation of smoke and there are now several standards that have to be met by modern commercial aircraft.

In general, to meet certification standards, the manufacturer must show that the design features of its transport aircraft are not "hazardous" or "unreliable." The cabin must have at least one door which can be opened from outside or inside, even if people are crowded against it. Furthermore, the door must be marked and located so that it can be found and operated in darkness. Ventilation must ensure that the crew and passenger compartments are kept free from harmful concentrations of gases or vapours even allowing for malfunctions. Those compartments which are not accessible by crew or passengers must have interiors that meet oxygen, flammability, and/or detection and protection requirements. Cargo and baggage compartments are also subject to fire safety regulations.

There are of course many more safety requirements that have to be met by manufacturers, far too many to list here but airlines also have to meet high standards with crew training and maintenance. In truth, the aviation industry's impressive safety record in recent decades is by and large, a result of technological developments introduced and refined in the second half of the 20th century. Subsequent generations of jet aircraft have generally proved to be safer than the one before. The piston-driven aircraft that dominated the world's airline fleet in 1950 and early 60s, had an accident rate of 27.2 accidents per million departures. The second generation of aircraft in the latter half of the 1960s and early 1970s, which included the Boeing 727 and the DC-9 jet airliners, had an accident rate of 2.8 accidents per million and the current generation of aircraft have an accident rate of 1.5 accidents per one million departures and that's pretty impressive.

Appendix

Chapter Thirteen

Appendix

Jackie Cochran

Jackie Cochran in 1943

Known to her friends as "Jackie" and maintaining the Cochran name, Jackie Cochran was the first woman to break the sound barrier in 1953. She was one of only three women to compete in the Mac-Robertson Air Race in 1934 and in 1937 she was the only woman to compete in the Bendix Trophy and worked with Amelia Earhart to open the race to women. That same year, she also set a new women's world speed record and by 1938, she was considered the best female pilot in the United States. She had won the Bendix and set a new transcontinental speed record as well as altitude records, she was also the first woman to fly a bomber across the Atlantic and she managed to win five Harmon Trophies. Sometimes called the "Speed Queen", at the time of her death, no other pilot held more speed, distance, or altitude records in aviation history than Jackie Cochran.

In the 1960s, Cochran was a sponsor of the Mercury 13 program, an early effort to test the ability of women to be astronauts. Thirteen women pilots passed the same preliminary tests as the male astronauts of the Mercury program before the program was cancelled,

In September, 1939, Cochran wrote to Eleanor Roosevelt with the proposal of starting a women's flying division in the Army Air Forces. She felt that qualified women pilots could do all of the domestic, noncombat aviation jobs necessary in order to release more male pilots for combat. She pictured herself in command of these women, with the same standings as Colonel Oveta Culp Hobby who was then the director of the Women's Army Auxiliary Corps (WAAC) that was given full military status on July 1st 1943, thus making them part of the Army. At the same time, the unit was renamed Women's Army Corps.

That same year, Cochran wrote a letter to Lieutenant Colonel Robert Olds, who was helping to organize the Air Corps Ferrying Command for the Air Corps at the time. In the letter, Cochran suggested that women pilots be employed to fly non-combat missions for the new command and in early 1941, Olds asked Cochran to find out how many women pilots there were in the United States, together with what their flying times were, their skills, their interest in flying for the country, and any personal information about them. She used records from the Civil Aeronautics Administration to gather the data needed.

Lieutenant General Henry H. Arnold, the Chief of the Air Corps knew that women were being used successfully in the Air Transport Auxillary (ATA) in England so he suggested that Cochran take a group of qualified female pilots to see how the British were doing. When Arnold asked Cochran to go to Britain to study the ATA, she asked 76 of the most qualified female pilots, identified during the research she had done earlier for Olds, to come along and fly for the ATA. Qualifications for these women were high: at least 300 hours of flying time, but most of the women pilots had over 1,000 hours anyway. A total of 25 women passed the tests and, two months later in March 1942 they went to Britain with Cochran to join the ATA.

While Cochran was in England, in September 1942, General Arnold authorized the formation of the Women's Auxiliary Ferrying Squadron (WAFS), under the direction of Nancy Harkness Love. The WAFS began at New Castle Air Base in Wilmington, Delaware, with a group of female pilots whose objective was to ferry military aircraft. Hearing about the WAFS, Cochran immediately returned from England. Her experience in Britain with the ATA had convinced her that women pilots could be trained to do much more than ferrying so she began lobbying Arnold for expanded flying opportunities for female pilots and he sanctioned the creation of the Women's Flying Training Detachment (WFTD) headed by Cochran. In August 1943, the WAFS and the WFTD merged to create the Women's Airforce Service Pilots with Cochran as director and Nancy Love as head of the ferrying division.

She received the Distinguished Service Medal (DSM) in 1945 for her wartime service. Her award of the DSM was announced in a War Department press release dated March 1st 1945 which stated that Cochran was the first woman civilian to receive the DSM, which was then the highest non-combat award presented by the United States government. (In actuality, however, a few civilian women had received the DSM for service during the First World War).

Captain Eric Brown

Captain Eric Melrose Brown

Captain Eric Melrose "Winkle" Brown, CBE, DSC, AFC, Hon FRAeS RN. (1919 – 2016) was a British Royal Navy officer and test pilot who flew 487 different types of aircraft, more than anyone else in history. He was also the most-decorated pilot in the history of the Royal Navy. He received the affectionate nickname "Winkle" from his Royal Navy colleagues, it being short for "Periwinkle" a small mollusc, the name was given to him because of his short stature of 5 ft 7 in. Brown partly attributed his survival of dangerous incidents to his ability to "curl himself up in the cockpit".

Brown holds the world record for the most aircraft carrier deck landings with 2,407 and a similar number of take-offs,2,271 of which were catapult launches. He achieved several "firsts" in naval aviation including the first landings on an aircraft carrier of a twin-engined aircraft, an aircraft with a tricycle undercarriage and also both a jet aircraft and a rotary-wing aircraft.

He also flew almost every category of Royal Navy and RAF aircraft: glider, fighter, bomber, airliner, amphibian, flying boat and helicopter. During and just after World War Two he also flew many types of captured German, Italian, and Japanese aircraft, including experimental jet and rocket planes, an astonishing achievement.

He first flew at the age of ten, sitting on his father's knee in a Gloster Gauntlet and in 1936 his father took him to the Olympics in Germany where he met and spoke to Hermann Göring and Ernst Udet, a former World War One fighter ace.

On the BBC programme "Desert Island Discs" Eric said that Udet later took him for a flight in a two-seater Bücker Jungmann and that Udet had made their final approach upside-down! only rolling back just in time to touch down.

After they had landed, Eric said that Udet had slapped him on the back and told him, "*You will make a fine fighter pilot, do me two favours, learn to speak fluent Garman and learn to fly*", both of which he did.

In September 1939 he was an exchange student in Germany and he was woken one morning to be told that Britain and Germany were at war. Brown was subsequently arrested by the SS but after three days he was escorted to the Swiss border in his MG Magnette sports car and released, apparently told that he could keep the car because there were no spares for it in Germany.

Once back in Britain, he joined the Royal Navy as a Fleet Air Arm Pilot flying a Grumman Martlet and distinguished himself by shooting down two Focke-Wulf Fw 200 Condor patrol aircraft.

Grumman Martlet, shown here with D-Day markings. Darren Harbar Photography.

When his ship, HMS Audacity was torpedoed and sunk on 21st December 1941 he was in the water with several other crew for a number of hours and when eventually picked up, Eric was the only one to have survived the cold.

Brown was awarded the Distinguished Service Cross for his service on Audacity, in particular "*For bravery and skill in action against Enemy aircraft and in the protection of a Convoy against heavy and sustained Enemy attacks*".

Following the loss of *Audacity*, Brown resumed operational flying, being seconded to the Royal Canadian Air Force to train pilots in deck landing techniques and after returning to the Royal Air Arm in 1943 he was transfered to Southern Italy to evaluate captured Italian and German aircraft.

On completion of these duties, his commander, being impressed with his performance, sent him back to the RAE with the recommendation that he be employed in the Aerodynamics Flight department at Farnborough.

Focke-Wulf Fw 200 Condor patrol aircraft.

During the first month in the Flight department, Brown flew 13 aircraft types, including a captured Focke-Wulf Fw 190, after which time, his experience with deck landings was sought by the Royal Aircraft Establishment at Farnorough, where he tested the new Sea Hurricane and Seafire aircraft.

Focke-Wulf Fw 190

Whilst taking part in carrier compatibility trials, Brown crash-landed a Fairey Firefly Mk I, Z1844, on the deck of HMS Pretoria Castle on 9th September 1943, when the arrester hook indicator light falsely showed the hook was in the "down" position, this was compounded by the batsman failing to notice that the hook was not down. The fighter hit the crash barrier, sheared off its undercarriage and shredded the propeller, but he was unhurt.

While at Farnborough as chief naval test pilot, Brown performed the first deck landing of a twin-engined plane, a Sea Mosquito, on the 25th March 1944.

During this time, the RAE was the leading authority on high-speed flight and Brown became involved in this sort of testing. Aircraft being flown were usually the Spitfire and it would be dived at speeds of the high subsonic and near transonic range. Figures achieved by Brown and his colleagues during these tests reached Mach 0.86 for a standard Spitfire IX, to Mach 0.92 for a modified Spitfire PR Mk XI flown by his colleague, Squadron Leader Anthony F. Martindale.

Brown was selected as the pilot for the Miles M.52 supersonic research aircraft programme, and he flew modified aircraft incorporating components intended for the M.52; however, the post-war government later cancelled the project in 1945 with the M.52 almost complete. On 2nd May 1944, he was appointed MBE "for outstanding enterprise and skill in piloting aircraft during hazardous aircraft trials."

In February 1945, Brown learned that the Aerodynamics Flight had been allocated three Sikorsky R-4B Hoverfly helicopters. He had never seen one of these tail-rotor machines, so a trip to Farnborough was arranged and Brown had a short flight as a passenger in one. A few days later, Brown and Martindale were sent to RAF Speke to collect two new R-4Bs.

On arrival, they found the American mechanics assembling the machines, and when Brown asked the Master Sergeant in charge about himself and Martindale being taught to fly them, he was handed a large orange-coloured booklet with the retort; "*Whaddya mean, bud? – Here's your instructor*".

Sikorsky R-4B Hoverfly

Brown and Martindale examined the booklet and after several practice attempts at hovering and controlling the craft, followed by a stiff drink, they set off for Farnborough. Brown and Martindale both managed the trip safely, if a little raggedly, in formation, although sometimes as much as a couple of miles apart.

During this period, Brown was asked by Brigadier Glyn Hughes, the Medical Officer of the British 2nd Army occupying the newly liberated Bergen-Belson concentration camp, on learning that he spoke fluent German, to help interrogate the former camp commandant and his assistant. Agreeing to do so, he interviewed Josef Kramer and Irma Grese, and later remarked on the experience by saying that, "*Two more loathsome creatures it is hard to imagine*" and further describing the latter as "*the worst human being I have ever met.*" Kramer and Grese were later tried and hanged for war crimes.

Being fluent in German, he helped interview several Germans after World War Two, but he described the interviews as being minimal, and limited to matters related to aviation, due to the need to begin the Nuremberg trials.

Over the course of his career Brown flew aircraft from Britain, the United States, Germany, the Soviet Union, Italy and Japan and is listed in the Guinness Book of World

Records as holding the record for flying the greatest number of different aircraft. The official record is 487, but this includes only basic types. For example, Brown flew 14 versions of the Spitfire and Seafire and although these versions are very different, they appear only once in the list and the list includes only aircraft flown by Brown as "Captain in Command".

Brown went on to achieve even more firsts and is almost certainly the most extraordinary pilot of all time and if the Ministry of Supply had proceeded with Ralph Smith's V2-based MegaRoc sub-orbital manned spacecraft, Brown would almost certainly have been the leading candidate for its projected 1949 first manned spaceflight. He died on 21st February 2016 aged 96.

Wind Tunnels

During the early years of aeronautical research, it became obvious to those doing the research that, because it makes no difference to the flow of air over a wing whether it is the wing or the air that is moving, it would be far easier for an observer to study the flow of air over a stationary wing and the wind tunnel was born.

English military engineer and mathematician Benjamin Robins (1707–1751) invented a whirling arm apparatus to determine drag and did some of the first experiments in aviation theory and Sir George Cayley also used a whirling arm to measure the drag and lift of various aerofoils.

However, the whirling arm does not produce a reliable flow of air impacting the test shape at a normal incidence. Centrifugal forces and the fact that the object is moving in its own wake mean that detailed examination of the airflow is difficult.

Francis Herbert Wenham (1824–1908), a Council Member of the Aeronautical Society of Great Britain, overcame these problems by inventing, designing and operating the first enclosed wind tunnel in 1871 and once this breakthrough had been achieved, valuable technical data was soon amassed. Wenham and his colleague John Browning are credited with many fundamental discoveries, including the measurement of lift to drag ratios, and the revelation of the beneficial effects of a high aspect ratio.

Konstantin Tsiolkovsk built an open-section wind tunnel with a centrifugal blower in 1897, and determined the drag coefficients of flat plates, cylinders and spheres and Danish inventor Poul la Cour applied wind tunnels in his process of developing and refining the technology of wind turbines in the early 1890s.

In a classic set of experiments, the Englishman Osborne Reynolds (1842–1912) of the University of Manchester, demonstrated that the airflow pattern over a scale model would be the same for the full-scale vehicle if a certain flow parameter were the same in both cases. This factor, now known as the Reynolds number, is a basic parameter in the description of all fluid-flow situations, including the shapes of flow patterns, the ease of heat transfer, and the onset of turbulence. This comprises the central scientific justification for the use of models in wind tunnels to simulate real-life phenomena. However, there are limitations on conditions in which dynamic similarity is based upon the Reynolds number alone.

Gustave Eiffel built a wind tunnel in 1909, powered by a 50 kW electric motor, at Champs-de-Mars, near the foot of his famous tower and conducted numerous tests in it before it was moved in 1912 to Auteuil, a suburb of Paris, where his wind tunnel with a two-metre test section is still operational today.

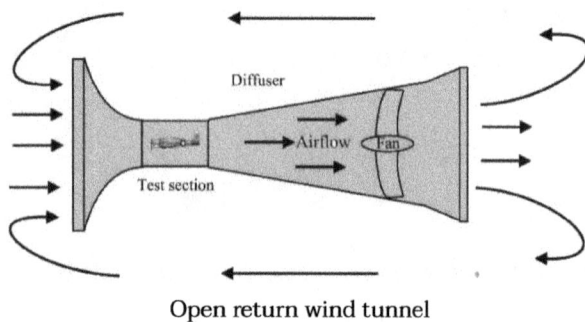

Open return wind tunnel

Eiffel significantly improved the efficiency of the open-return wind tunnel by enclosing the test section in a chamber, designing a flared inlet with a honeycomb flow straightener and adding a diffuser between the test section and the fan located at the downstream end of the diffuser, an arrangement now followed by a number of wind tunnels; in fact, the open-return low-speed wind tunnel is often referred to as the Eiffel-type wind tunnel.

Both the open and closed wind tunnels have their advantages and disadvantages. The open tunnel has lower construction costs and is better for the use of smoke to see airflow. One of the major draw-backs to the open design however, is that the airflow can be affected by outside influences such as nearby objects or weather and with an open system the fan has to continually accelerate the speed of the incoming air.

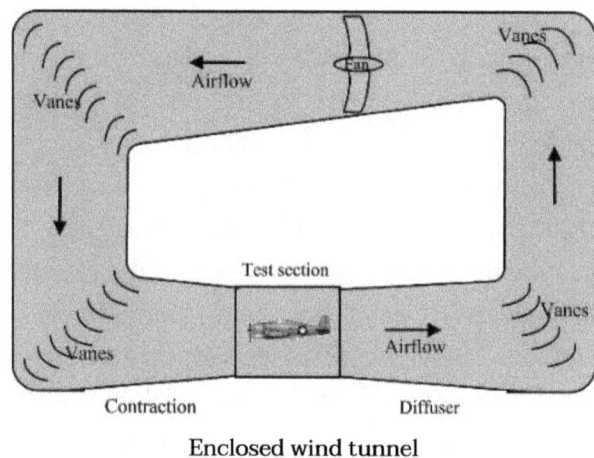

Enclosed wind tunnel

The advantages associated with the closed return tunnel are the better flow quality in the test section and the fact that once the air is circulating in the tunnel, the fan and motor only needs to overcome losses of speed along the wall and through the turning vanes, the fan does not have to constantly accelerate the air. The drawbacks to the closed system are, the higher construction costs because of the vanes and ducting, the fact that the tunnel must be designed to purge exhaust products that can accumulate during testing and it is an inferior design for propulsion and smoke visualization.

Until World War Two, the world's largest wind tunnel, built in 1932-1934, was located in a suburb of Paris, Chalais-Meudon, France. It was designed to test full-size aircraft and had six large fans driven by high powered electric motors. The Chalais Meudon wind tunnel was used by ONERA (The Office National d'Etudes et de Recherches Aérospatiales) which was the French national aerospace research centre until 1976 in the development of the Concorde. Today, this wind tunnel is preserved as a national monument.

During the Cold War period, wind tunnel testing was considered of high strategic importance in the development of supersonic aircraft and missiles. Also after the war, wind tunnel study came into its own, when the effects of wind on man-made structures or objects needed to be studied, such as when buildings became tall enough to present large surfaces to the wind, and the resulting forces had to be resisted by the building's internal structure. Determining such forces was required before building codes could specify the required strength of such buildings and these tests continue to be used for large or unusual buildings today.

Today, even new cars are tested in wind tunnels to determine ways to reduce the power required to move the vehicle on roadways at a given speed. In these studies, the interaction between the road and the vehicle plays a significant role and this interaction must be taken into consideration when interpreting the test results. In an actual situation the roadway is moving relative to the vehicle but the air is stationary relative to the roadway, but in the wind tunnel the air is moving relative to the roadway as well as the vehicle, while the roadway is stationary relative to the test vehicle. For this reason, automotive-test wind tunnels have incorporated moving belts under the test vehicle in an effort to approximate the actual condition, and very similar devices are used in wind tunnel testing of aircraft take-off and landing configurations.

Wind tunnel testing of sporting equipment has also been prevalent over the years, including golf clubs, golf balls, Olympic bobsleds, Olympic cyclists, and race car helmets. Helmet aerodynamics is particularly important in open cockpit race cars. Excessive lift forces on the helmet can cause considerable neck strain on the driver, and flow separation on the back side of the helmet can cause turbulent buffeting and thus blurred vision for the driver at high speeds.

Advances in computational fluid dynamics (CFD) modelling on high-speed digital computers has slowly reduced the demand for wind tunnel testing, however, CFD results are still not completely reliable and wind tunnels are used to verify CFD predictions.

Aircraft Carriers

On 12th July 1849, the Austrian Navy ship SMS Vulcano was used for launching incendiary balloons in the form of small hot air balloons intended to drop bombs on Venice. Although the attempt largely failed due to unfavourable winds which drove the balloons back over the ship, one bomb did land on the city.

It was inevitable that balloons being launched from ships would lead to the development of balloon carriers, or tenders during World War One, by the navies of Great

Britain, France, Germany, Italy, Russia, and Sweden. About ten such "balloon tenders" were built, their main objective being aerial observation posts.

The first purpose-built seaplane to put in an appearance was the French Fabre Hydravion, built by Louis Ferdinand Ferber, a canard configuration monoplane with a pusher powerplant, it was the first aeroplane to take off from water under its own power in March 1910.

The pilot sat astride the upper fuselage beam. The aircraft was equipped with three broad floats: one at the front of the aircraft, the other two mounted on struts extending down from the wing, and the pilot sat astride the upper fuselage beam.

The Fabre Hydravion.

It successfully took off and flew for a distance of about half a kilometre (a third of a mile) on 28th March 1910 at Etang de Berre, Martigues, Bouches-du-Rhône, France, despite Fabre having no previous flying experience.

He flew the floatplane successfully three more times that day and within a week he had flown a distance of 3.5 mi (5.6 km) but the aircraft then became badly damaged in an accident.

These experimental flights were closely followed by aviation pioneers Gabriel and Charles Voisin who were eager to construct a floatplane of their own. The Voisins subsequently purchased several of the Fabre floats and fitted them to their Voisin Canard.

mpression of a Voisin float plane.

The Voisin Canard was an aircraft developed by the Voisin brothers during 1910 and first flown early in 1911. It was originally flown as a landplane but after the addition of floats it became one of the first floatplanes to be used by the French Navy.

These trials with floatplanes inevitably led to development of ships to carry aeroplanes. Commissioned as a torpedo boat supply ship in 1896 the French ship Foudre underwent several changes of role, becoming first a repair ship and then a minelayer in 1910. In 1912 a flight deck was constructed above her bow and a hanger, together with a crane to lift seaplanes from the water, to the rear of her funnels. In November 1913 an improved 10 metre launch deck was fitted for use with a Caudron G.3 seaplane and a successful launch was conducted on May 8th 1914.

In that same year both the Royal Navy's HMS Hermes and the US Navy's USS Mississippi were also converted to carry seaplanes, however HMS Hermes was sunk by a

German submarine in October 1914 but in 1919, the first purpose built British carrier was built and was also called HMS Hermes, unfortunately she was eventually sunk by the Japanese in 1942.

The first successful sea-launched air attack took place in 1914 and was launched from the Japanese seaplane carrier "Wakmiya" against German forces during the Battle of Tsingtao.

Launching a Maurice Farman from the deck of the Wakamiya.

The Maurice Farman floatplanes used in the raid were lowered into the water by crane and retrieved back from the surface in the same way afterwards.

The Wakamiya was initially the Russian freighter Lethington, built by Duncan in Port Glasgow, United Kingdom, laid down in 1900 and launched on 21st September 1901. She was captured on a voyage from Cardiff to Vladivostok by a Japanese torpedo boat during the Russian – Japanese War in 1905. Acquired by the Japanese government she was renamed Takasaki-Maru until given the official name of Wakamiya-Maru on 1st September, and from 1907 she was managed as a transport ship.

In 1913 she was transferred to the Imperial Japanese Navy and converted to a seaplane carrier, being completed on 17th August 1914. She was a 7,720-ton ship, with a complement of 234 crew with two seaplanes on deck and two in reserve.

Artist's impression of the Cuxhaven raid.

On the Western front, the first naval air raid occurred on 25th December 1914, when twelve seaplanes from HMS Engadine, Riviera and Empress, all of which were cross-channel steamers converted to seaplane carriers, attacked the Zeppelin base at Cuxhaven.

The attack was not a complete success however, although a German warship was damaged and the raid at least demonstrated the feasibility of attack by ship-borne aircraft to the world and showed the strategic importance of this new weapon.

After the war a great many cruisers carried a seaplane for reconnaissance that was launched from a flat deck by catapult and recovered by crane from the water after landing.

During World War Two these vessels had some notable successes, such as with the HMS Warspite's float-equipped Fairy Swordfish during the Second Battle of Narvik in

1940, which spotted for the guns of the British warships, helping to sink seven German destroyers, and also sank the German submarine U-64 with bombs.

Eugene Ely became the first pilot to launch from the deck of a stationary ship in 1910. The light cruiser USS Birmingham was fitted with an 80 feet long wooden platform erected on the bow.

Eugene Ely taking off from the deck of USS Birmingham in 1910.

His Curtiss aircraft, which had been fitted with floats under the wings, just in case, rolled off the edge of the platform nose down, then settled and briefly skipped off the water, slightly damaging the propeller. Ely managed to stay airborne however and landed 2 ½ miles away on the nearest land, Willoughby Spit.

Taking off from a ship having been accomplished, albeit precariously, Ely was now ready to try landing on one. He and the Curtiss team were scheduled to fly in San Francisco in January and arrangements were made for the attempt on the west coast.

The armoured cruiser USS Pennsylvania was prepared and anchored in San Francisco Bay. This time a longer platform was erected, 120 feet long with ropes and sandbags stretched across to serve as a crude arresting system for landing. There was also a canvas awning at the end to catch the aeroplane if the ropes and sandbags were not sufficient. With longer wings and hooks on the landing gear on the plane and Ely donning a padded football helmet and bicycle inner tubes around his body in case anything went awry, all was ready on the morning of January 18th 1911.

Eugene Ely landing on the deck of USS Pennsylvania in 1911.

Crowds lined the shore and boats collected in the harbour to witness the daring flight. At 11:00 a.m., Ely took off from nearby Tanforan Race Track and headed for the Pennsylvania. To the delight of thousands of spectators, he managed to make a safe landing, the arresting equipment working perfectly. After lunch with the ship's captain and after a few photographs, the platform was cleared and the Pennsylvania was pointed into the wind. Ely took off, flew past the crowd, and landed safely back at Tanforan.

On 9th May 1912 during the Royal Fleet Review, Commander Charles Rumney Sampson of the Royal Navy became the first pilot to take off from a moving ship. He took off in a Short S.38 from the deck of the battleship HMS Hibernia while she steamed at 15 knots. The first pilot to land on the deck of a moving ship was Royal Navy Squadron Commander E. H. Dunning when he landed his Sopwith Pup on HMS Furious on 2nd August 1917. Commander Dunning was tragically killed five days later attempting another landing on the Furious.

The first carrier to have a full-length flight deck was the Royal Navy HMS Argus completed in 1918 and the American Navy followed suit in 1920 with the USS Langley.

The first purpose designed carrier to be laid down was HMS Hermes in January 1918 and the following year Japan started work on the Hōshō. Although the Hermes was the first to be started the Hōshō was the first to be commissioned in December 1922. HMS Hermes was not commissioned until 1924 due to several changes to her design after she was launched and was the first carrier to have an off-set control tower. HMS Hermes has all the appearance of a modern carrier with the exception of an angled flight deck with squared off prow.

Japanese Navy's Hōshō.

The Hermes was also the first carrier to have what is known as a "Hurricane bow" that is a bow that is sealed up to the flight deck.

The introduction of jet fighters with their faster landing speeds meant that changes had to be made and various trials took place. The first ever deck landing of a jet aircraft was, unsurprisingly, performed by Lt Cdr Eric Brown in December 1945 when he landed a modified de Havilland Vampire onto the deck of HMS Ocean.

With the introduction of jet aircraft, the risk of damaging propellers was no longer an issue and it was recognised that eliminating the landing gear of carrier borne aircraft would improve their flight performance and range, since the space taken by the landing gear could be used to hold additional fuel tanks.

These ideas led to the concept of a deck that would somehow absorb the energy of landing, although take off would require some sort of launching cradle.

After his successful jet landing on HMS Ocean, Commander Brown carried out more tests with the de Havilland Sea Vampire, this time testing a "flexible deck" fitted to HMS Warrior. The deck consisted of a rubberised sheet fully supported on multiple layers of pressurised fire hose that would absorb the energy of landing and eliminate the need for an undercarriage. The flexible deck idea was found to be technically feasible but was abandoned anyway, mainly because there were always doubts about the ability of an average pilot to land in this way.

The Angled Deck

In the 1950s the Royal Navy introduced the angled flight deck, an idea conceived by Captain D.R.F. Campbell RN and Lewis Boddington of the Royal Aircraft Establishment at Farnborough.

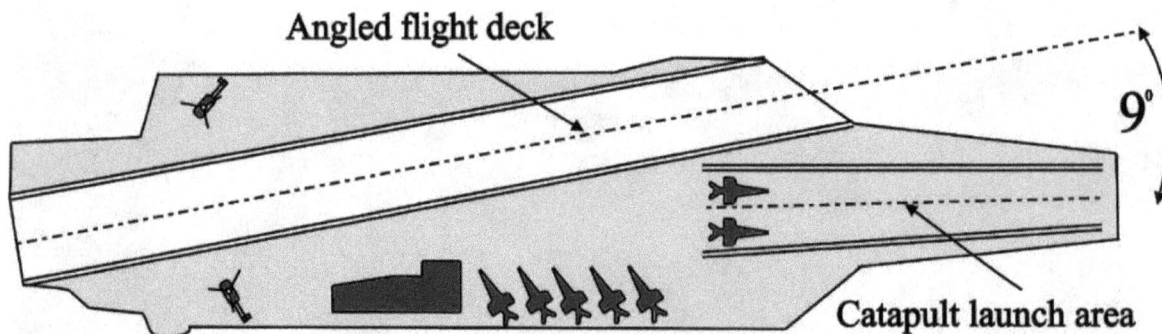

Modern US type carrier with angled deck for landing and catapult launch.

With the runway canted at a few degrees from the longitudinal axis of the ship, any incoming aircraft that missed the arrester cables could simply apply full throttle and get airborne again without hitting any aircraft parked on the fight deck. Tests with painted angled deck markings on HMS Triumph proved the angled deck's worth and in February 1955 HMS Ark Royal became the first carrier to be designed and built with an angled flight deck, closely followed by HMAS Melbourne and USS Forrestal.

Optical Landing System

The first of the Optical Landing Systems was another British innovation. The Mirror Landing Aid invented by Lieutenant Commander H. C. N. Goodhart RN. was a gyroscopically-controlled concave mirror, replaced in later designs by a Fresnel Lens landing system, on the port side of the deck. On either side of the mirror was a line of green "datum" lights. A bright orange "source" light was directed into the mirror creating the "ball" (or "meatball" in later USN parlance), which could be seen by the pilot who was about to land. The position of the ball compared to the datum lights indicated the aircraft's position in relation to the desired glidepath. If the ball was above the datum, the plane was high; below the datum, the plane was low; between the datum, the plane was on glidepath. The gyro stabilisation compensated for much of the movement of the flight deck due to the sea, giving a constant glidepath. The first trials of a mirror landing sight were conducted on HMS Illustrious in 1952. Prior to OLSs, pilots relied on visual flag signals from a Landing Signal Officer to help maintain proper glidepath.

The Ski-jump

Yet another British innovation was the ski-jump ramp as an alternative to contemporary catapult systems. The ski-jump ramp at the end of a runway or flight deck allows an aircraft which makes a running start to convert part of its forward momentum into upward motion. The intent is that the additional altitude and upward-angled flight path from the jump provides extra time until the forward airspeed generated by engine thrust is high enough to maintain level flight. STOVL aircraft also use their ability to direct some of their thrust downwards to give them additional lift until required airspeed is attained.

The latest British carrier, HMS Queen Elizabeth is designed to operate with the short take-off and vertical landing F35B and therefor has a ski-jump for take-offs but does not require an angled flight deck for landings as there is no chance of the aircraft overshooting the landing area.

HMS Queen Elizabeth has a straight flight deck and ski-jump.

Sea Harrier using a ski-jump for take-off : Darren Harbar Photography.

What of the future

Although aircraft in 2020 have the same basic structure and outworld appearance of those built in the nineteen fifties and sixties there has been a steady stream of advances in design, materials and avionics spurred on by the competitive nature of the industry, however the expectations and demands of the public seems to be changing. Along with the call for ever greater speed there is now demand for the industry to be environmentally friendly and to go about its business without polluting the atmosphere.

Airlines are now looking at promoting how environmentally friendly and economical they are. One is temted to point out that they have always strived for economy, largely at the expense of the paying customer. There has also been a tendency in recent years for airlines to prefer twin engine passenger jets rather than the three or four engined craft they used to buy. Why use four engines when it's cheaper with just two? With the increase in engine power and reliability there has been a relaxation in ETOPS, (Extended Range Operation with Twin-Engined Aeroplanes, later shortened to just, Extended Operations) that stipulated how far two-engined jets were allowed to fly away from designated diversion points.

It may not be long now before the majority of cars on the road will be fully electric and aircraft for short haul flights may not be as far behind as you think. Perhaps electric tilt-rotors will become a common sight, certainly there are several well established projects underway at the moment looking at electric powered aircraft including the Airbus, "City Airbus", the hybrid-electric aircraft being developed by "Zunum" a manufacturer start-up backed by Boeing Horizon X and JetBlue Technology Ventures, and distributed propulsion projects like the NASA X-57 Maxwell.

On the military front things seem to be ever moving towards pilotless drones which begs the question, will the electric commercial aircraft be piloted or remote control? Well maybe that's still a little way off.

And what of long-haul lights? A start-up in Silicon Valley, "Boom Supersonic" is developing an aircraft that is expected to fly at Mach 2.2 at lower costs than Concorde and the Aerion AS2 is another civilian supersonic project under development.

Perhaps those still in school at the moment we will see a time when short and medium haul flights will be electric powered and long-haul journey being taken in space with sub-orbital flights. Who knows what the future holds?

Glossary
of
Terms

Chapter Fourteen

Glossary of Terms

Adverse yaw	When the nose of an aircraft turns away from the direction of turn.
Altitude	The vertical distance of the aircraft above the ground
Aerofoil	The shape of a surface such as a wing, blade, turbine or rotor that generates lift from air passing over it
Aileron	Control surface on the trailing edge of a wing to control roll or bank
Angle of attack	The angle made from the chord line of an aerofoil and the direction of the air that strikes it.
Camber	The degree of curve in an aerofoil.
Canard	An arrangement wherein a small forewing is placed forward of the main wing of a fixed-wing aircraft. The term "canard" may be used to describe the aircraft itself, the wing configuration, or the forewing itself.
Chord line	An imaginary line on an aerofoil from the leading edge to the trailing
Cowling	Removeable covering for an aircraft engine
Crosswind	Wind that blows in a direction not parallel to the course.
Delta wing	Triangle- A shaped wing that looks similar to the shape of the uppercase Greek letter, delta.
Dihedral wings	Wings which slope upwards towards the wing tip. If the wing slopes down it is an Anhedral wing.
Downwash	In aeronautics, the term describes air that is deflected downwards by the aircraft wing or a rotor blade on a helicopter.

Drag	A force on the aircraft as it moves through the air. The force runs parallel and opposite to the aeroplane's direction of travel
Flaps	Moveable surfaces added to the trailing edges of the wing. These change the curve of the wing and allow the pilot to adjust lift and drag so the plane can safely fly at a lower speed.
Flight deck	Another name for the cockpit, which is located at the front of the aircraft and holds the pilot and instruments
Glider	A fixed-wing aircraft that is supported in flight by the dynamic reaction of the air against its lifting surfaces, and whose free flight does not depend on an engine.
Horizontal stabiliser	A lifting surface on the tail of an aircraft, also known as the tailplane or elevator, that provides stability.
interdictor aircraft	An interdictor aircraft, also sometimes known as deep air support (DAS), is one that uses preventive tactical bombing attacks against enemy targets, often well inside enemy lines, that are not an immediate threat, in order to delay, disrupt, or hinder later enemy engagement of friendly forces
Joystick	Also known as the control column, the joystick is the main device in the cockpit for controlling the aircraft.
Leading edge	Front surface of a wing or aerofoil
Longeron	A longeron is a load-bearing component of a framework. The term is commonly used in connection with aircraft fuselage where they are used in conjunction with stringers to form structural frameworks
Longitudinal axis	A direction of orientation; an imaginary line that passes horizontally through the centre of gravity, from the head to tail of an aircraft.
Nacelle	Housing for an aircraft's engine or powerplant
Pitch	A motion about an aircraft's lateral axis (which runs from wing to wing) that causes the forward end to rise or fall.
Powerplant	All the components of an aircraft's engine including any propellers.

Propeller	A rotating blade powered by the engine that produces thrust to propel the airplane through the air.
Pusher configuration	Aeroengine with the propeller behind the engine to push it forward.
Quadraplane	A type of aircraft that has four wings of similar spans
Roll	Motion on an aircraft along its nose-to-tail axis, also called bank.
Rudder	A vertical control surface in the tail of an airplane, which controls the side-to-side movement (YAW) of an aircraft.
Slots	A narrowing gap at the leading edge of a wing to increase airspeed.
Spoilers	Devices intended to increase drag.
Stall	An aircraft condition when the angle of attack is so great that the air no longer flows easily over the aerofoil.
Tail	The aerodynamic surfaces located at the rear of an aircraft.
Thrust	An aerodynamic force produced by a propeller or engine that pushes an aircraft forward.
Torque	A force that aims to produce rotation.
Tractor configuration	Aeroengine with the propeller in front of the engine to pull it forward
Trailing edge	Back edge of a wing or aerofoil.
Trim	To trim an aircraft is to set the control surfaces so that the aircraft maintains the set attitude without any further control input.
Ventral tank	A tank carried on the fuselage centre-line in such a way that it either forms the underside of the fuselage or is flush against it. It may be fixed or jettisonable.
Vertical Speed Indicator	A panel instrument that measures the rate of climb or descent in feet-per-minute, by sensing the change in atmospheric pressure, also known as a variometer.
Yaw	The side-to-side movement of an aircraft about its vertical axis.
Yoke	The control wheel of an aircraft, similar to a car steering wheel.

INDEX

Other books by Colin Holcombe

A History of Firearms (Black and white edition)	ISBN: 978 1787233300
A History of Firearms (Full colour interior)	ISBN: 978 1987591453
Samuel Colt. The Man Behind the Gun	ISBN: 978 1787234031
Cabinet Making	ISBN: 978 1787233393
Antique Furniture Restoration an Illustrated Guide.	ISBN: 978 1787233522
The Care and Repair of Antique Furniture	ISBN: 978 1516899081

Colin Holcombe is a retired antique restorer and conservator who has had a lifelong interest in aviation. His father worked on Beaufighters during World War Two, and growing up in Bristol he was never far from aircraft factories and airfields. Although never actually working in the aviation industry himself, he was surrounded by freinds and family who did and took up gliding as a passtime at the age of 18, qualifying as a solo glider pilot at the age of 21.

After working under an Italian restorer for nine years he started his own restoration business and counted Bristol Museum and Art Gallery, Harvey's Wine Museum and Lord Wraxhall amongst his clients.

He taught furniture restoration and French polishing at an adult nightschool for over twenty years. During his time running a business he wrote books on antique furniture restoration, woodwork and marquetry. In retirement he started writing again, determined to put all his interests into print and also have a go at writing some fiction which has resulted in four crime thrillers.

Apart from family, Colin's interests have always been, antique furniture and weaponry, aviation, magic, tennis and golf but not necessarily in that order